Our Lord's
Pattern for
PRAYER

Our Lord's Pattern for PRAYER

by
Adolph Saphir

Foreword by
Warren W. Wiersbe

KREGEL PUBLICATIONS
Grand Rapids, Michigan 49501

Our Lord's Pattern for Prayer by Adolph Saphir.
Copyright © 1984 by Kregel Publications, a division of
Kregel, Inc. All rights reserved.

Library of Congress Cataloging in Publication Data

Saphir, Adolph, 1831-1891.
    Our Lord's Pattern for Prayer.

    Reprint. Originally published: The Lord's Prayer.
4th ed. London: J. Nisbet, 1872.
    1. Lord's prayer. I. Title.
BV230.S255   1984   226'.9606   84-9710
ISBN 0-8254-3748-2

Printed in the United States of America

CONTENTS

FOREWORD

On Sunday, February 17, 1839, Andrew A. Bonar wrote in his journal: "I have been somewhat unsettled by the occurrence of a proposal in Edinburgh to send Robert McCheyne and me, for six months, to inquire about the Jews throughout the Continent of Europe and even round Jerusalem." This concern among Scottish Presbyterians for Israel was partly the result of a new interest in biblical prophecy, and the mission was strongly promoted by Dr. Robert Candlish, minister of Free St. George's Church in Edinburgh.

Bonar and McCheyne were joined by Dr. Hugh Black, Professor of Divinity in Aberdeen, and Dr. Keith, minister at St. Cyrus; and the deputation sailed from Dover on April 12, 1839. They returned on November 6, and from their experiences grew a strong mission to the Jews both in Great Britain and on the Continent.

Drs. Keith and Black returned to Scotland via a different route that took them through Budapest, where there was a large Jewish community. In that community was a merchant named Saphir, and, as a result of the Mission, he and his family became believers.

The son, Aaron Adolph, grew up in a Christian home. He was born in 1831, educated at Berlin, Glasgow, Aberdeen, and Edinburgh, where he was licensed to preach in 1854. For a short period, he ministered among the Jews in Hamburg, and in 1856 he became pastor of the Presbyterian Church in South Shields, Glasgow. In 1861 he moved to St. Mark's Presbyterian Church, Greenwich, serving for eleven fruitful years, his longest pastorate.

In 1872 he accepted a call to Notting Hill, London, and it was there he presented his wonderful series of studies on The Book of Hebrews.

Ill health forced him to leave the pastorate in 1875, and for the next five years he held no regular pastoral charge. He served the Belgrave Presbyterian Church in London for only one year (1887-88), and in 1891, he died of a heart attack.

"Mr. Saphir always has something to say worthy of the attention of spiritual minds," wrote Charles Haddon Spurgeon. "His mind finds a track of its own, but he is never speculative."

Because of his Jewish background, Saphir was able to shed much light on the Scriptures and make them meaningful to his Gentile listeners and readers. Next to his *Expository Lectures on the Epistle to the Hebrews* (now available from Kregel Publications as *Epistle to the Hebrews*), his *Divine Unity of Scripture* is his best-known book. But I rejoice that another of his fine works, *Our Lord's Pattern for Prayer,* is now available to a new generation of Bible students.

Originally published as *Lectures on the Lord's Prayer,* this book is one of the best on that very special portion of Scripture. There are many volumes written by various authors on this prayer, but too often they go to one of two extremes: either they are so "devotional" that they are doctrinally shallow, or so "technical" that they never touch the heart. Saphir manages to blend pastoral warmth with good exegesis to produce a book for both the head and the heart. I especially appreciate the insights he gives from Jewish lore and custom.

Best of all, Saphir magnifies the Person of our Lord Jesus Christ, so that the reading of this book is almost an experience of worship. I commend it to you, not only for personal study, but for personal growth in grace.

Back to the Bible Broadcast
Lincoln, Nebraska

WARREN W. WIERSBE

1

PRAYER AS REVEALED IN CHRIST

"And it came to pass, that, as He was praying in a certain place, when He ceased, one of His disciples said unto Him, Lord, teach us to pray, as John also taught his disciples." — Luke 11:1.

WE possess a twofold record of the model prayer which the Lord bequeathed as a precious legacy to His Church.

At the commencement of His ministry, in the Sermon on the Mount, after His warning against the false view of the heathen, who think they will be heard for their much speaking, Christ taught His disciples the seven petitions which combine the greatest brevity with exhaustive fulness; while in the invocation, " Our Father, which art in heaven," He revealed the basis and starting-point of all true and spiritual worship, the assurance of divine love and favour, which all worship which is of human invention, and prompted by the legal spirit, regards as the end to be merited and obtained.

Towards the end of His ministry, one of His disciples asked Him, " Lord, teach us to pray, as John also taught his disciples."   What gave occasion to the expression of this desire was the circumstance, that the Saviour had been praying before His apostles. Doubtless, as they listened to the prayer of the Lord, the only-begotten of the Father, they felt that never man spake unto God as this Man; that in Him the filial spirit of prayer had found its perfect expression; that He was the true High Priest, who entered into the very presence of God. John the Baptist had taught his disciples to pray, for the object of all God-sent teachers is to bring souls into communion with God. But the master cannot give more than he possesses; and the disciples of Jesus felt that all previous instructions on prayer must yield in depth and power to the teaching of Him whose nearness to God infinitely excelled the position of the most favoured saints of old. Then they themselves, through one of their number, requested the Saviour to teach them to pray. Their desire was, that the great High Priest should show them how they might become priests with Him, approaching and worshipping God in His Spirit with that liberty and confidence which He possessed. They wished to breathe the same atmosphere of divine love; though as yet they did not understand how Jesus would grant their desire more abundantly and fully than their boldest hope anticipated. For Christ, by His Holy Spirit dwelling in our hearts, prays in us; it is the Spirit of the Son of God who in our hearts cries now, Abba, Father.

Jesus teaches not merely what and how we are to

pray, but He teaches prayer. He is the revelation of prayer. The mystery of prayer is made manifest in Him, who is our Mediator and interceding High Priest, who from all eternity was appointed by His Father to be the beginning of the creation, the redeemer of sinners, and the heir of all things. When we understand the mystery of mediation, manifested in the incarnate and now glorified Son, but existing in the purpose of God from all eternity, prayer loses its enigmatic and isolated character; it no longer appears as an after-thought, there is no longer any discord between it and the unchangeableness of God; but it is seen as having its root and beginning in the blessed Trinity, its fountain in the eternal counsel of salvation.

The Messiah says, in one of the prophetic psalms : *I am prayer.** During His pilgrimage on earth, His whole life was communion with God; and now, in His glory, He is continually making intercession for us. But this does not exhaust the idea, " I am prayer." He not merely prayed and is now praying, He not merely teaches and influences us to pray, but He *is* prayer, the fountain and source of all prayer as well as the foundation and basis of all answers to our petitions. He is the Word in this sense also. From all eternity His Father heard him, heard Him as interceding for that world which, created through Him, He represented, and in which, through Him, divine glory was to be revealed. In the same sense,

* Psalm cix. 4.

therefore, in which He is light and gives light, in which He is life and resurrection, and therefore quickens, Jesus *is* prayer. Sympathy has, in like manner, its eternal origin in the Son of God. The Father loved and pitied us, but the mind, which was in the Son of God, was to humble Himself, and to take upon Him our nature, to learn obedience, and to be made perfect through suffering; that He might be a compassionate and merciful High Priest.

Jesus teaches prayer. This is the sum and substance of His teaching; the object of His life and death. He came to bring us unto God; He died for our sins, that the love of God may now come freely and fully into our souls, and that eternal life may be ours. He became man, that we, through Him, might obtain the adoption of sons. He is a High Priest, that we, gathered round Him, should be priests unto God and His Father. That His disciples may pray in Christ's name, as one with Him, as standing in a filial relation to God through Him, this is the high end of the incarnation and of the sufferings of the Son of God,—this is the glorious fruit of His resurrection and of the Pentecostal gift. For prayer is not one among many manifestations of spiritual life; it is not even enough to say that it is the first and most important. It stands by itself, and pre-eminent. It is *the* manifestation of our personal relation to God; it is the essential and immediate expression of our filial relation in Christ

to the Father.*   " Behold, He prayeth," is the begin-
ing of the new life; " Abba, Father," is the first word
of the regenerate.   And as the spiritual life commences, so is its continuation.   Thus it is true that
Jesus teaches to pray, and that the sum and substance, the summit and crown of the teaching of
Jesus, is *prayer* in His name.

Guided by the central fact, that the Lord Jesus is
seen praying, and bearing in mind the Saviour's
teaching, which, in connexion with the perfect model
He gave on prayer, let us consider :—

I. Jesus Praying—The Revelation of Prayer.
II. Prayer in Relation to Life.
III. The Spirit of Prayer, and Stated Seasons
    for Prayer.
IV. Difficulties and Experiences in Prayer.

I. Jesus Praying—The Revelation of Prayer.

We often read in the gospel narrative, that Jesus
prayed ; and besides this fact, we possess also the
petitions, which on several occasions He offered to
His Father, in the hearing of His disciples and the
people.

What is usually called the Lord's Prayer is not
such in the sense that Jesus offered it in His own
person as the expression of His wants.   Not merely
was it impossible for Him, who was sinless, to use
the fifth petition, but we never find that the Lord,

---

* Hofmann, " Schriftbeweis," ii. 321.

in addressing God, or speaking of Him, uses the
expression " Our Father." He invariably says either
"Father," or " My Father," or " Your Father." For
even, when He gave to Mary Magdalene the assurance that the disciples were His brethren, He carefully reminded her that He is the *only*-begotten, and
that His relation to the Father is essentially different
from ours. But there are several prayers of Christ
recorded in the Gospels, and they are an invaluable
treasure and comfort to the Church.

The first word recorded of Jesus as a child, reveals
to us that the days of His childhood were days of
prayer and meditation. Afterwards we read, that,
" being baptized and *praying*, the heavens were
opened, and the Spirit descended on Him." * Again,†
that He withdrew Himself from the great multitude
who came to hear and to be healed ; and went into
the wilderness and *prayed*. Before He chose the
apostles, He went out into a mountain to pray,
and continued all night in *prayer* to God.‡ And
before He asked His disciples, " Whom say the
people that I, the Son of man, am ? " He had been
alone praying. It was while He prayed on the
Mount, that the fashion of His countenance was
altered. At the grave of Lazarus, He thanked God
for having heard Him ; before He fed the multitude,

---

* Luke iii. 21.   † Luke v. 16
‡ The words of Martha (" I know, that even now whatsoever thou
wilt ask of God, God will give it thee") show that the Saviour's
life of prayer was well known to His disciples.

He lifted up his eyes to heaven and gave thanks; before He healed the dumb man, He sighed to God; teaching us, that all His miracles were preceded by prayer to the Father, even as they were wrought in Him.*

But we possess also the very words of Christ's prayer. Thus, when He thanked the Father for having revealed those things to babes. And on the last day of His public teaching, when His soul was moved deeply with the thought of His approaching suffering, and the glory that should follow, He prayed in the hearing of the people : " Father, glorify Thy name."† We know, also, that He prayed for Peter, that his faith might not fail. But our thoughts hasten to the last evening with His apostles, when, after He had spoken to them the words of consolation, revealing to them " plainly " the mystery of His union with the Father, and with His believing people, He lifted up His eyes and prayed for Himself, for His disciples, and for the whole Church. His prayers also in Gethsemane and on the cross are recorded for our instruction ; and though all Christ's words are holy, and infinite, we regard these words as the inmost sanctuary of Scripture.‡

When we contemplate the praying Christ, we realise most fully His humanity. In no gospel are we so constantly and clearly taught the subordination

---

* Luke vi. 12.   In Him, comp. John xiv. 10, 11.

† Luke vi. 12. ; ix. 19, 28, 29.   John xii. 27–29.

‡ There are more than a hundred prayers of our Lord recorded in Scripture.   Where ? you ask.   In the Psalms of David, and in the prophets.— *Kohlbrügge.*

of the Son to the Father, his constant dependence on
Him that sent Him, as in that very gospel which
most emphatically dwells on His eternal Sonship
and glory, that gospel which is so full of the declarations of His divinity, in which Jesus so often says,
I Am.   A striking harmony exists between the
Gospel of John and the second portion of the
prophet Isaiah, for in the latter, too, the position
of the Messiah as servant, His prayerful, humble,
confiding, and obedient attitude, is combined with
the declaration of His divine majesty.   He was
sent, yet He, different from angels and men, of
His own will came; He obeyed, and yet he is
one with the Father; He prayed—the *Son of God.*
For although His humility, His obedience, His
prayer, reveal to us most clearly His humanity,
showing us that he lived by faith, and that the perfection of His humanity consisted in His living by
the Father, yet we can never lose sight of His
divinity.   We believe in Christ, God and man,
two natures but one person.   We cannot separate
His divinity from His humanity.   *The Word* was
made flesh, and dwelt among us.   That sacred
humanity is a creature, yet inseparably united
with the eternal Word, revealing God perfectly.
Thus, when we think of Christ praying, we think of
Him as God and man,* and therefore the true

---

* On the prayer of Jesus very vague views prevail.   Some think
He prayed chiefly to show us an example; some, that He prayed
only according to His humanity; others, again, believing He

Mediator between God and us; and though we know that, while He was on earth, He was in the form of a servant, and had laid aside the glory which was His both before His incarnation and after His ascension, yet believing that Jesus Christ is the same yesterday, to-day, and for ever, we feel sure that His prayer on earth was a manifestation both of His prayer after His exaltation, and of His prayer before He was incarnate.

1. His prayer after His exaltation. His prayers were not ended on the cross; in one sense, His prayer commences with His ascension and session at the right hand of God. He is even now our High Priest

---

prayed as God-man, are at a loss why He should need to pray, as all things were given to Him of the Father from all eternity. This vagueness arises from a defective view of the doctrine of the Trinity, as revealed in Scripture. We do not realise sufficiently the distinctness of the persons in the unity of the Godhead. The eternal life of God is the communion of the Three blessed Ones; "Each divine person"—to use the words of Schmieder,—"working in His peculiar sphere in original and creative glory, that which the other persons could not work and express in the same way" (*Hohepriesterliche Gebet*). Thus the Son spoke from all eternity to the Father, and the Father answered and gave; and herein is the Father's glory and joy, as well as the glory and joy of the Son. We hesitate sometimes to speak of the three persons in the language of Scripture—to use the plural, as is done in Gen. i. 26, xi. 6, 7; Isa. vi. 8; where the divine persons speak as a communion of several; as Jesus says, *we* will come and make *our* abode with him. Elohim is the expression of plurality, which yet is unity; Jehovah of unity, which includes plurality. It is worthy of notice that the apostles, in speaking of the Father, the incarnate Son, and the Holy Ghost, seem to be neither afraid of offending the monotheistic Jews, or of being misunderstood by their converts from Polytheism.

interceding for us. The prayers of believers, and of all who are coming unto God, must be viewed as connected with His prayer. Christ, whom we worship, is also the first of worshippers. The Father regards Christ and the Church as one. Jesus identifies Himself with us, and thus His prayer and our prayers are united; the Father, strictly speaking, hears only one voice, the voice of the Son, whom He heareth alway. On the other hand, Jesus, identifying Himself with the Father, sends the Spirit into our hearts, and it is no longer we that pray, but Christ in us—the Spirit, as the representative of Christ, enabling us to pray in Christ's name.

The intercession of the Lord Jesus Christ is based on His obedience, death, and resurrection.* He is our advocate as our righteousness; but he is our advocate also as our head and representative; His intercession is therefore inseparably connected with the gift of the Holy Ghost. Thus do we by the Spirit call Jesus Lord; and one with Him, we say to God—Father.

2. But while we have no difficulty in seeing the connexion between Christ's present intercession and our union with Him, the God-man, as the essence and power of our prayer, may we not also look back to the centuries before His advent, and to " the beginning," and to the eternity " before the foundations of the world "? Let Scripture only be our guide. Did not all the saints of God pray in the

---

* Rom. viii. 34.

name of the Mediator? True, it was to them a
mystery, seen dimly; but Jehovah, the God of the
covenant, who condescended in grace and for redemption, and whom they expected finally to reveal
His glory manifestly among them,—the messenger,
in whom was God's name and God's countenance,
was He not the same who was afterwards born in
Bethlehem? Was not He their representative, surety,
and advocate? And did not He say to the Father,
during all these ages, "Lo, I come; in the volume of
the book it is written of me, I come to do Thy will."

And going still farther back: Is not He the
beginning of the creation of God? Are we not
taught, that all things are made by Him and for Him,
and that in Him all things consist? He is represented
as the Word, "in the beginning with God," and as
upholding all things by the word of His power.* He
also, as God-man, is appointed heir of all things.
Creation, providence, or history, and the final glory,
are thus connected with Christ, as the Mediator, as the
Word.† But we know that the eternal purpose of

---

* John. i. 1–3.   Col. i. 16, 17.   Heb. i. 3.   Rev. iii. 14.

† "God's ways are His works *ad extra*, wherein He purposed to
go forth and manifest Himself towards creatures. Now, in the
beginning of these ways, and the first thoughts of them, did God
possess Christ, God-man, in His foreknowledge, as the richest
treasure of all His glory to be manifested in His creation, without
which He would not have proceeded to any other work, or have
walked forth in any creation-way, but rested in that blessed
society of the three without them. And it is not said *in the
beginning of His way*, but it is also further added that He possessed
Him before His works of old."—*Goodwin on the Knowledge of God.*

redemption is the primal and central thought in God. Christ is not merely the Word, but the *Lamb* foreordained before the foundation of the world. For the manifestation of God's glory *in Christ*, the world was created, upheld, and redeemed. In Christ, and for Christ's sake, the love of the Father and the power of the Spirit descend to earth. And thus we can and must conceive of the prayer of the Son of God *as eternal ; from all eternity the Son spoke unto the Father on behalf of the world, on behalf of the manifestation of God's glory in His love.* And in answer to this eternal prayer, all things became and all things are ordered.* Creation and history proceed from Christ's eternal prayer. It is the imperfect

* " That there might be a glory given the Son from everlasting is clear from this, that there was the highest and freest mutual converse held between the Three Persons amongst themselves from everlasting, when no creature was ; and in that converse they drove and carried on designs of what was to come, and gave the glory to one another, of what each of them was, or should be, or do, in their several activities, to all eternity. They spake one to another, and one of another, as Heb. x. : The Son of man said to the Father, ' A body hast thou prepared me ; ' and the Father to the Son, ' Thou art my Son, this day have I begotten thee.' And this latter was from everlasting in the decreeing of it, spoken to Him ; for the words before are, *I will declare the decree.* Whereof that speech, therefore, was the matter. Likewise there were mutual engagements and promises passed between them : Tit. i. 1, 2. Eternal life was promised afore the world began. And there must be an intercourse of persons promising, and that received and accepted the promise. And in like manner in their converses they glorified one another : John xvi. 14, *The Spirit shall glorify me,* says Christ. He says it indeed of His glorifying Christ to us, but if He doeth it to us, much more among themselves."—*Goodwin on the Knowledge of God.*

time-clothed manifestation of an eternal fact, when it is said in the second Psalm to the true David, whose kingship is based on His Sonship : *Ask of me*, and I will give thee the heathen for thine inheritance, and the uttermost ends of the earth for thy possession.

God, in hearing His Son, heard only the echo of His own will. As we distinguish the persons, we hold fast the unity of the Godhead. The Father's will and the Son's prayer are one : yet was the Son's prayer real. Even as now Christ assures us that He prays for us ; and again, to remind us of His oneness with the Father, He adds : I say not I will pray unto the Father, for the Father himself loveth you.*

There is no antagonism between prayer in time and the unchangeable will of God in eternity, for Christ is the bridge, the solution of all problems, the peaceful light in our darkness. He reveals prayer as a mystery, but a mystery of light, dark by excess of brightness. Jesus is the archetype of prayer. We are made the sons of God in Him, and our great High Priest enables us to enter with Him into the Holy of Holies. We pray because Christ is in us, and the Father is in Christ.† Even before His incarnation, and before Pentecost, the saints of God prayed, anticipating the revelation of the mystery of union. " David prayed in Christ, and Christ in him, so that Christ could adopt the words of David's

---

* John xvi. 26.   † John xvii.

prayer, which He himself by His Spirit had wrought in David's heart." But as the revelation of God increases in clearness, the union with His people increases in depth. Jesus, the Son of man, who lived, suffered, and died, exalted at the right hand of God; that same Son whom God hath appointed the heir of all things, by whom He made the world, who being the brightness of His glory, and the express image of His person, and upholding all things by the word of His power, by Himself purged our sins, is the Word in whom God spake unto us,—He is the Word in whom we speak unto the Father. Praying in the name of Christ, we pray according to the eternal purpose of God, and we are lifted above sin and death, and all the imperfections of the creature ; we are beyond the clouds of time, in the bright region of divine love. " The Father loveth the Son, and hath given all things into His hand."* In this element is our life, for Christ has declared, and by His Spirit is always declaring unto us, the Father's name, "that the love wherewith Thou hast loved me, may be in them, and they in me." †

II. Prayer and Life.

The Lord's Prayer, which stands in the heart of the Sermon on the Mount, forms part of our Lord's teaching on prayer. And this, again, is but a section

---

* John iii. 35.

† John xvii. 26. A similar view of prayer is advocated by Löber, "Lehre vom Gebet." Erlangen, 1860.

of our Lord's teaching on almsgiving, prayer, and fasting. These three will be found to exhaust all the manifestations of spiritual life, to represent it in all its aspects.* They embrace our relation to man, charity; our relation to God, prayer; our relation to ourselves, self-discipline. They show us man looking around him, in his relation to the world, looking upwards to God, and looking within into his own heart. They correspond to the threefold description of the discipline of grace, that we should live soberly, righteously, and godly in this present world. (Titus ii.)

Prayer is thus connected with our whole life. The sincerity, spirituality, and strength of our prayer, is the measure of our self-discipline and of our walk; our attitude towards God determines our attitude to man; and our realisation of things unseen is the source of our self-denial and victory over the world.

In the Lord Jesus Christ we see most clearly the union of prayer and life, the harmony and continual interpenetration of the two spheres of life—communion with God and the work of earth. The Son of man, while He lived on earth, was in heaven and in uninterrupted fellowship with God; He glorified the Father on earth by word and deed. Always in communion with the Father, He thought it no interruption when His disciples or the people demanded His help or His teaching; and without

---

* Beck, Reden, vol. v. p. 18, following Calvin, Inst. III. 20.

any effort, He passed from quiet retirement to activity, and from the activity and tumult of life to the more direct and special act of prayer. Nor must we forget that, sinless as He was, He had a work not merely in regard to the world round Him, but also with regard to Himself. We shrink from applying the word self-discipline to Him whose humanity was free from all sin and imperfection. But we read of Jesus that He came not to do His own will. Looking up to God,—that is, by prayer, —He continually kept all that was within Him in harmony with the Divine will. For the joy that was set before Him, He endured the cross, painful as it was, despising the shame, which He felt as such.

We are to be conformed to Christ: as He was, so are we in the world. It is in virtue of our union with Him that we pray aright, and that our prayer becomes the centre and power of our whole inner and outer life.

Hence the parallelism, that as we pray in the name of Christ, we are commanded by the apostle, "And whatsoever ye do in word or deed, do all in the name of the Lord Jesus, giving thanks to God and the Father by Him." We pray and live in Christ's name. As one with Christ, we appear before God; Christ the great High Priest does not merely intercede in our behalf, but by His Spirit He prays in us, and our union with Jesus is the very soul of prayer. As one with Christ, we are to appear before the world—

in our character and conduct representing not ourselves, not man in his natural condition,* but the Lord
Jesus, the Son of man, the first-born among many
brethren. Both our prayer and our life are viewed as
the offering of thanksgiving unto the Father, whose
joy it is to see and love the Church, which is the
body of Christ. As therefore good words and works
have no value or power except as the manifestation
and fruit of our communion with the Father in
Jesus, the whole energy of the Christian is concentrated on one point. It is, to abide in Christ ; to
live, yet not he, but Christ in him. This concentration is the reason why His words and works are
according to the will of God : it is the very principle
and power of expansion.†

Prayer and activity are not antagonistic. It is
false to view them even as existing merely side by side,
as if prayer ceased when activity commenced. They
exist for and in each other. One with Christ, we live,
as He lived ; abiding in the Father's love, we keep
His commandments.

Praying in the name of Jesus is absolutely essential for life in His name. A life representing Christ
must be a life in conformity with the Father's will.
And how can we even know what is His good and

---

* 1 Cor. iii. 3.

† Martha and Mary are often viewed as representing two equally
legitimate manifestations of life.   But it is clear that the Lord
rebukes Martha, and commends Mary. The concentration of Mary
must precede and accompany the manifold activities of a loving
faith.

holy will concerning us without prayer? As the Saviour said of Himself, that the Lord had given Him not merely the tongue of the learned, but quick and sensitive hearing, so that every morning He listened to the voice of the Father; so it is by prayer that our hearts and consciences are enlightened and established, and that we learn not to do our own will, but the will of God, and to live in the good works which God hath before ordained that we should walk in them.

Good words and works have no vitality and power without prayer. We may apparently walk in the path of godliness and of useful activity; and yet there may be little blessing on our word, and little fruit from our labour. But if we meditate on God's law day and night, we shall be like a tree planted by the rivers of water, that bringeth forth his fruit in his season, his leaf also shall not wither, and whatsoever he doeth shall prosper. The Word of God abiding in us makes us fruitful at the right time, keeps us cheerful and fresh within; and our works being done in God, are made manifest in the beauty and strength of divine blessing.* While Sardis has the name, that it liveth and is dead, the weakest words and most insignificant works of Smyrna, animated by prayer, live for ever and obtain an everlasting reward.

He, who lives with God, prays often without being conscious of it. "For the life of the soul is deeper than our consciousness." Moses received a divine

---

* Löber, l. c.

answer to a prayer of which we do not read that it was offered. The prophet Elijah appeared before Ahab with the declaration: "As the Lord God of Israel liveth, there shall not be dew nor rain these years, but according to my word." In the Epistle of James we are told that this announcement of faith was the result of fervent prayer. Thus all words and works of faith will be recognised on that day as connected with prayer.

If prayer is the germ of Christian activity (taking this expression in the large sense of self-discipline as well as conduct), the element of *work* must be in *prayer* itself. For the seed contains the plant. One reason why the connexion between prayer and life is so often viewed superficially (either as a mere subjective connexion, or as a mere mechanical co-ordinate relation), is because we do not sufficiently recognise that prayer is work; it is the most concentrated energy of the will, it is connected with meditation, self-examination, self-conquest; the words we utter must be spirit and life.

Our Lord's advice on prayer sets this clearly before us, for He warns us against hypocrisy and insincerity; He insists on our praying "in secret," realising the presence of God; and He implies the necessity of self-examination, when He connects the pardon of our sins with a merciful and forgiving spirit.

Sincerity in prayer presupposes a great mental and moral activity. It implies that we understand the nature, and feel the need, of the spiritual bless-

ings we ask; and that we are determined to receive
and to cherish them, when sent by God in answer
to our supplication. An earthly parent often waits
to see whether a child's request even for a good
gift be a mere passing fancy, a mere imitation of
what he has noticed somewhere else, or a true and
heartfelt wish. God need not wait until time
reveals the true character of our petitions—past
and future are before Him in an everlasting *now;*
and he recognises immediately whether we "pray
in praying." *

There may be meditation without prayer, but
there can be no prayer without meditation. Communion with God cannot be without communing
with our own heart. He who says, "O my God,"
frequently says also, "O my soul." We look upward and inward; when we pray—heaven is not
merely above us, but within us is the temple of
God.†

---

* James v. 17.

† When Jacob awoke from his dream, he said within himself
(Gen. xxviii. 20-22), that if God would be with him, Jehovah should
be his God; but as he spoke thus within himself before God, his
soliloquy became prayer, and he concluded by saying, "And of all
that *Thou* shalt give me, I will surely give a tenth unto Thee."
Thus he interrupted the prophetic address to his sons by exclaiming, "I have waited for Thy salvation, Jehovah," expressing
before God the thought of his heart, that he expected salvation,
not from anything in his descendants but from God. . . . Prayer
is as manifold as the emotions of the human heart. Thus, in the
19th Psalm, David first sees God's glory in nature, then in the revealed Word, then in his own heart, seeking forgiveness and cleansing, and the whole Psalm he calls, Speech of his heart before God.

In the Lord's Prayer there are six petitions for spiritual blessings; only one refers to our temporal wants. What discipline is constantly needed, if we are to enter sincerely into the spirit of this proportion! By nature our idea is, that God should be our earthly benefactor and protector; but if we pray in the name of Christ, then, being risen with Him, we seek the things which are above. "What seek ye?" is the question Jesus addressed to the disciples whose footsteps He heard behind Him. "What wilt thou, that I do unto thee?" He asked those who appeared before Him as suppliants. To answer this question is work for the heart, conscience, and will.

How definite are our petitions when they refer to some temporal blessings or difficulties. We know what we ask; we understand our position. We have often considered it, and by careful and diligent thought, discovered where the evil lies. We ought to have as distinct knowledge and definite desires in spiritual things. We ought to know as clearly the things which hinder our spiritual prosperity, which undermine our soul's health. Notice the prayers of Paul for the Ephesians; he is able, not merely to assure them in general that he prayed for them, but he had such a definite view of the spiritual blessings he desired for them, that they

---

Heman was all sorrow and anguish when he wrote the 88th Psalm, but he poured out his heart before God, and therefore the cry of anguish is worthy to be part of the Psalter.—*Condensed from* HOFMANN, *Schriftbeweis*, ii. 324.

remained vividly impressed on his conscience. Alas, as Chrysostom said, how can we expect God to remember our petitions when we ourselves forget them! The weakness of memory is the necessary result of the faintness of our desires.

Prayer is work. It is true that work is prayer; for he who prays carries the spirit of prayer into his daily work. He is always a child of God, a soldier of the cross, a stranger and a pilgrim, a servant and follower of Christ. But prayer is work. It is not merely the spontaneous overflowing of the heart—it is spiritual labour. It is not merely the expression, but the discipline of feeling; not merely the offering up of our desires, but also the offering up of our old man for crucifixion. In every true prayer there is death and resurrection.

Prayer calls forth "all that is within us." The heart must be united; all powers of the soul must be brought into harmony, none remain behind, none remain separate, but all with one accord be lifted up to God, and to His heavenly gifts.*

And because of this its solemn character of energy, prayer is continuous. "Praying always with all prayer and supplication in the spirit, and watching there-

---

* "Believe me," said Coleridge to his nephew, two years before his death, "to pray with all your heart and strength, with the reason and the will, to believe vividly that God will listen to your voice through Christ, and verily do the thing He pleaseth thereupon,—this is the last, the greatest achievement of the Christian's warfare upon earth. Teach us to pray, Lord."— Coleridge's *Table Talk*.

unto with all perseverance." Life culminates in prayer. All experiences lead back to it. We watch for the blessings which we ask, and as the work or the trial comes for which we implored wisdom and strength, patience and victory, the heart recurs to its petition, renews it, and receives the answer. Time is thus connected with eternity; it possesses a rhythm which gives us light and courage; we know when "the hour is come," day is linked to day, the alternations of seed-time and harvest, waiting and receiving, silence and testimony, rest and labour, are viewed in their connexion with prayer: "The golden thread of prayer goes through the life of the just, excluding what is evil and false, securing what is pure and good." *

III. The Spirit of Prayer, and stated Times of Prayer.

We have seen that it is the characteristic of the Christian to pray without ceasing. But do we need special times of prayer?

Our spiritual life is so weak, and is beset by so many hindrances, interruptions, and hostile influences, that periods of retirement, for collection of thought and renewed uplifting of the heart to God, are absolutely necessary. There is so much noise and dust on the road on which we journey, that we must seek from time to time, in private prayer, the green pasture and the still waters. And what

---

* Nitzsch.

shall we say of our sins ; of unholy thoughts and
desires ; of unkind and selfish words and deeds, which
need confession and sorrow and the divine pardon ?
Or again, when are we to seek guidance, or to ask for
the spiritual blessings we need, or to implore the
grace of God for our friends and the Church ?

The example of our Saviour places this necessity
in the most striking light.   If even He, whose communion with the Father was perfect and uninterrupted,
whose inner life of prayer knew of no pause, who was
always beholding the countenance of His Father, and
whom nothing ever separated from fellowship with
God,—if even He set apart special times for prayer,—
if He whose whole life was, in the truest sense, a dwelling in the secret place of the Most High, a life of
solitude with God,—if even He went up into a mountain apart, to be alone with God, how much more do
His disciples need frequent seasons of private prayer ?
If we resemble the Lord Jesus in the spirit of constant prayerfulness, shall we not also be like Him in
the habit of special prayer at stated times ?

Let me remind you of the example of the saints of
God, as recorded in Scripture.   We read of David,
" Seven times a day do I praise Thee, because of Thy
righteous judgments;" and of Daniel, "that he kneeled
upon his knees three times a day, and prayed, and
gave thanks before his God."   This had always been
his habit, a habit dear to him as life, for he would
not relinquish it even at the risk of death.   Nathanael
was most probably in prayer under the fig-tree when

our Saviour saw him. Peter had fixed hours for prayer : we read of his going up to the house-top to pray, about the sixth hour.

These examples are very striking, especially when we notice the character and circumstances of the men. Take the case of Daniel. He was a man in a most prominent position, filling a place of the greatest responsibility. In one of the greatest empires which this world has ever seen, he held the chief ministry ; pre-eminent among the presidents who ruled over the hundred and twenty princes who governed that vast monarchy. What a burden must have been upon his mind ! How little leisure could he have enjoyed ! And yet he found time to pray three times a day. He was determined to secure it ; for he knew that prayer is a gain of time, an increase of strength, the safeguard and prosperity of work.

And thus we learn this great lesson, that regular private prayer is compatible with an active and busy life ; that we cannot excuse ourselves by pleading the onerous character of our work, or the incessant claim that our occupations have on our time. The examples of diligence and regularity in prayer are taken from the chambers of the most active men of the world ; who, though not of the world's spirit, yet belonged to the world's sphere and engagements. The men who prayed most have done most work ; they were not slothful in business, because fervent in spirit.

The influence of this habit on the life of Daniel

shows how the Father, which seeth in secret, rewards openly. The king and all the nobles noticed there was an excellent spirit in Daniel. The world may not be able to appreciate orthodoxy of religious opinion, or fervour of religious sentiment; it may not be able to see the height of your lofty doctrine, or the depth of your spiritual affections ; but the world notices the excellent spirit of a man,—his tone, the tenor of his life, his unfeigned humility, his unostentatious love of good works, his kindliness of heart, his integrity, his firmness and consistency : they recognise the man who is actuated by an inward principle and a heavenly influence.

This illustrious man had nothing to facilitate, but everything to obstruct, his spiritual life. In a heathen land, among a court worldly and opposed to the faith of Israel, far from the Temple of Jerusalem, and without the cheering influences of congregational life, he was exposed to temptations of doubt and despondency, in which it was easy to fall into languor and lukewarmness. Many envied him ; not one sympathised with him. And yet they could find no fault in him. No inconsistency in life or temper, no injustice, no harshness, no pride ; his only fault was " concerning the law of his God." He was a worshipper of God, fearing and loving Him. This was the only fault which jealous and watchful enemies could point out. What an illustration of the power of prayer !

Solitude is the appropriate expression of our

mental collectedness, and it is a very important aid to devotion. True, we may, even though alone, be filled with the memories and thoughts of the world; our heart may be a noisy and crowded thoroughfare, where earthly plans and desires pass to and fro, instead of a quiet and calm sanctuary, from which prayer ascends to the Lord. But if we seek to be alone with God, outward solitude, as the Saviour commands, is most helpful. Solitude itself is dangerous, and often leads to sin; but solitude with God is salutary. The Pharisees said their private prayers in public; the Christian's great aim is to be in secret, even when he prays in the congregation; he seeks loneliness with God.

Morning and evening are the most natural seasons of prayer. Each day we rise, let us bless God. As every morning is a renewal of our natural life, let it be also a renewal of our true life, which is hid with Christ in God. Jesus speaks of our taking up our cross daily; does not this imply a daily dedication of ourselves unto God?* It is good to see the face of God ere we see the face of man, and to breathe the atmosphere of eternity, before we commence our earthly and transitory occupations. It is good to commend ourselves to that love and care which condescends to our smallest troubles and duties, and to be reminded that we are called to eternal blessedness, and to glorify God in our daily

---

* " Room to deny ourselves, a road
   To bring us, daily, nearer God."

work. He who has sought divine light and peace is prepared for the day's work and trial; he is not afraid of evil tidings; while he remembers that we know not what a day may bring forth, he is assured that all things work together for good unto them that love God. And some divine promise, some spiritual truth, having been most probably impressed on his mind during prayer and the reading of Scripture, his soul has a nourishment " that the world knows not of."

Evening prayer has a retrospective character. It is a time of looking back on the past day; of confessing sin and praying for forgiveness; of giving thanks for blessings received, for work done by God's aid, of collecting and fixing our heart, which may have been scattered during the day; and of committing ourselves, in childlike faith, and with perfect peace, into the hands of our heavenly Father; thus learning—

> " To dread
> The grave as little as our bed."

The morning and evening sacrifices, which were offered in the temple by the priest in the name of Israel, are fulfilled now in the intercession of our Saviour at the right hand of God; and it is a blessed thought that, while Christ is praying for us from morn to eve, and from eve to morn, we unite more especially our supplication and worship with His at the beginning and conclusion of the day.

And need I say that we ought to remember our

morning prayer, expecting and ready to recognise God's gracious answer during the day; and that between the morning and evening prayer there will thus be a bridge of frequent though brief mental prayer and thanksgiving?

Life does not always run on smoothly; its course is not uniform. Sometimes we are elated by success, sometimes depressed and desponding; seasons of affliction and conflict alternate with times of peace and mirthfulness. There are dark days of storm, and bright days of sunshine. As James expresses it, at times we are afflicted, at times merry. Now, prayer ought never to be interrupted by these seasons of excitement, whether it be the excitement of grief or joy. Is any man afflicted, let him pray. Is any merry, let him sing psalms. *All our emotions are to issue in worship,* and for a threefold reason. For this very purpose are they sent us, to rouse us to more fervent praise and more earnest supplication. In these special seasons God is very near us, and His purpose is to intensify our gratitude and love, to increase our faith and courage, to test and purify our submission and hope. The second reason is, because in all these emotions and excitements there is a danger of error and of sin, there is a disturbance of our spiritual health; prayer is the only safeguard and remedy. Mirth, which is not moderated and hallowed by praise, will soon deprive us of that true joy which alone is secure; sorrow, which is not relieved by humble and submissive prayer for consolation and help, will soon embitter or overwhelm the soul. And thirdly, all these experiences, whether joyous or grievous, are sent that *afterwards* they may yield peaceable fruits of righteousness; and this important purpose, which contains germs for eternity, is only fulfilled in them that are "exercised" by these dealings of God, or, in other words, that seek the divine influence and training by prayer.

We are to pray always; and it may be helpful and salutary for us to view prayer not exclusively as a privilege, but also as a duty. He who prays merely from a sense of duty cannot have tasted yet that the Lord is gracious. Yet it is good to bear in mind that when we neglect prayer, we not merely forego a privilege, but neglect a duty and commit sin. How strange is it that we avail ourselves so rarely of the inestimable right of drawing near unto the Most High! This convinces us more than anything else of the worldliness and hardness of our hearts. But God in His Word demands that we should take, as it were, also a lower and sterner view of the neglect of prayer; for He rebukes His people severely for not seeking Him diligently, and calling upon Him in earnest and persevering prayer. He who gives up regularity in prayer deprives himself of the emblem and safeguard of submission and obedience to God. The bowing of the knee before the God and Father of our Lord Jesus Christ is both the symbol and nourishment of the spirit of filial obedience, of the surrender of our will and the

dedication of our energies to God. We should therefore view prayer not merely as an enjoyment, but as
a sacrifice in which we present ourselves to God,—
" a sacrifice living, holy, acceptable unto Him, which
is our reasonable service " (Rom. xii.)

IV. Difficulties and varied Experiences in
Prayer.

The deeper our view of prayer is, the more are we
often oppressed with difficulties in prayer. Sometimes the Christian feels as if, instead of gaining
greater facility and strength in prayer, he finds
the road of prayer more steep and arduous as he
progresses. He also imagines that he is singular in
this experience ; and hearing much about the joy
and fervour of Christians in prayer, he begins to
despond or to grow apathetic. Let us remember
that the apostle Paul includes *himself* when he
speaks of " our infirmities " in connexion with this
very subject.* And let us seek aid, as he directs us.
We may be so disheartened and alarmed at our
irreverence and coldness, at our wandering thoughts
and languid desires, that we almost give up prayer
in despair. How can we approach the great and
holy God, when we feel so little love, and when we
realise so little the presence in which we profess to
have come ; when we have so little interest in the
things which are for God's glory and our holiness ;
when we cannot keep our thoughts from running

---

* Rom. viii. 26.

to and fro, even to things vain and sinful? We are shocked at our irreverence, at our weakness of faith, at our worldliness, at our insincerity.

If we feel this, let us descend still lower, and humble ourselves still further. Let us kneel down to prayer *as to a work far above us;* let us then throw ourselves entirely on the intercession of Jesus Christ and on the help of the Spirit. Let us commit our imperfect, sinful, defiled prayers to Christ, that He may present them to the Father, pure, perfect, and prevailing; let us wait on the aid of the patient and gentle Spirit, to breathe in us holy desires and good petitions. The less pleased we are with our prayers, the more truly do we pray; God hears for Christ's sake, and the Spirit maketh intercession for us when we are sincerely conscious of our need of His aid.

The feeling ot our wretched imperfection in prayer has induced some to stop short of going to God himself. They think about prayer; they feel they ought to pray; they meditate and consider also what are desirable blessings; they read about God's grace; they hear others pray—but they do not pray to God! Such is the state of some among us; under different training they would seek the intercession of Mary and the angels and saints. You discern the vast distance between God and you, but you dare not stop at any resting-place by the way. Great is the height where God is enthroned, but there is no intermediate station where you can find refuge. Rejoice, then, to know that

Christ Jesus, man and God, is the Mediator ; that
He has consecrated, by His death, a new and living way to the Father, which sinners may use in
humble peace and sure hope ; and that while on
account of His perfect sacrifice He has entered the
Holy of Holies, He is there the great High Priest,
presenting us and our petitions to the Father.
Relying on His intercession, pray to the Father.
Come as you are; say what you feel; ask what you
need.

And be not unduly discouraged by your difficulties
in fixing your attention, in excluding inappropriate
thoughts; unduly, in the sense of being alarmed and
desponding.   Do not be tempted to attribute the
inequality of your feeling to the supposed arbitrary
coming and going of the Spirit of God ; rather rest
in the assurance that, grievous as your apathy,
waywardness, and fitfulness are to the Holy Ghost,
He yet, in divine and perfect love, abides with you,
indefatigable in His gracious aid ; supplying you
continually with renewed life, instead of quenching
the smoking flax.   Thus believing in a faithful
Saviour above, who presents your person and
prayers without guilt and blemish, and in a faithful
and indwelling Spirit within you, who perseveres
with you through all failures and provocations,
continue in prayer ; though your soul cleaveth to the
dust, go on diligently and earnestly seeking and
asking His light.

There are times when prayer is easy—when the

heart is full, when God's Spirit is drawing us with
special power and sweetness.   Sometimes in the
depth of repentance and humiliation.   Then, as in the
51st Psalm, there is confession of sin, accompanied
by an intense faith in the mercy of God.   Or in the
loneliness of the soul, longing and thirsting after
God; as in the 41st Psalm, when, as the hart panteth
after the water-brooks, David's soul cried after God,
and in hope anticipated the coming joy in the presence
of his Lord.   Sometimes on some sunny height of
prosperity, when the soul sings, and all within us
makes melody unto our God.   Even in our Saviour's
life, there were such special concentrations of spiritual
feeling and prayer.   He rejoiced in the Spirit and
prayed.   At such times God allows us to gain some
deep insight into His Word, to gain some higher
position whence our view is enlarged and brighter.
God may do this after we have been faithful in
some self-denial and temptation ; or before some
difficult trial or work ; or it may be, that when
we have been cold, and his Fatherly love sees
this as the best method to restore us to a more fervent life ; sometimes it happens in our ordinary
reading, meditation, or partaking of the Lord's
Supper.   After long and perplexing difficulties, God
sends such elevating and consoling experiences ; as
we see in the 73d Psalm, when Asaph at last was
able to say, Yet God is good to Israel !   Such special
seasons are to be received not merely with gratitude,
but with great caution, as a treasure intrusted to us,

not so much for present enjoyment, but to be laid out on usury, as new strength and light bestowed to fit us for greater and more devoted service to God in our daily life. The experience of such moments is of importance for subsequent years; it begins a new era in our history.

Let us also remember that sometimes we are near God and offering true spiritual prayer, although depressed by a sense of languor and conviction of our unworthiness and deadness. Likewise may there be excitement of feeling, warmth of emotion, rapture and a vivid glow of imagination, exuberant expression and joy—and yet the grace of God, the influence of the Holy Ghost, may be altogether wanting. Beware of such prayers, false prophets, which come to you in sheep's clothing, but inwardly they are ravening wolves,—wherefore by their fruit ye shall know them. If this very enlargement in prayer leaves you more humble and lowly, more meek and forgiving, stronger for God's work, more patient in tribulation, and more loving to the brethren, then was it a visitor from the heavenly sanctuary.

But let us not, waiting for such seasons of refreshment, suspend the habit of regular prayer and meditation. The apostolic Christians continued steadfast in prayer, as well as in doctrine and fellowship and in breaking of bread. Every habit is in danger of degenerating into routine—we must therefore watch; but when we give up a good habit, we have ceased watching, and yielded to the enemy of our souls. Continue in prayer with thanksgiving.   The Spirit of Christ is in you as a well of water.   Blessed symbol of His indwelling—"the most refreshing thing in nature, a perennial thing; not stagnant, yet not boisterous; transparent and spontaneous; springing up in the morning and at noon, and at eventide and in the night watches.*

---

* Phelps, "Man's Renewal," p. 207.

2

THE MODEL PRAYER

"After this manner therefore pray ye." — *Matt. 6:9.*

THE model prayer which the Lord Jesus gave to His disciples has been a precious and most cherished treasure of the Church up to this hour.* Since those gracious words—words of infinite wisdom and infinite love—flowed from the lips of the Son of man, the saints of every age and every language have used them, and found in them the perfect expression of their deepest feelings and truest need, as well as the high ideal and standard of spiritual life, which on this

---

* Although we have no direct evidence that the Lord's Prayer was used in the apostolic Church, we can scarcely doubt it. Bengel has pointed out the very striking parallelism between the Lord's Prayer, especially in its first petitions, and the first Epistle of Peter. (Gnomon,1 Peter i.) According to the testimony of Tertullian and Cyprian, it was the usual prayer of the congregation. The former calls it the prayer taught by God, upon which all other prayers are to be founded, and by which they are to be sealed, the sum of the gospel and compendium of Christ's discourses. Augustine states that at baptism the Catechumens were taught this prayer: "Receive now this precious jewel and keep it; receive the prayer which God himself has taught us to bring before God." Of the Reformers, perhaps none had so deep an insight into this prayer, and such profound affection for it, as Luther, who constantly alludes to it, and always with peculiar warmth and enthusiasm.

1. Bengel's New Testament Commentary, Kregel Publ. p. 725

side of the grave remains ever above our actual attainment. In uttering these petitions, we realise our communion with all saints, whether they have entered into their rest or are still sojourning on earth. We are strengthened and elevated by the thought that we are members of an innumerable and glorious company, part of which has already obtained the victory ; we are comforted and tranquillised by the remembrance that God has been the dwelling-place of His people in all generations,—that the same sorrows and difficulties, the same petitions and thanksgivings as ours, were brought before the throne of grace.

It is a model prayer, and as such commends itself to the most superficial glance,—approves itself at once to the conscience of man.* It is beautiful and symmetrical, like the most finished work of art. The words are plain and unadorned, yet majestic ; and so transparent and appropriate that, once fixed in the memory, no other expressions ever mix themselves up with

---

* From personal experience I know how the Lord's Prayer commends itself to the mind and conscience of a devout Israelite. The following anecdote, mentioned by Arndt ("Vater unser," p. 166.) still further illustrates this point : " A traveller in the East '(Hay) was pitching his tent near an Arab village, when he was surrounded by an excited crowd, who cursed him as an atheist. He addressed a venerable man, whom he supposed to be a priest. How can you say that we do not believe in God ? Listen to my daily prayer, and then judge. He repeated the Lord's Prayer. The people listened with amazement. At length the priest exclaimed, 'Never will I speak against the followers of such a faith ; your prayer shall be mine till my hour of departure comes. Repeat it, I beg of you, O Nazarene, that we may learn it and write it in golden letters.'"

them; the thought of substituting other words never enters the mind. Grave and solemn are the petitions, yet the serenity and tranquil confidence, the peace and joy which they breathe, prove attractive to every heart. The prayer is short, that it may be quickly learned, easily remembered, and frequently used; but it contains all things pertaining to life and godliness; in its simplicity it seems adapted purposely for the weakness of the inexperienced and ignorant—and yet none can say that he is familiar with the heights and depths which it reveals, and with the treasures of wisdom it contains. It is calm, and suited to the even tenor of our daily life,—and yet in times of trouble and conflict the Church has felt its value and power more especially, has discovered in it anew that it anticipates every difficulty and danger,—that it solves every problem, and comforts the disciples of Christ in every tribulation of the world.* It is the beloved and revered friend of our childhood, and it grows with our growth, a never-failing counsellor and companion amid all the changing scenes of life. And as in our lifetime we must confess ourselves, with Luther, to be only learning the high and deep lessons of those petitions, so it will take eternity to give them their answer.

The disciples who asked Jesus to teach them to pray belonged to Israel, and had been brought up in

---

* As a recent illustration, I noticed that during the Revolution of 1848, Tholuck in Halle, and Maurice in London, preached on the Lord's Prayer with special reference to the times.

an atmosphere of prayer. In the true sense of the word, worship is offered to God only by His people, who know His name and who believe His promises. The need of all God's creatures, uttered or unexpressed, may be viewed as a prayer ascending to His throne, as an appeal to infinite benevolence, wisdom, and power. In this sense Scripture speaks of the young ravens crying unto God, who provideth for them food,* and of the eyes of all creatures waiting upon Him, who openeth His hands and satisfieth the desire of every living thing.† Man, created in God's image, though fallen, feels his dependence on God; where there is conscience, there must be prayer; supplication is as old and wide-spread as our race, and the Psalmist expresses the universality of prayer co-extensive with the frailty and helplessness of man, when he says: " O Thou that hearest prayer, all *flesh* shall come to Thee."‡ Scripture acknowledges frequently and with great tenderness the longings of man after God; it often gives us glimpses into the mysterious region of heathenism, unillumined by direct revelation, assuring us that even there God left Himself not without witness, and that the worship offered to the unknown God in ignorance proceeded from depths which He alone could fathom. §

---

* Job xxxviii. 41.   † Ps. civ   ‡ Psalm lxv.

§ A very interesting analysis of the cultus of the Greeks and Romans, as contrasted with Christian worship, is given by De Quincey (Works, ix. 234). His result is that, strictly speaking, the ancients never prayed ; that their supplications were of the nature of mercantile contracts ; that there was no *doctrinal* part in their

Still nearer the kingdom, and at the very entrance, stand the contrite, convinced of their sin, longing after God's pardon and peace, after the enlightening and renewing grace of the Lord; from whose hearts ascend to God the solemn questions: What shall I do to be saved? Show me Thy way, make known to me Thy salvation!

But we speak of the worship of God by His children, who know, love, and serve Him, who have been brought into fellowship with Him, and are now living the life of faith.

Prayer in Israel possesses the same fundamental characteristics as prayer in the Church of Christ. Scripture abounds in statements concerning this great subject; we have a full insight given us into the spirit of Jewish prayer.

Most significant is the fact, that in the law of Moses we find no direct command, and no specific regulations, concerning prayer. For prayer is not so much a duty as a privilege, and, strictly speaking,

---

religion; and that all their moral theories were utterly disjoined from their ceremonial worship. This is no doubt true; strictly speaking, as Coleridge observes, revealed religion is a tautological expression, religion presupposes the idea of God, and this must be revealed, given from above. Still there are, even in the darkness of heathenism, some faint and touching glimpses of light: "Sometimes the suppliants, to give emphasis to their prayer, mention the relationship in which they stand by their birth and ancestors to the god; and the exiled remind Apollo that he had tasted the sorrows of banishment, that he therefore knows the feelings of the stranger. God did not leave Himself without witness to them."—LÖBER, *Vom Gebet*, 60, 97.

belongs not to the law, but to the gospel.   The law, revealing to us God's righteousness and our sin, declaring to us God's justice and our guilt, and announcing to us the condemnation and curse of a holy and just God, silences man.   It takes from us all hope.   It freezes and paralyses the heart.   Love only can speak;   where fear reigns, the voice of prayer is hushed.   And the law worketh wrath;   it rouses sin instead of banishing it;   it calls forth opposition;   it brings to sin, as Paul says, in bold yet true paradox, new life, new vitality and power — "the law is the strength of sin."   But the promise of the grace of God brings both the light and the life of sunshine.   The soul is quickened and encouraged.   We respond to the joyful sound of salvation.   "When thou saidst, Seek ye my face, my heart said unto thee, Thy face, Lord, will I seek."   The Jews prayed because they knew the gospel. Dimly, perhaps, and in the spirit of servants, kept as children under the schoolmaster, but not the less truly and deeply.   And as the gospel came before the law, and Israelites are not the children of Moses but the children of Abraham, we find from the very commencement of the chosen people prayer as the response of divine promise.

We have the records of many prayers in Scripture. What a treasure do we possess in the prayers of Abraham, the friend of God ; of Jacob, who became Israel ; of Moses, whom the Lord called emphatically "My servant ;" in the thanksgiving of Hannah, whose silent supplication and trembling lips were changed into joyous praise and jubilant song; the soul-communings of David, the man after God's heart, so wonderful in their breadth, the variety of outward and inward condition which occasioned them, and in their depth, the intensity of their feeling; the prayers of Daniel, the man of strong and fervent desires heavenward; and of Jonah, and Isaiah, and Jeremiah; nor ought we to forget, as belonging to Israel, the song of praise uttered by Mary, true daughter of believing Abraham and royal-hearted David; and the praise of Zachariah the Aaronite, who served God in uprightness and humility. What a stream of prayer! flowing through so many centuries, amid scenes so grand and varied, until it reaches at last that blessed Fulfilment, which is also its source—Jesus, at once the answer and the Teacher of all prayer. Considering these prayers, offered as it were during the moon-lit night and the early dawn of morning, by men not favoured as we with the full light of the Incarnation and the accomplished Redemption and the Pentecostal ministrations of the Spirit, we cannot fail to notice, among others, the following peculiarities of Jewish or true prayer:—

First, They were spiritual. Spirituality is not so much an inherent subjective quality; it is the reflection of the object worshipped: as the God, so the worshipper. God is Spirit; God seeketh worshippers in spirit and truth, who adore Him as the Father.

But the most refined and elevated men cannot find
the true God; and what they worship, ethereal and
ideal as it may be, is not spiritual, but carnal. Notice,
then, the spiritual idea Israel had of God. Their
dispensation was an elementary one, and they themselves were carnal, and fell continually into idolatry. The more striking is it, that the idea of God
revealed in their Scriptures, and uninterruptedly maintained by their leading men, is so pure, so exalted,
so perfect. God reveals himself, but they are to
remember that they had seen no shape, no image.
God chooses a place where He is to be worshipped;
but David finds God near him in the wilderness,
Jonah in the belly of the whale, Daniel in Babylon.
God is holy, and yet it is His glory and delight to
fill the whole earth with His majesty and love. His
righteousness and His justice are declared with
special solemnity; but where can we find more
touching and tender assurances of the pity, the
mercy, the compassion, the yearning affection, the
burning love and jealousy of God towards His
people? The greatness of God, His ineffable glory,
His incomprehensible majesty, the pavilion of
darkness round about Him, are here so beautifully
blended with simplicity, condescension, familiarity,
and confidential friendship, that while they adored
with awe, they also loved and trusted Him as if
He were indeed among them, their King and
Friend. Their prayers were spiritual because they
knew God; and they knew God because He had

revealed himself to them : " We know what we worship." *

Notice, secondly, Their reverence. Without love there may be fear, awe, dread ; but there can be no reverence. "There is forgiveness with Thee, that Thou mayest be feared," is the secret of the reverence of the ancient saints. "The Holy One of Israel *and* thy Redeemer." This "and" is full of depth ; it explains why that word holiness is so full of sweetness. Their humility is deep, unfeigned, and therefore constantly manifesting itself. When their petitions seem boldest, and their confidence most childlike, their consciousness of sin and weakness, and of God's greatness and holiness, is evidently most vivid. Man is proud, and the strength of his pride may be measured by this—that no punishment, no failures, no difficulties, not even the torments of hell can humble him. The love of God alone clothes us with humility.

Notice, thirdly, Their faith. They were the children of Abraham, who staggered not at the promise of God through unbelief, but were strong in faith,

---

* " Think of the religions of antiquity. Where do we seek and find the sanctuary of true, deep, manifold, and eloquent prayer ? where the language and grammar, where the scale of all notes of supplication, typical for all humanity and all the ages ? Where, except in the assemblies of the worshippers of Jehovah, in the courts of that service which knew no image of the unseen, in that temple whose God, in His sublime spiritual presence and reality, transcends all human thought, who for centuries since, and through all coming ages, fills and guides the heart of all believers."—*Nitzsch Predigten.* vi. 31.

giving glory to God, fully persuaded that what He had promised He was able also to perform. They appealed to God's word and promise ; to that which underlies the divine word and promise—God's character. With the confidence of a child, of a loyal friend, of a like-minded, sympathising friend, they uttered their petitions.

And let us remember, fourthly, Their unselfishness in prayer. They were men who sought God's glory, whose deepest affections and most constant thought was God's honour; for Thy name's sake was their constant plea, the manifestation of God's glory was their profoundest desire.

Such prayer was in Israel ; such was the spirit which God had given unto His servants of old ; such the exalted and blessed influence of His presence, of His revelation, of His dealings with his chosen people. For the hypocritical, self-righteous, narrow, and carnal prayer which characterised the Pharisees was an apostacy, not merely from God, but from the true nation, the kernel, the Israelites indeed. Rather must we study the spirit of the blessed Virgin, of Zachariah, of aged Simeon, if we would know what Jewish prayer was ; and John the Baptist, who summed up Moses and the Prophets, who preached the law primarily, but with direct reference to the gospel, pointing to the Lamb of God, taught his disciples to pray according to the Divine mind, no doubt showing them that the repentance and renewal which he demanded was the gift of God and the baptism of the Spirit, and that they should ask of Him the fulfilment of His great promise, the manifestation of His Christ.

Thus in an atmosphere of prayer was the request made of the Lord Jesus by His disciples—Teach us to pray, as John also taught his disciples.

None can teach us to pray like Jesus.

To be a perfect teacher of prayer two conditions require to be fulfilled : a perfect knowledge of God's character and purpose, and a perfect knowledge of man's condition and wants. Jesus alone possesses this knowledge, and therefore He alone is the true Mediator. Who knows God the Father but the only-begotten Son, the true and faithful Witness, who is himself the brightness of His glory, the revelation of His name and will ?—He who was with the Father from all eternity, reveals unto us God, and, possessing the full and perfect knowledge of the Father's will and character, is able to teach us what petitions are according to God's will and to God's glory.

In like manner Jesus only knows us. To know man, every man, all that is in man, is only possible to One who is perfect man. He must be the true representative of man, the exponent of humanity, the embodiment of the divine idea of man. None but Jesus can justly call himself the Son of man. Of none else can we say what we say of Him—"The Man Christ Jesus." Separate He was from sinners, and yet for that very reason His knowledge of our state, our heart, our wants, our difficulties, our sorrows, our temptations, our destiny, is perfect. And as His knowledge is perfect, His sympathy is perfect, His love infinite, His tenderness unspeakable. For He *suffered* in taking our position, in visiting our prison-chamber, in coming into our hospital, in entering in our stead into our darkness and death.

What a wonderful Teacher of prayer ! He is God —and hence we can have no doubt that the petitions He teaches are acceptable unto God, in accordance with His holy and loving nature, and with His gracious and world-wide purposes. He is man—and He knows our need better than we ourselves.

And remember this Mediator is given us of the Father. How willing is God to hear us when He sends His own Son to teach us the petitions we are to offer ! and how full may be our assurance that God will answer when Jesus is our Advocate, who presents our petitions as His own desire for us, as the very prayer which He has instructed us by His word, and empowered us by His own Spirit, to offer ! And this leads me to notice some misconceptions of the true significance and value of this prayer as a model.

On two occasions, separated by an interval of years, the Lord gave His model of prayer, not without slight verbal variations, but the sàme in substance, in sequence of petitions ; a circumstance which shows, if additional proof were needed, that this prayer is so perfect and so truly expressive of the inmost mind of the Saviour, that it possesses an eternal character all-comprehensive and exhaustive.

Jesus often spake to His disciples about the manner of prayer; but here He teaches us, not how, but *what* to pray. And this is very important. Our ignorance of God, and our alienation from Him, are so great, that we not merely do not know *how* to approach the throne of God, but that we even are ignorant as to what petitions are according to God's mind, as well as necessary and salutary for us. It requires no great humility to acknowledge our ignorance and infirmity, as to the manner of prayer. " Be not rash with thy mouth, and let not thine heart be hasty to utter anything before God; for God is in heaven, and thou upon earth; therefore let thy words be few. " * But that we do not know what to ask, shows a far greater mental and moral weakness than we are ready to admit. So great is the difference between the region of earthly wisdom and heavenly. We know how to give good gifts to our children; but we require divine teaching to enable us to ask the Holy Spirit of our Father in heaven. The Saviour supplies this want by putting petitions in our mouth. It is in similar condescension and adaptation that the Lord says, in the prophet Hosea, " Take with you words, and turn to the Lord, and say unto him, Take away all iniquity, and receive us graciously."

Is a form of prayer in harmony with the free and spiritual character of New Testament worship? Even in the more elementary dispensation of the

* Eccles. v. 2.

law, there was no form of prayer given. The high priest confessed the sins of the people in such words as he felt most appropriate. It is worthy of notice that, even among the Jews, before the Spirit was given as an indwelling Comforter, under an economy of literal and minute regulations, prayer, private and public, was left free. The only form of prayer given for perpetual use is the one in Deut. xxvi. 5–15, connected with the offering of tithes and first-fruits, and containing in simple words the important elements of prayer, acknowledgment of God's mercy, self-dedication, and petition for future blessing.* To this may be added the benediction which Aaron and his successors were to pronounce. Nor does this strictly come under the category of prayer, rather was it the objective announcement of the covenant-blessing of the Triune God. We have therefore every reason to value our freedom from prescribed forms of prayer, and to abide in fellowship with the Church of the first centuries, in whose assemblies the presiding minister prayed in the name of the congregation as the Spirit of God enabled him.

But when the Lord Jesus says, " After this manner pray ye," He evidently refers to the spirit, the scope, the contents, the order of the petitions. This is to be our model.

Yet surely we are at liberty to use the very words; nay, it would be unwise and ungrateful not to use

---

* Smith's Bible Dict., Prayer.

words so perfect and beautiful, consecrated by the lips into which grace was poured, and endeared by the experience of thousands and tens of thousands who are now in the presence of Jesus.

Some have felt difficulty in using this prayer, because they did not recognise its evangelical character. They think it was not intended for the Church of Christ. They point out that the name of Jesus does not occur in it, and that there is no special reference to the Atonement. We must consider these difficulties, because the solution lies simply in a truer understanding of the words of Christ, and of prayer in general.

The Lord's Prayer is a prayer for Christ's people; it is prayer in Christ's name.

True, His name is not mentioned; nor the atonement of His death, and His intercession as the great High Priest. In all Christ's teaching (with the exception of His last words to the disciples) there was this necessary reticence. We might as well say, the parable of the prodigal is not a gospel parable, because the mediation of the Saviour is not directly mentioned, though, as has been quaintly said, the father's kiss is the symbolic representation of the mystery of God manifest in the flesh; the best robe, the ring, the shoes, and the fatted calf, are, in like manner, emblems of the gospel gifts, righteousness, adoption, obedience, and spiritual joy in fellowship with God. All the prayers of the Jewish saints were gospel-prayers. " For Thy name's sake " means Christ. They all prayed relying on the covenant grace of that Jehovah whose full manifestation is in the Lord Jesus. Hence, we may say the real and full meaning of the Lord's Prayer was only disclosed after Pentecost; it remained in the disciples as seed dormant until the Spirit descended.*

But, besides, if you will receive it, this prayer is the *only* prayer which is perfectly in Christ's name. The simplest, and at the same time the highest, exposition of prayer in Christ's name is surely this: Prayer, offered not merely in reliance on Christ's mediation, but prayer such as Christ directs and authorises us to offer. I ask petitions in Christ's name when I can say of them: These blessings Christ wishes me to obtain; they are not merely my desires, but His desires for me. I claim them from the Father, as Christ's representative, as sent by Him. Hitherto, says the Lord to His disciples, ye have asked *nothing* in my name, that is, you have not offered what are *my* petitions.

---

* "It cannot be deemed strange that Jesus does not represent the forgiveness of sin in the fifth petition, and the deliverance from the devil in the seventh, as effected through His mediation (through the Hilasterion of Christ, and relatively through the gracious influences of the Spirit), since the knowledge of His mediation and faith in it had to be left to the *future* development of the disciples. Afterwards (after Pentecost) this mediation was necessarily understood as implied, without being expressed. . . . In like manner it was reserved also to the future, to use the words of the invocation ' Our Father' in the specific Christian manner; and accordingly the Lord depended, in the whole of this prayer, on the approaching baptism of the Spirit (John xiv. 26), by which they were to be enabled to pray *in His name* (John xiv. 13, 15, 16 ; xvi. 2)."— *Meyer Commentar*, i. 186.

And in this sense (the only one in which praying in Christ's name, praying according to God's will, and praying in the Holy Ghost are seen to be essentially and inseparably connected)* the Lord's Prayer is the true prayer in Christ's name; here are the petitions which He desires us to offer and the Father to grant; and hence, instead of saying the Lord's Prayer is not in Christ's name, it would be more correct to say that no prayer is in Christ's name except that which harmonises with this model prayer.

But do you not see Jesus in every word of the Lord's prayer? This prayer has well been designated as the condensed substance of all previous prayers. Here all the desires, petitions, hopes, of God's servants are summed up; all the strings of David's harp, all aspirations of patriarchs and prophets, are blended in perfect harmony. And if the Lord's Prayer were only this, would it not necessarily be full of Christ? How full of Christ are the Psalms! But here is more than the Psalms. Here is the Son of God, there only longed for, and seen from a distance,—Jesus, the great Immanuel, the mouth of God speaking, the very heart of the Father revealing to us the fulness of divine love.

"Our Father which art in heaven." The very invocation is Pentecostal. It is based on the cross, and it breathes the air of the resurrection-morn. "I ascend to my God and to your God, to my Father

---

* Comp. remarks on " Amen."

and to your Father," "the God and Father of our Lord Jesus Christ." "He is not ashamed to call us brethren. Ye have received the Spirit of adoption, crying, Abba."

"Hallowed be Thy name." Jesus is the messenger in whom is God's name. He that hath seen Him hath seen the Father. And the name of Jesus is the name above every name given unto the Son, as our Redeemer, who was obedient unto death, even the death of the cross.

"Thy kingdom come." Is not Jesus the King, the Son of man, who shall come with the clouds of heaven, and to whom shall be given dominion and glory, and a kingdom, that all people, nations, and languages shall serve Him?

"Thy will be done on earth as it is in heaven." Christ is the only one who fulfilled God's will, and through whom this petition will find its realisation. We are sanctified by that will according to which Christ offered Himself.

"Give us this day our daily bread." "I am the Living Bread, which came down from heaven." The bounty and forbearance of God are for the sake of Christ and His salvation.

"Forgive us our debts.". Here we behold the sufferings and the death of Christ. If any man sin we have an advocate with the Father.

"Lead us not into temptation." This is the petition taught and offered by the High Priest, who was tempted in all things as we are, yet without sin; whose sympathy is perfect, and whose prayer for us, when Satan desires to have us, that he may sift us as wheat, is that our faith fail not.

" Deliver us from evil." Here is the great Conqueror, who bruised the serpent's head, and shall yet bruise Satan under our feet.

" For thine is the kingdom, and the power, and the glory for ever." " And the seventh angel sounded, and there were great voices in heaven, saying, The kingdoms of the world are become the kingdoms of our Lord and of His Christ, and He shall reign for ever and ever.

" Amen." The very name by which the Saviour calls himself: " These things saith the Amen, the faithful and true Witness, the Beginning of the creation of God."

Think of the prayer again, and behold Christ throughout. In the invocation, Christ the Son, the only-begotten of the Father, and yet the first-born of many brethren; the exalted Saviour at the right hand of God in heaven. In the first petition Jesus, the name of God, the Revelation of the Father. In the second, Jesus the King—once crucified, but coming again in glory. In the third petition see Jesus in Gethsemane, the perfect embodiment of obedience; see Jesus ruling in the hearts of His people by His Spirit. In the fourth, regard Jesus, both the manna, and the channel of " all things " good and needful to the Father's children.. In the fifth, see Calvary. In the sixth, see the High Priest interceding, the Shepherd guiding and restoring. In the seventh, see the Saviour welcoming all who have overcome to sit down with Him on His throne.

Well has one of the Church Fathers called the Lord's Prayer the gospel abbreviated. It is, indeed, the epitome of the evangel. The more fully we enter into the liberty and the comprehensive character of the gospel, the better shall we understand, and the more heartily shall we love, this perfect prayer.

Let us consider now the *structure* of the prayer.

God's works in nature and revelation are perfect; there is nothing superfluous or defective. All is arranged in wisdom and beauty. There is a divine order and symmetry. In trying to discover this order, we must avoid two errors. The one is, an arbitrary and fanciful method, introducing divisions of our own. Good and wise men, fervent in feeling, and of an imaginative and spiritual mind, have erred in this way; and their very reverence for Scripture has betrayed them into what is surely irreverent, forcing the meaning of divine and infallible words. On the other hand, and this is perhaps the danger to which we are more liable at present, there is the tendency to forget the perfection of God's Word, even in its arrangement, structure, and detail. We can never overestimate the fulness, the manifoldness of Scripture. We, and all generations before and after us, can never see all that is in

Scripture. "Every word of His is full of instruction, looking many ways." Hence even the number of petitions and their sequence must not be regarded as accidental.

The Lord's Prayer evidently consists of two parts. In the first, we are struck with the threefold occurrence of the word *Thy:* Thy name, Thy kingdom, Thy will. In the second, the pronouns which occur are *our* and *us.* In the first we have three petitions referring to divine things—God's name, kingdom, will; in the second, we have four petitions referring to human things—bread, sin, temptation, evil. In the first three petitions there is no conjunction used—co-ordinate, equal are the three blessings. In the four petitions of the second division, one follows the other, joined by conjunction—*and* forgive us, *and* lead us not, *but* deliver us. And lastly, the first and the second divisions have a parallelism. There is a comparison in each. In the third petition, we ask God's will to be done on earth *as* in heaven; and in the fifth, we ask God to forgive (in heaven) *as* we forgive them that trespass against us.

These peculiarities may be observed even by a cursory glance at the external structure of the prayer.

Let us learn some lessons from these facts. All Christians have noticed that the Lord's Prayer consists of two parts. We first ask God to enrich us with His blessings; we then ask Him to come down to our earthly condition, and take from us our need.

We first ascend to God, and in Him we find all good, and nothing but good; we then ask Him to visit us, and with us He finds nothing but want and evil. So far the prayer corresponds exactly to the divinely-taught petitions in Hosea,—" Take away all iniquity, and give good,"—only that the order in the Lord's Prayer is the true and perfect one ; the high order to which God's forgiven and renewed children are raised by the Spirit.

Now, what are the blessings God gives ? God gives Himself. The gift of the covenant is—" I will be their God." There is no other God but God the Father, Son, and Holy Ghost ; no other God of salvation, no other living and loving God for the children of men. God above us—the Lord himself revealed to us by His name ; God with us—the kingdom which He sends us, righteousness, peace, and joy in the Holy Ghost ; God in us—the indwelling of the Father and the Son by the Spirit. God's name— that is, God the Father, revealed in Christ ; God's kingdom—that is, the grace and salvation of God by His Son ; the will of God—that is, the indwelling of Father and Son by the Spirit. In each petition we ask to be blessed with God himself. In each petition we therefore see the Trinity, while one person of the Trinity is more prominently brought forward. The name is the Son revealing the *Father ;* the kingdom is the Father beheld and loved in the *Son ;* the will renewed is the *Holy Ghost* fulfilling in us what the Father ordains and Christ mediates. In

these three petitions there is no sequence—they
are coequal, co-ordinate—hence there is no conjunction.*

In the second division we find man's wants. He
wants bread, he is a dependent and needy creature,
whose life is not in himself; and, as he needs daily
bread, he needs daily forgiveness. And even with
his wants supplied and sins pardoned, he is in a dangerous and difficult path, and needs guidance, and
in this guidance deliverance from evil around and
within. Bread, pardon, guidance, deliverance, are
what *he* needs, whose only property is want, and sin,
and danger, and misery. First we ascend to heaven
—God gives us all, even Himself, the Triune God;
then we descend to earth—God supplies all our wants,
and takes from us our evil.

This consideration will prepare us to understand
the meaning of the numbers. There are seven petitions, of which the first three refer to God, and the
last four to man. Of symbolical numbers in Scripture, there are none whose meaning is so certain and
obvious as the numbers three, four, and seven.
Three is the number of God, as in the threefold
blessing which the high priest pronounced, the threefold "holy" in the song of the seraphim, and in
various passages. The mystery, most clearly expressed in the institution of baptism and throughout

---

* Only try and pray, Hallowed be Thy name, *and* Thy kingdom
come, *and* Thy will be done on earth; you would at once perceive
that it is not correct.

the epistles is contained in germ in all the manifestations of God unto His people.

The number four is evidently the number of the
world, of the manifold mundane relationships of
creation in its fulness and variety. This symbolism
finds its expression in nature—the four directions in
space, the four corners of the earth, the four winds,
from which all the elect shall be gathered. It is to
be noticed in the Tabernacle, the measures, curtains,
colours, and ingredients, where it denotes regularity
and completeness. With this corresponds the facts
that we have a fourfold account of the life of Christ,
and that the creaturely life and perfection is represented by the four living Beings.*

Seven is the number symbolising God manifesting
Himself in the world. From the very first chapter
of Genesis to the closing Book of the inspired record,
this number is invested with a special dignity and
solemnity. The seventh day is not merely the day
of rest, but the day on which are *completed and perfected the works of God.*† Seven is the number of
clean animals which Noah was commanded to bring
into the Ark. Seven branches had the golden candle-
stick in the holy place of the Tabernacle; seven
days lasted the great festivals in Israel; on seven
pillars was built the House of Wisdom; walking
amid seven golden candlesticks Jesus is represented
in the Apocalypse; seven spirits are before the throne;

---

* Comp. Herzog. Encypl. Zahl., Bâhr's Symbolik, i.
† Gen. ii. 2.

seven words the Saviour uttered from the cross ; seven petitions He gives to His people.

The very structure of the Lord's Prayer is full of instruction and encouragement. The number seven teaches us, that God is in the midst of us. The work of the Lord is perfect, His gifts are all-comprehensive. The number three, in its preceding the four earthly petitions, shows that we must begin with God, who, in the infinite plenitude of His covenant-salvation, is our portion ; while the number four points out that God will supply all our earthly needs.

Of equal importance is the invocation—" Our Father which art in heaven." It is both entrance and basis, commencement and compendium. Our union with Christ, and the election, love, and power of the Father, are here opened to us ; the key-note is here struck, filial, brotherly, heavenly. It is sustained in every petition, both by the promise of God, and the praying heart. The conclusion returns to the eternal, unchanging, and peaceful Origin and End— the glory of God and the Amen, the seal of God, in which all promises are secured, even his Son Jesus Christ.

What encouragement does this prayer give us! It presupposes nothing in us, but that we are poor in spirit ; it takes us at once away from earth and man, from our own exertions, and from legal demands, to the fulness of the blessing of the gospel in Christ. It gives us all good, and takes from us our evil. Thus would Jesus have you pray—thus does

Jesus himself pray for you ; for this purpose has the
Father given us Jesus, His own Son.

Nor let us forget the two pillars on which the
two great divisions of the prayer rest. Earth is to
be like heaven, heaven is to descend to earth. But
how ? We know the time is coming when God's will
shall be done on earth, when the nations shall walk
in righteousness and rejoice in peace. But what is
the method by which this harmony is finally to be
realised, and by which God's children are to anticipate it now ? It is by our living in the atmosphere of
mercy. In no other way can we bring down heaven
to earth, but by forgiving as God for Christ's sake forgives us ; and, therefore, we promise (the only vow in
this prayer) to put on, as the elect of God, bowels of
mercy, compassion, gentleness, forgiving and forbearing one another. When the love of Christ constrains
us, when we are conformed to the image of the Son
of man, who came not to judge but to save, whose
delight was in forgiving and healing, it is then that
we reproduce on earth that Apostolic Church which
was, like the Garden of Eden, a prophecy and pledge
of the coming glory. Let us think of these golden
chains of love and mercy, by which, after the separation of sin, the redeeming God has re-connected
heaven and earth.

I conclude with a remarkable saying of a cabalistic
work, which contains a most beautiful, though unin-
tentional, summary of the Lord's Prayer.

" When the Schechina—that is the glory of the

Lord—is in His Temple, all the Prophets ascend to Him, knock at the door, and say: Lord, open Thou my lips! (Ps. li. 17). The first three petitions which they then offer are in reference to the soul, that through them they may be brought to the Origin of all things, for in this consists the life of the soul. The middle petition refers to the supply of our bodily wants. The last three obtain from the King the turning of evil unto good. And before all these petitions there is a Hand which writes, and after all these petitions is a Hand which seals."*

May the Lord Jesus Christ, by His Holy Spirit, teach us to pray "after this manner." AMEN.

---

* Sohar, quoted by Schöttgen.

3

THE DOCTRINE OF THE INVOCATION

"Our Father which art in heaven."

OUR experience in prayer is somewhat similar to that of the man sick of the palsy. He and his friends believed in the power and goodness of the Lord Jesus. Their great difficulty was how to gain access to Him and reach His presence. But when this difficulty was overcome by the energy of their faith, all was easy. Their petition did not even need utterance ; Christ, with the quickness of infinite love, saw immediately their desire and faith, and granted them His merciful help.

Thus we sometimes feel our great difficulty is to enter the Divine presence, to force our way through the crowd of distracting thoughts, worldly cares, sinful desires, and to realise that God is, and that He is the rewarder of them that diligently seek Him ; to fill our mind and heart with the thought, we are before " our Father, which is in heaven."

Without faith we cannot come to God. We must know the character of Him whom we approach, and the relation in which we stand to Him. And for this reason the Saviour has taught us the invocation, " Our Father which art in heaven." These words are simple, yet all our lifetime we are but spelling them, and eternity alone can unfold all their meaning. More striking even than their simplicity is their sweetness. Let this first impression remain the deepest and the most prominent. God wishes to fill our hearts with childlike confidence and love, that we may approach Him, to use Luther's expression, as dear children go to their dear father.

The words are very comprehensive. Their height is that they mount to the very throne of God, high above all heavens, where Christ, His blessed Son, has gone. Their breadth—they comprehend the whole family of God. Their depth—that they enter into the very deep things of God, the eternal love of the Father to His Son, and to believers in Him. Their length—that they embrace all petitions; for if God is our Father in heaven, we hallow His name, we have entered His kingdom, we submit to His will, and all needful earthly gifts will be bestowed by paternal goodness and mercy. The night before his death, Dr Chalmers was walking in his garden, and was overheard by one of his family, in low but very earnest tones, saying, " O Father, my heavenly Father ! " Well might the result of a life, even of such profound thought and great service in the Church of Christ, be summed up in these simple but all-comprehensive words. And what more do we need to strengthen us in the valley of the shadow of death? A little Jewish child, who had been taught this prayer, used to say, " At night, when mother puts out the candle, I pray, ' Our Father which art in heaven.' " It was childish to be afraid in the dark, but the feeling of safety and peace in a Heavenly Father was true faith; and when the light of our earthly existence goes out, and we enter that unknown eternal world, may we be like little children, exclaiming in their helplessness, with perfect trust and confidence, " Our Father which art in heaven."*

The words may be compared to the entrance leading to a building. As in the porticoes which lead to a grand temple or magnificent palace there are often many things remarkable and beautiful which attract and rivet our attentive gaze, so this introduction contains many sublime and consoling truths, many salutary and elevating thoughts, and the Christian delights to pause here in devout and grateful meditation.† " It is good to be here."

Comparing these words to an antechamber or portico of a beautiful building, is, however, a very defective and inadequate illustration of the relation

---

* " There have been times, and there will be times again, when we can only say, but it will be quite enough to say, ' Our Father which art in heaven.' "—Rev. J. VAUGHAN, *of Brighton.*

† Veith, " Vater Unser," ii.

in which they stand to the subsequent petitions.
Rather should they be compared to the key-note
which the Divine Master strikes, and which runs
through the whole prayer, meeting our ear and
heart in every petition we are taught to bring before
God's throne. It is the golden thread on which all
the precious pearls are strung. As a man's soul
expresses itself in his countenance, and specially
beams forth in his eyes, so the life and essence, the
soul and spirit, the sum and substance of this prayer,
manifests itself in the introductory words. And thus
it frequently happens, that the first words of the
prayer are its countenance. "Out of the depths" is
the commencement of that psalm of repentance and
profound knowledge of sin; "Have mercy upon
me," of that prayer of contrition and intense faith
taking hold of the grace of God; "Bless the
Lord, O my soul," of that hymn of praise and
exulting thanksgiving. Most significantly has this
prayer been called the "Paternoster," and, with
perhaps deeper and sweeter feeling of its fatherly
character, by the German Christians, the "Vater
Unser."

If we understand and possess these opening words,
we have the key to the whole prayer.

God is Father, God is our Father, He is our
Father in heaven; to know Him as Father is to be-
lieve; to know Him as our Father is to love; to know
Him as our Heavenly Father is to hope.

At present we confine ourselves to the doctrinal

aspect of the invocation, while in a subsequent lecture our attention will be directed to its experimental and practical teaching.   We notice—

I. God is the Father of our Lord Jesus Christ, and in Him the Father of all who believe in the Saviour.

II. Jesus is the First-born among many brethren, Head of the Church, the Centre of union.   In Him we say, " *Our* Father."

III. Jesus has opened to us heaven, the holy of holies ; and, risen with Christ, we seek now the things which are above, we pray to our Father *in heaven.*

IV. It is by the Holy Ghost, who is given to us as the Spirit of the Son, that we cry Abba, and call Jesus Lord.

The words " Our Father who art in heaven," contain the doctrine of the Father, Son, and Holy Ghost.   Redemption and adoption are the two pillars upon which they rest.

I. It may be objected that men who deny the divinity of the Lord Jesus, and who do not acknowledge the influence of the Holy Ghost, admire and use the words of the text.   We welcome the objection, for it leads to an earnest and thoughtful consideration of the question.   Let us exclude then from our thought for an instant, the Divine Mediator, the great work which was accomplished on Golgotha, and the fulfilment of the Father's promise on Pentecost.   Let us view the words in the light of reason, conscience, and the law. Is God our Father—may He not claim our reverence, humility, trust, love, and obedience? Has He nourished and brought up children—what term is strong enough to describe the guilt of their rebellion? Is He a Father—where is His honour? Is He a bountiful and beneficent Father—how justify or excuse the abuse which we have made of His gifts? The inference from the word *Father*, which reason draws, which the conscience ratifies, which the law proclaims, is, "Thou shalt love the Lord with all thy heart, and with all thy soul, and with all thy strength." And if God is *our* Father, and we are brethren, the question arises—Have we felt, spoken, acted, and lived as brethren? Have we been unselfish, generous, kind? Have we fulfilled the commandment, Thou shalt love thy neighbour as thyself? Thus, while the word *Father* contains the first table of the law, the word *our* epitomises the second; and, in the sight of our transgressions, who can utter the words without self-condemnation? But whereas the words *our Father* condemn us for what we have done, the words *which art in heaven* condemn us on account of what we *are*. Is God in heaven, in light, in holiness, truth, and blessedness, —where are we? What is the element in which we live? What is the character of our heart? If only the heavenly-minded can be citizens of heaven —if God is of purer eyes than to behold iniquity— if without holiness no man can see God—who can say

" Our Father which art in heaven " without feeling that he is guilty on account of his disobedience, banished on account of his iniquity ?

Who can say it, who does say it, in truth, in peace, in power—believing not merely that God is our Creator, and that He is full of benevolence and compassion, but believing that He loves us as His children, that He regards us as the dear and accepted members of His household, and the appointed heirs of His glory, and that we resemble Him in spirit and in character? None but they who have obtained the adoption, who have experienced the grace of the Lord Jesus Christ, and the love of God, and the fellowship of the Holy Ghost.

God is not merely called Father; He *is* Father. Fatherly feelings and dispositions are not merely attributed to Him; but the earthly fatherly relation is only a shadow of His eternal Fatherhood—Jesus Christ is the only-begotten Son of God.

Jesus is the only one who, in the full sense of the word, calls God Father. The Fatherhood of God is never seen except in the only-begotten Son. When Jesus says Father, the word reveals the whole mystery of godliness, the counsel of redemption. For it is by virtue of His filial relation to the Father that Jesus became the First-born among many brethren, and the everlasting Father of an innumerable multitude.

God, as Creator, may be called Father. The angels are called the sons of God: " The morning stars sang together, and all the sons of God shouted for joy." *   God, who has chosen Israel, is called Israel's Father.   Thus the Lord says to His people, " Is not He thy Father that hath bought thee ? hath He made thee and established thee ? " †   And Israel responds, " Doubtless Thou art our Father." ‡   And again : " But now, O Lord, Thou art our Father ; we are the clay, and Thou art the potter ; and we all are the work of Thy hand." §   To Israel pertaineth the adoption. ‖   But the true and real Fatherhood of God, and the true and real Sonship, are revealed to us in the dispensation of the Spirit ; when we look up to heaven, we behold Jesus, the Son of God, at the right hand of His God and our God, His Father and our Father.   God has a Son, eternal, Light of Light, God of God—begotten, not created ; He is His only Son, and all real Sonship is in Him. We are the sons of God, through and in Christ. And this not merely legally, but really, for through the indwelling of the Holy Ghost, we are one with the Son of God.   A mystery which, while it condescends to our lowest estate, and dawns upon us with rays of mildest peace, lifts us into the heavenly sanctuary, and brings us not merely near to God, but into union with the eternal and divine Son.

We stand here on sacred ground.   We draw near with reverence, but with the assurance of peace. The mystery of eternity is unveiled, and there is

* Job xxxviii. 7.   † Deut. xxxii. 6.   ‡ Isa. lxiii. 16.
§ Isa. lxiv. 8.   ‖ Rom. ix. 4.

no dazzling splendour to overpower our weakness. Mount Sinai was most terrible, and yet there God revealed only His will, His law. Here we are to behold the very heart and mind of God. And what do we behold?

We see a child lying in the manger of Bethlehem. An infant, feeble and helpless. In this Child we behold the Word made flesh, the only-begotten of the Father in our nature. Here is the Son of God, and He is ours; for He is Son of man.

Israel knew that a great Redeemer was to come *from among them.* Israel also knew that the Lord Jehovah was to come down *from above.* What did they know of the Son of man? What did they know of the Son of God?

They knew Him as seed of the woman; Son of Abraham according to the promise; miracle-born, even in the person of Isaac; Shilo from Juda's tribe; David's Son, beloved of God, and Friend of the people; Solomon, in wisdom, peace, and wide-spreading glory; Virgin's Son, Immanuel; Servant of the Lord, who dealeth prudently; delight of God, meek and lowly; despised, and rejected, suffering unto death, and exalted; Shepherd of the flock; perfect Servant of God, possessing the fulness of the Spirit; true Man, in humility, in obedience; suffering, dying; pleasing God, and yet forsaken; His delight, and yet put by Him to grief; the sword awakes against the Shepherd—even the Man who is my equal, saith the Lord.

This Son of man, and equal of Jehovah, cometh afterwards with the clouds of heaven, and receiveth dominion, and a kingdom everlasting. He is the Son of David, yet He comes unto Israel as the eternal King,—He is the pierced One, yet the exalted Fountain of the Holy Ghost. Is this Son of man, who from below ascends on high, the Son of God who is seen coming down from heaven?

For that He is Lord, and yet different and distinct from God; divine, and yet sent; eternal, and yet appearing in time; uncreated, and yet manifest in creature form: this also was gradually unfolded in Israel. As Abraham's guest, as Israel's guide; as the Messenger of God's name, countenance, and covenant; Captain of the Host of the Lord; Pele or Wonderful, He appeared unto the fathers; Jehovah, God, and yet different from the God who sent Him, whom He represented, and with whom He is one. They knew also that He was from before the beginning of the world. In Israel existed faith in God, the Creator of heaven and of earth. That fundamental truth, without which God cannot be apprehended as God, above all, had been revealed to them: God created all things. But into the region before creation the mind of man seeks to penetrate, and seeks to find there a *living* God; and cannot find a living God, if it only knows of a lonely God. And God revealed to Israel that He was a living God before creation; not lonely, not quiescent, but in fulness of life, love, communion. *Wisdom* * saith, " The Lord possessed me in the beginning of His way, before His works of old. I was set up from everlasting, from the beginning, or ever the earth was. When there were no depths, I was brought forth . . . when He brought forth the heavens, I was there . . . then I was by Him, as one brought up with Him, and I was daily His delight." They knew the Christ also, though dimly, as the *Son.* " Who hath ascended up into heaven, or descended? Who hath gathered the wind in His fists? Who hath bound the waters in a garment? Who hath established all the ends of the earth? What is His name, and what is His *Son's name*, if thou canst tell?" Thus asked Agur.† And in order to combine the two

---

* That " Wisdom " is not a mere personification, has been satisfactorily proved, among others, by Nitzsch (in his celebrated article on the Trinity, Theologische Studien, 1841), and by Dr M'Caul (" On the Eternal Sonship of the Messiah "). Wisdom is a person, because attributes and actions are ascribed to her ; she is described as eternal ; she invites the simple to make a covenant with her, using the same expressions which in Isaiah are ascribed to God ; she promises to " pour out my Spirit," and declares that she will execute judgment upon those who refuse to hearken. " Our Rabbis have said, Beginning is nothing else but wisdom;" and therefore it is translated in the Jerusalem Targum, " By wisdom God made the heavens and the earth." Wisdom is also spoken of by the Jews as the First-born, and as the Schekinah, or Divine Person who dwelt in the Holy of Holies (comp. John i. 1-3; Col. i. 15 ; Matt. xi. 19). The passage in Prov. xxx. shows that a knowledge of the name of the Son of God is an essential part of the knowledge of God, and that man can attain this knowledge only by revelation (comp. Matt. xi. 27).

† " True, this is the only passage of the Old Testament where, quite apart from typical persons, the eternal Son of God is

lines—the upward line, from Israel to God, from earth to heaven—and the downward line, from God to Israel, from heaven to earth—the beloved David received this promise, that the future Messiah was to be, in a special sense, *the Son*, who would say unto God, my Father! And the word came: "Thou art my Son; this day have I begotten thee." Thus was Israel prepared for the coming of *the Son of God*. But *we* see the fulfilment, and, in the blessed light of day, we now adore the revealed mystery.

Jesus is the Son of God. The Father sent the Son, and the Son became Man. His Sonship is eternal. His humanity begins in time. Jesus is the true God and eternal life, the eternal Son of God, the I Am before Abraham was, the Word and Wisdom before the world was made. He truly became man. He did not *appear* in flesh; He *was made* flesh; He was

---

spoken of; but this is in accordance with the searching spirit of Solomon."—STIER, "Politik der Weisheit," p. 22. Speaking of the Old Testament statements, Dr M'Caul says: "Every term that the Hebrew language affords to express filiation in the proper sense has been employed—offspring, branch, first-born, Son, begotten, brought forth;—and every form of expression that can convey the idea of proper eternity applied—before the creation of the sun, before the formation of the mountains, before the existence of chaos, the beginning of God's way, from everlasting, from the beginning or ever the earth was. And these expressions are not confined to a single passage, but interwoven through the whole of the sacred volume. Surely, then, we have no alternative but to believe that Messiah is the eternal Son of God, or to believe that the language of the Bible has been constructed for the purpose of deceiving and misleading those who study most its modes of speech."

true man, body, soul, and spirit; God with us; God among us: nay, more, God planted into our race, the branch coming out of our earth; yet a new Adam, a new creation, a new Divine beginning in the power of Spirit.

I see Him an infant, and I am meant by God to see Him as an infant. God does not—like short-sighted men—conceal from us the true and full *incarnation* of His Son. As a child, the Father watches over Him, through the love of Mary, and the conscientious guardianship of Joseph. The angels are sent to point the way to Egypt, for He also was one of those little ones over whom the angels watch (and yet were they His from of old). As a child, I behold Him in the temple of Jerusalem, asking questions— (and yet He had the key of David). I am told by the inspired Evangelist that Jesus grew in stature and in wisdom, and in favour with God and man. The flower unfolded. He was always sinless, but He was capable of growth, for He was man. And He knew more of God and of man, and became stronger in love and in zeal for God. " *My Father,*" he said; no man had ever uttered this word in Israel, Not even David, wonderful as was his personal relationship to God from his childhood. The temple of Jerusalem was His Father's house, the written Word, in which, as every Jewish child, He was taught, His Father's Word, and that which temple and nation only typified, was here in blessed reality, the Son of God, the temple of the Holy Ghost.

And when the time was fulfilled, in perfect consciousness of His Sonship, He came ; and on Jordan's bank He called God Lord, and as the servant He obeyed. But the Lord called Him *Son,* my Son, "my beloved Son, in whom I am well pleased." Jesus heard in these words His eternal glory before the world was, His present possession of the Father's love and delight, and His future sacrifice as the Isaac of promise.

The three years of His prophetic life are over. He had manifested God, declaring His name. He had finished the work. The last evening had come. He is now to return to the Father. In the twofold consciousness of the eternal glory out of which He had come, and the glory to which He was now returning, He washed the disciples' feet, He ate with them the Passover, He sang with them the song of praise, He spoke to them of what He was to them, and would be in them. *All* is now summed up in His use of the word *Father.* *

Now the disciples understood clearly, and felt in their inmost soul as they were listening to the words and prayer of Jesus : Here is the Son of God, the only-begotten of the Father. He who had taken such deep root on earth, was the Son of the Most High. He who called them friends was the ever-blessed Jehovah. That Vine, into which, by faith, they were grafted, was Himself, essentially and eternally one with the Father. And it was God's will and glory, that

---

* John xiv.–xvii.

the Son should become man, and be united for ever with the children of men.

When Jesus says Father, He stands alone.   He is the Only-begotten.   When Jesus says Father, He abideth not alone ; we are sons of God through Him, and shall abide in the house for ever.

For He returns to the Father not as He left the throne of glory.   Even from eternity He was the Christ, and we were loved in Him.   He is the Lamb slain from the foundation of the world.   And during the centuries preceding His advent, He came and appeared unto the fathers, and the Lord dealt with Israel through Him.   But when He became man, *God gave Him unto us for ever.   As Son of man* He ascended.   His pierced hands were uplifted, blessing His disciples, when He was taken up.   As Son of man, standing at the right hand of God, He appeared unto Stephen ; as Son of man, speaking the Hebrew tongue unto Saul of Tarsus.   John, the beloved apostle, saw Him in His celestial glory as the great Royal High Priest of the Church, as the Lamb in the midst of the throne ; heard Him call himself the root and offspring of David ; and as Son of man He is waiting now for " the hour," and His feet shall stand upon the Mount of Olives, when mourning and repenting Israel shall see the Messiah whom they pierced, and shall receive from Him the spirit of grace and supplication.

Only once was His communion with the Father interrupted.   When He was made sin for us, and bore the curse, He cried, " My God, my God, why hast Thou forsaken me ? " It was then, that identified with the transgressors of the law, God made Him, who knew no sin, to be sin for us. And as we were one with Him on the cross, so we rose with Him in His resurrection. He who is the Only-begotten from all eternity, He who was born of the Virgin Mary in the fulness of time, had a third birth when He rose from the dead, the First-begotten of the dead, the First-born among many brethren. Hence His resurrection is viewed as our regeneration. " Blessed be the God and Father of our Lord Jesus Christ, who, of His abundant mercy, hath begotten us again by the resurrection of Jesus Christ from the dead, to an inheritance incorruptible, undefiled, and that fadeth not away, reserved for us in Heaven." God created us according to His goodness and love. God begat us again according to His abundant mercy through the sacrifice of His Son. Our first creation was a transition from non-existence to life. Our regeneration is a triumph over death, the penalty of the law. Our first birth connects us with Adam ; sin and death are before us. Our second birth connects us with Christ, *after sin and death are behind Him.* Thus we begin a new life, as forgiven and accepted children, who have nothing before them but the inheritance.

How blessed to call God Father, because we are one with Jesus, the risen Saviour !

II. When Jesus enables us to say *Father*, He also

teaches us to say *Our*. The body has many members, the flock consists of many sheep, the temple is built of many stones; and union with Christ necessarily implies union with all that are His. As we have met in the eternal counsel of God, when we were chosen in Christ; as we have met on the cross of Christ, when the iniquities of us all were laid upon Him; as we have met in the resurrection of Jesus from the grave, and as we are to be together with the Lord for ever; so even now we are one in the love of the Father, in our union with Christ the Head by the indwelling of the Holy Ghost.

Jesus is the centre; He fulfils the divine purpose of bringing us unto God. We were not merely far from God, but we were also estranged one from another; without the bond of love we had lost our true unity. As there is only one God, so there is only one source of love; and men cannot love one another except they be united in the love of the Father. The sheep who err from the shepherd's fold and guidance, cease to be a *flock;* and, as the prophet confesses, we have turned every one to his own way. Men seek to find centres of union, but their method being carnal and not spiritual, their remedies superficial and not radical, we find that their attempts result rather in augmenting and deepening the discord which they hope to heal. Babylon, instead of being the centre of union, is the starting-point of divergence and confusion.

Men can only be gathered by being brought unto

God in Christ. Through the fall of Adam sin and disunion had entered, so that humanity ceased to exist as a body, a community in the truest and highest sense of the word. A new beginning was necessary, the second Adam. For this reason,—the glorious series of believers in the 11th chapter of Hebrews does not commence with Adam, for the Father of the chosen generation and royal priesthood is the second Adam, the Saviour and Strength of God's people.

How clearly did Jesus manifest Himself as the centre of humanity. He was above all, and yet near all. He touched and cleansed the leper; He attracted the publicans and sinners; the common people, whom the scribes despised on account of their ignorance, heard Him gladly. While He became the self-invited guest of Zaccheus, He kept not aloof from the homes of Pharisees. He opened to the woman of Samaria the Fountain of living water, and the kingdom of heaven to the dying thief. His love broke every barrier down. It embraced the little infants whom maternal tenderness brought unto Him for His benediction; it understood the meaning of children's Hosannahs, it rescued the depraved, and broke the chains of the possessed. He gathered all round Him, but especially the poor in spirit, the quiet God-fearing ones in the land, the true Israelites without guile, who waited for redemption.

And after such a life of love came the night " *in which He was betrayed!* " It seemed as if He

gathered—only against Himself: Herod and Pilate,
Pharisees, scribes, and the multitude of the people
were united—but to crucify Him: even His own
disciples were scattered; Jesus was left alone.

And we know that He descended into a still more
awful loneliness on the cross, and that, as the Substitute of sinners, He felt the bitterness and curse of
that separation and desolateness which sin deserves
according to the law of a holy God.

This awful isolation and death were necessary for
the most glorious expansion of divine love and communication of eternal life. "Except the corn of wheat
die, it abideth alone; but if it die it bringeth forth
much fruit." The Church of Christ, like Eve from
Adam, is taken out of His pierced side—she sprang
out of His dying love. The vitalising power, the
indwelling Spirit, could be sent only from His glorified humanity.

How rare is true, unselfish friendship. So rare,
that when it appears in the course of centuries,
as in the case of Damon and Pythias, of David
and Jonathan, history takes note of it, and the
memory thereof is handed down to succeeding generations. And this proves, that, rare as it is, it is
good and precious in the estimation of humanity.
Jesus came not to destroy, but to fulfil; and in Him
and His Church we find the idea of communion
realised. The separating power of sin is most strikingly illustrated by the fact that, even when there
were only two human beings in existence, linked to-

gether, as never again two could be, by ties the most
solemn and tender, no sooner had sin entered, than
the sweetness of love departed—Adam was willing to
cast the burden of guilt on Eve, of whom he coldly
speaks, "the woman which Thou gavest me." What
contrast to that first poetic utterance of delight, the
first and deepest erotic poem, "This is now bone of
my bone, and flesh of my flesh!" Christ alone is the
Restorer of unity. In Israel we have presented to
us on a grand scale, though with many grievous
failings, the idea of a community whose centre was
God; most beautifully, and nearest to the great
ideal, in the time of David, the type of Him whose
kingdom is yet to come. The son of Jesse, beloved
of God, and the beloved of the nation for the sake
of God, was king by Divine grace, in the full sense
of the word; given to the nation by the Most High,
a ruler and yet a brother. His influence was spiritual, and the pillars of his throne were the loyal and
loving hearts of the people, especially the faithful of
the land. Because of his personal relation to Jehovah, he became the centre of the nation. His whole
strength was in God. It was the attractive power of
his piety, the influence of his godly spirit, the overflowing tenderness and comprehensive deep sympathy
of his soul, that riveted all hearts, and made Israel
a nation of brothers, of which brotherhood Jerusalem
was the centre as well as symbol. "Jerusalem is
builded as a city that is compact together," (brotherly,
neighbourly), "whither the tribes go up, the tribes of

the Lord, unto the testimony of Israel, to give thanks unto the name of the Lord. For there are set thrones of judgment, the thrones of the house of David. Pray for the peace of Jerusalem : they shall prosper that love thee. Peace be within thy walls and prosperity within thy palaces. For my brethren and companions' sakes, I will now say, Peace be within thee. Because of the house of the Lord our God I will seek thy good " (Ps. cxxii.)

The typical significance of David in his relation to Israel is plainly the future glory of Him, over whose cross was written, King of the Jews. But symbolically viewed, it is a picture of the union of believers in Christ, who is not ashamed to call them brethren. And this union was never so beautifully manifested as in the first apostolic Church at Jerusalem. What a commentary is that Church on the words of the apostle : " Whosoever believeth that Jesus is the Christ is born of God, and every one that loveth Him that begat, loveth him also that is begotten of Him." When we say *Father*, we can also say *Our ;* when we rejoice in Christ, we feel that we are members one of another ; when the Spirit descends from the great High Priest, brethren dwell together in unity.

III. Christ teaches us to say " Our Father which art in heaven ; " only in Him we see the heavens open.*

---

* On heaven as a place, compare the remarks of next chapter.

Man was created to look upwards. Even the heathen saw in this something symbolical of man's dignity and greatness. But sin has degraded man. It has fixed the eyes of his mind downward ; it has deprived him of the winged love which soars aloft; it has chained him to the ground by the dark weight of guilt. The kingdoms of the world are represented in the symbolic vision as four beasts, because their character is of the earth, earthy ; their motives, methods, resources, and aims are material, selfish, carnal. They can look around them, but they cannot look above ; their level is fallen creation, nature, experience. They cannot lift up their eyes to the hills, to the eternal heights from which light and strength come down to all angels, and to all the children of the Most High. The reign of the Son of man will be heavenly in its character, and therefore truly human

Israel was taught to lift up his eyes to heaven. God appeared unto Abraham, and commanded him not merely to see the visible sky with its innumerable stars, but to lift up his heart and to live by *faith*. God taught His people that there was a sanctuary, a holy of holies, where His glory was revealed between the cherubim. Christ the Lord has revealed heaven,* and through faith in Him we have access into the very presence of God. Heaven is very near unto us.

We behold now the Saviour at the right hand of

_____

* John i. 52.

God. We see Him as the custodian and dispenser of the spiritual blessings which He has purchased for us and obtained from the Father. We are assured that He presents there our petitions and our works, and the sacrifice of our faith, cleansed from all imperfection and sin, and perfumed with the incense of His intercession. And thus our home is in heaven. *There* is our righteousness and our strength, there are our spiritual gifts and the weapons of our warfare. There is, as it were, the result of our soul's life and work, securely garnered, treasure laid up, which we shall receive with usury. Every time we pray, whenever our souls feed on Christ and are strengthened by God, we are lifted up to heaven. We are seated with Christ in the heavenlies. As the high priest in Israel had the tribes engraven and secured by golden chains on his shoulders and breastplate ; as the shepherd had the saved sheep resting securely on his shoulders when he returned home to his sympathising friends, so are we with Christ in the Father's sanctuary, where sin, condemnation, and death cannot enter. And as a tree is rooted in the earth, deriving strength and nourishment from the soil, we are rooted in Heaven, deriving light and guidance, strength and growth from thence, the pure river, clear as crystal, which proceedeth from between the throne and the Lamb making glad the city of our heart.

But the Lord teaches us to say, " Our Father which art in the heavens." God is His own heaven, and

Christ is ascended above all heavens. "Behold," said Solomon, "the heaven and heaven of heavens cannot contain Thee." Thus, while Scripture teaches the locality of heaven, a real and true tabernacle of God, a holy of holies, the throne of God and of the Lamb, surrounded by His angels, we are also taught the most spiritual view of God's omnipresence. We think of God in the realm of His infinite perfections, in His omnipotence, in His wisdom, in His boundless love, in His never-failing faithfulness. What vastness of space is to the eye, this is to the soul. This is the boundless ocean which fills our heart with adoration and satisfies our longing. These are the many mansions filled by the great I AM—and in all these heavens He is—our Father in Christ. We dwell on the manifold manifestations which He has given to us in His Word and in His works, we behold in all, the same Father in Christ, Creator and Redeemer, the only true and living God.

Thus, whenever we realise God, we are in heavenly repose, we are breathing the heavenly atmosphere, we are replenished with heavenly life-powers. The Saviour calls it being "in secret." "He that dwelleth in the secret place of the Most High shall abide under the shadow of the Almighty." In the midst of this world we are living in the heart of another. Well may we sing :—

> "How full of sweet content
> I pass my years of banishment.
> To me remains nor place nor time,
> My country is in every clime ;

> I can be calm and free from care
> On any shore, since God is there.
> While place we seek, or place we shun,
> The soul finds happiness in none ;
> But with a God to guide our way,
> 'Tis equal joy to go or stay."

IV. We say, *Our Father*, because the Holy Ghost is given unto us, as the Spirit of adoption.

All covenant gifts and blessings, proceeding from the love of God the Father, and purchased by the blood of Christ the Son, in whom they are also secured for us in heavenly places, are bestowed by the Holy Ghost. This is seen pre-eminently in our adoption. The fountain of this blessing is the Father, who chose us; the channel is Christ, the Only-begotten, in whom we become the sons of God. But except we be born from above, of water and of the Spirit, except we be converted and become as little children, except we be renewed by the Holy Ghost, we cannot enter into the kingdom of God. Jesus brings us to the Father, the Spirit brings us to Jesus.

We are not merely called God's children, but we are in *reality* and *nature* His children, born of God.* There is perhaps no subject on which the Lord and His apostles have left a fuller and more varied testimony than the subject of regeneration. The Saviour, in His conversation with Nicodemus, teaches the absolute necessity of the new birth, and that it is from above, the work of the Holy Ghost ; while, at the same time,

---

* John i. 12, 13.

He shows that to believe in the Son of God as the Saviour is to be born of God. John, who narrates this interview, gives his comment in John i. 12, 13, and 1 John v. 1. In both passages he dwells on the supernatural, heavenly, divine character of the change, as well as the simple and easy method by which we are made the subjects of it—believing in the grace of the Lord. Faith is not a small thing—for to believe is to be born of God; regeneration is not inaccessible, for to be born again is to trust in Christ.

Paul represents regeneration as the ingrafting of the soul into Christ; if any man is in Christ, he is a new creature. By faith we become one with the Saviour; and being thus brought into union with the second Adam, old things, the condemnation and spiritual death of our former state, are passed away, Christ is now our righteousness and strength.

Peter connects regeneration with the resurrection of Christ (as Paul also implies when he calls Christ the First-born from the dead). In the death of the Lord Jesus, and in His burial, we were one with Him; and now, having suffered and died in Him for our transgressions, we are raised with Him into a new life, full of peace and light.

James connects regeneration with the will, the energy, and purpose of God, as the cause, the word of truth as the instrument, and the glory of the Father as the great end.*

* 2 Cor. v. 17 ; 1 Pet. i. 3, &c. ; Eph. ii. 1, &c. ; James i. 18.

In the discourses of Christ recorded by John, as well as in his Epistles, the eternal election of God's children, their essential difference from the "world," their real sonship, their being of God, born of Him, having His seed in them, is most prominently brought forward.

It is evident that "adoption" has a very special and deep meaning in Scripture, and that by the children of God are meant those who, chosen by God out of the world, are regenerated by the power of the Holy Ghost through faith in Jesus Christ, by which faith they are brought into a vital and eternal union with the Saviour. They are called God's children, viewed and treated by Him as such, and they are in reality God's *children* (and not merely His *creatures*), by virtue of their second birth.

If we wish to have a full assurance of our adoption, we must dwell on the mystery of our union with Christ by the Holy Ghost.

"God hath sent the Spirit of His Son into our hearts, crying, Abba, Father." It is therefore not our spirit only or primarily that calls within us, God, Father. It is the Spirit of God, as Christ's Spirit. Jesus was the Anointed; He received the Spirit in full perfection, and from Him, as the risen and glorified Saviour, the Spirit is now sent into our hearts. The second Adam is a quickening Spirit. And as the Spirit comes from Jesus, as our Head and Mediator, so He comes as Christ's representative and substitute. His indwelling is not merely the pledge, but the earnest of our inheritance, for when the Spirit of God dwells in us, Christ and the Father have their abode in our hearts.

We distinguish, according to the Divine Word, between the indwelling of the Spirit and His influences within us; as we distinguish between the person of Christ and His work. "The love of God is shed abroad in our hearts by the Holy Ghost, which is given unto us." Here we have the person who is given unto us, distinguished from the gracious influence He exerts. "The Spirit himself beareth witness with our spirit, that we are the children of God." Here we have a clear distinction between the Spirit of God, our spirit, and the testimony borne to our spirit by the divine, eternal, infinite Spirit, co-equal with the Father and Son.

The indwelling of Christ's Spirit brings us into a state new and marvellous. According to the Father's will, the Spirit unites us with His Son. If any man is in Christ, he is a new creature; old things are passed away, behold, all things are become new, and all things are of God; what is born of the Spirit is spirit; we who are the children of Adam, and were once the children of wrath and disobedience, are now the children of Christ, the everlasting Father. Thus, Christ, who here teaches us to pray "Our Father," knew that these words could not be fully understood, until the Spirit was given. Now we understand them as indicating our oneness with Jesus. He indeed is the Only-begotten, eternal, infinite. In one sense He can never pray with us ; in another sense He is not merely the Lord adored, but the chief singer of Israel, as He says, " I will declare Thy name to my brethren; in the midst of the Church I will sing praise unto Thee."   We are one with Him, He lives in us ; by the Spirit we are joined unto the Lord, and the Spirit teaches us to pray in His name ; for what is the cry of the Spirit ?   He utters the same prayer as Jesus had taught : Abba, *Father.*

The Spirit of Christ creates within us the filial spirit.   He conforms us unto Christ, so that we seek God's glory, are zealous for His honour, long for His kingdom, and desire not to do our own will but His.   He works in us that calm believing rest in God, who supplies our daily want and delivers us from the feverish anxiety and timorous thought of the future ; He makes us forgiving, patient, and gentle towards all men, and dreading and hating nothing but temptation and evil. Or, in other words, *He prays and fulfils in us the Lord's Prayer.*

Notice, secondly, how the Spirit gives and sustains in us the assurance of our adoption.

Himself beareth witness with our spirit that we are the children of God.   We are not left in uncertainty. We build not on our own feelings and the evidence of our life, but on the testimony of that Spirit which is truth.   We do not persuade ourselves, taking a partial and self-complacent view of our condition and of our good works ; there is another, who is our Comforter and Advocate, who pleads our cause in the judgment-chamber of the conscience, who encourages the faint and timid heart, as Jesus comforted His disciples while He was yet with them. Thus have we not merely the Scripture, but His Word, by the Spirit, abiding in us.

The Spirit enables us, *as children*, to pray in the name of Christ, without doubt and wavering, without fear and dread, but with confidence, knowing that God will hear us. Here is no presumption, but humility; we rejoice in the abundant grace of the Father and of our Saviour; we hide ourselves in Christ; we appear before the Father with the humility of the prodigal, increased and deepened by that regal robe in which we are clothed, Christ's blood and righteousness.

Thirdly, As the Spirit enables us to say *Father;* He enables us also to say *Our*. A new spirit must be given to us if we are to fulfil the royal law. And the affection which is to bind together the children of God does not flow from nature and the flesh, it is the work of the Spirit. " Endeavouring to keep the unity of the Spirit in the bond of peace; there is one body and one spirit." " God is my record, how greatly I long after you all in the bowels of Jesus Christ." " If we love one another, God dwelleth in us, and His love is perfected in us. Hereby know we that we dwell in Him and He in us, because He hath given us of His Spirit."

Lastly, The Spirit of God is within us a spirit of

hope, waiting for the full manifestation of our adoption, the redemption of our body.   And He continually directs the thought, desire, and hope of our heart heavenward.

He, who is the earnest of our inheritance, will comfort and strengthen us during all the evils and sorrows of time ; and, finally, all who are strangers and pilgrims on earth will be gathered in heaven, where Christ will present them to the Father: Behold I and the children which God hath given me.

4

THE SPIRIT OF THE INVOCATION: FAITH, LOVE, AND HOPE

"Our Father which art in heaven."

THE invocation contains mysteries. When we say "Father," we think of the mystery of the Father and His Son Jesus Christ; we remember the great mystery of godliness, God manifest in the flesh; and we rejoice with thanksgiving in the mystery of our new birth by the word of truth.

When we say "our," we think of the mystery of the Church, the body of Christ.

When we say "who art in heaven," we think of the citizenship of the children, whom the world knoweth not, and of the inheritance reserved for them; we think of the anchor, which has entered within the veil, and of the sanctuary, where the eternal High Priest is enthroned.

Thus the very simplest words which we can utter are full of high and august mysteries; wonder and awe must always mingle with our gratitude and joyous confidence. Nor do we feel revealed truths a

burden, because they are beyond our understanding;
" we rather welcome them and exult in them, nay,
and feel an antecedent stirring of heart towards them
for the very reason that they are above us." For we
delight to say with David, " O Lord, my God, Thou
art very great ! "

High as are the mysteries revealed, they are full of
power influencing our daily life. We live not merely
in the knowledge, but in the spirit of these mysteries. The word " Father " appeals more directly to
our faith ; " our," to our love ; " in heaven," to our
hope. More directly, but not exclusively, and bearing this general division in mind, not observing it
rigorously, let us consider the filial, the brotherly, the
heavenly spirit of the believer.

1. We have received the spirit of adoption, whereby we cry, Abba Father. Dwell on the trustful-
ness and the peaceful confidence of children to
their father. We " cry," says the apostle, " to express the spontaneousness, the strength, and the
exuberance of filial emotion." * Be not afraid to
transfer to God all you know and have felt and experienced of an earthly father's love and pity, faithfulness and kindness. Let us not weaken the force
of Bible comparisons. God speaks to us in human
language, and the inadequacy of the vehicle consists
in this, that God's love, tenderness, pity, joy, are not
less real than ours, but excel our feeling infinitely in
purity, strength, and tenderness. We are afraid to

_____
* Dr D. Brown *in loc.*

speak of God's feelings, but Scripture does not hesitate to say of God that He is not able to give us up, that His bowels of mercy and compassion are yearning over us. We see Him rejoicing over the returning prodigal ; * we hear Him sigh when He exclaims, " O that they had hearkened to my voice ! " " All the exquisite feelings of sympathy and love that inhabited the bosom of the humanity of Jesus Christ, inhabit the bosom of Deity, and to Deity they must be traced." † Beholding in Jesus the image of the invisible God,—believing that God is indeed our loving Father, let us cultivate a simpler trust, a more loving confidence, a more bright and sunny calmness in prayer and meditation. Let the word " Father " be to us not so much the exponent of a scriptural and theological dogma, but the utterance of a peaceful and radiant heart.

This filial spirit rests on the Fatherhood of God, as the source of all blessings. It is not because God has given us life and health, temporal and spiritual benefits, that we infer that He is our Father, and

---

* " Greater than the joy of an earthly parent at the first stammering attempt of his child to call him father, is the joy of God in heaven, when sinners have confidence in Jesus to call Him Father." —Löhe, *Vater Unser.*

" That man hath most profited under His restoring dispensation in whom the [primeval] feeling of the love of God hath been restored in largest, sweetest, most assured experience, so that he feeleth it like a child to its parent, and speaketh it with the simplicity of a child who knoweth it, and knoweth nothing beside."— E. Irving.

† Howels, " Lord's Prayer," p. 31.

that we owe Him gratitude and love: in Christ Jesus we have gained a higher position and truer insight. It is because He is our Father that we expect good gifts from Him, and that we trace all the light and love of past days to His paternal forethought and mercy. "If I could only truly believe it," said Martin Luther, "that God, the Creator of heaven and earth and all things, is my Father, I would conclude that Christ is my brother, and that all things are mine, Gabriel my servant, and Raphael my charioteer,* and all the angels ministering to me in my necessities, and sent to my aid by my heavenly Father."

"If I could truly believe it,"—and we all acknowledge that we do not fully and constantly rest in the fatherly love of God. We are often discouraged. It is good to be humbled; but it is not good to doubt the inexhaustible and unchangeable love and grace of God. As "Father" is the most endearing name of God, so it denotes also a relation most enduring and immutable. As the God and Father of the Lord Jesus Christ, He is our Father. Between the heavenly throne and us clouds may sometimes intervene, but there is never a cloud between the Father and our Saviour Jesus Christ. "The Father loveth the Son," this is the high and bright region of love, into which the Spirit of God lifts up our souls; nothing can separate us from the love of God, which is in Christ Jesus our Lord. "The Father loveth

---

* Notice how children say of all that belongs to their father, "our," "our house," "our garden."

the Son, and hath given all things into His hand."
" All things that pertain unto life and godliness"
are ours, and all dangers and foes are under His
control.

As the remembrance of our sin need not in-
terrupt our communion with God, so our weakness
is only an additional plea.* In His family there are
new-born babes; there are little children, there are
young men and experienced fathers; but they are
all chosen and adopted in Christ Jesus, renewed by
the Holy Ghost.†

This confidence is full of reverence and holy adoration. ‡ As in heaven so in earth, love and reverence
are blended in the worship of God. God's glory is
the manifestation of His grace. The more we realise
that He is our Father, the more we behold His
majesty; the greater insight is given us into the
mystery of our redemption and the high end of our
calling, the more shall we adore the Lord, of whom
and through whom and to whom are all things. It
is unto God as unto the Father of our Lord Jesus
Christ, that Paul and all saints bow their knees in
lowly and reverent worship.

Not that the feelings of reverence and confidence
alternate; still less that one neutralises the other.
It is not that when we adore our trust is not so

---

* Ps. ciii. 13, 14. † 1 John ii. 12–14.

‡ The centurion, whose faith was greater than any faith in
Israel, said, " Lord, I am not worthy that Thou shouldest come
under my roof." Only *believing* humility is truly precious.

implicit; or that when we rely confidently on the grace of God we do not worship Him with awe and reverence. Our confidence is reverential; our worship filial. We love Him whom we adore; we adore Him whom we love. When Jesus reveals His condescension, then, as Thomas, we behold His glory, and exclaim, " My Lord and my God !"*

And our confidence is not merely reverential. This is the attitude also of angels who have never sinned. Our reverence is not merely in humility, but also in contrition. We call God Father; but it is because we are brought nigh by the blood of Christ. Jesus is not ashamed to call us brethren; though there is every reason why He should keep aloof from us, who, like Joseph's brothers, sold him into Egypt.

2. The filial spirit is a childlike spirit. In receiving the spirit of adoption, we are not only admitted into the family of God, but we are converted, and become as little children. It is a restoration of childhood, or rather the realisation and fulfilment of that of which childhood is an emblem and intimation.

---

* To Mary Magdalene the risen Saviour said, " Touch me not." His word unto Thomas was, " Reach thither thy finger, and behold my hands; and reach thither thy hand and thrust it into my side." But in the former case, Christ not merely reminds Mary of His majesty, but adds, in wonderful grace, " Go to my brethren, and say unto them, I ascend unto my Father and your Father, and to my God and your God." In the latter case, by revealing His mercy and condescending compassion, He fills Thomas with such awe and reverence, that he exclaims, "My Lord and my God ! "

There is in all of us a secret feeling of reverence and affection towards the days of our childhood. In the life of the unconverted there is no period which more resembles the new life of faith and love. Then we were free from care and anxiety; ambitious thoughts did not then alternate with despondency and fear; sin had not yet become a tyrant, exercising dominion over us; there was a certain peace and purity and contentment, which return to us not in the course of nature, but by the gift and new creation of grace.

Christ the Lord often dwells on childhood.* In bringing before us the mind of little children, the Lord at once avails Himself of a principle in our nature, which makes us regard our childhood with tenderness and a reverent affection, while He makes it easy for all to study the characteristics of the true believer.

The influence of the world is to lead us far away from the spirit and temper of childhood. I do not speak of open and flagrant sins, which degrade man, and which the wicked themselves feel to be so

---

* It has often been remarked that pagan antiquity had no knowledge of the Christian idea of humility, and scarcely a word to express it. God's people knew what was meant by the "poor in spirit;" David describes the meekness of a lowly and believing heart in the 131st Psalm. But the full revelation of humility and of the childlike spirit came in Jesus, who was meek and lowly in heart. It is significant that He was the first who set a child in the midst of His disciples as an emblem of the heavenly mind. Once the great thought was uttered, the conscience and heart of humanity instinctively received it as a true and beautiful revelation.

opposed to that sacredness with which God has invested little children, that their presence is to them as the very rebuke of a holy Judge. But the pursuit of wealth, daily labour and emulation, the very position we gain in society, the importance and responsibility attaching to us, the disappointments, as well as the successes in our career, all tend to fill us with a certain self-consciousness, very different from the humility and unassuming guilelessness of children. A child is docile. It is constantly instructed, corrected ; faults are pointed out, rules and regulations given ; it receives all willingly ; it requires no effort to remember that it is yet inexperienced, in need of teaching and training ; the constant influence of a superior mind, instead of raising a wall of separation, or infusing a spirit of bitterness, becomes rather a link of sweet and tender affection, which subsequent years cannot break or enfeeble. How different are we in our riper years ! How unwilling to be taught,—how slow to learn,—how reluctant to admit the interference of divine law and teaching with our thoughts, words, and habits ! With what bad grace, to say the least of it, do we become disciples !

A child is earnest. It is true a child is playful and fond of mirth, and not anxious about the morrow. But it is equally true that there is an intense earnestness and solemnity in childhood. With what earnestness and awe does a child listen to any description of something grand, or to any tale of sorrow, self-sacrifice,

or love !   How ready is he to believe things unseen !
How reverential his spirit when he hears of God and
of heaven !   How simple and intense is his immediate
application of divine truth to the wants and duties of
the present,—his expectation of answers to prayer,—
his eager desire to do what God commands !   Alas !
what a change comes over us afterwards !   Unreal,
vague, sceptical, undecided in the things of God ;
credulous, eager, engrossed, intoxicated with the
things of the world.

A child is unsuspicious and frank.   It is ready to
trust ; it cannot conceal its thoughts or disguise
its feelings.   Its yea is yea, and its nay is nay.   It
knows not why it should pay deference to wealth
or talent; it recognises in all kind and simple
children and men friends and play-fellows.   It is
hearty.   There is no false gloss of refinement ;
there is no crust of mammon-worship.   It breathes
the pure, fragrant air of the wood, not the sickly
perfume of civilisation.   A child is not ashamed to
confess its ignorance and helplessness ; there is a
clearness, an unconscious, pure, silvery note in
its voice when it asks a question or a favour.   Humility is not yet an effort.   To stoop and to sit
at the Master's feet is easy.   Thankfulness is not
felt as a burden.   A child lives in the present.
Trouble is soon forgotten ; care is unknown.   The
under-current of its life is a joyous rest in parental
love.

A child submits to discipline in faith.   It rarely

misunderstands the loving motive and salutary purpose of severity. A child will return, after rebuke and punishment, with full and loving confidence. It has also a keen sense of justice, of moral right and wrong, and is disappointed when, in a story, the wicked are not punished, or the moral equilibrium restored by the reformation of the transgressor.

But why analyse still further what we all know, or at least may easily see and recognise around us?

Now Christ would have us be as little children: free from pride, self-importance, self-assertion; docile, believing, flexible, and sensitive to good influence, ideal, that is, heavenly minded, unworldly, frank, ready to ask of God what we need, joyous in thanksgiving, free from care and anxiety, living in the enjoyment of a Father's love, in chastisement mingling sorrow and contrition with confidence and hope.

It need scarcely be added that the features of childhood, on which we have dwelt, do not exist in children in perfection, even as they are not found existing by themselves. We know from Scripture, and from our own experience, that folly is bound up in the heart of a child,—that as we are born in sin, sin manifests itself in our lives from the very earliest days of our existence. But, as has been well and beautifully remarked:* " What we were, when children, is a blessed intimation, given for our comfort, of what

* Newman, Sermons, vol. ii. 61. Compare Wordsworth's ex-

God will make us if we surrender our hearts to the guidance of His Holy Spirit, a prophecy of good to come, a foretaste of what will be fulfilled in heaven. And thus it is that a child is a pledge of immortality; for he bears upon him in figure, those high and eternal excellencies in which the joy of heaven consists, and which would not be thus shadowed forth by the All-gracious Creator, were they not one day to be realised."

We must also learn from the very imperfection and limitation of childhood. We derive from it a twofold lesson. The first is brought before us in that most beautiful and touching hymn (the thirteenth chapter of Paul's Epistle to the Corinthians) in which the great preacher of faith describes the essential necessity, the pre-eminence and the characteristics of love. Referring there to his childhood (what a theme for a poet's imagination, the childhood of Paul !), he says: " When I was a child, I spake as a child, I understood as a child, I reasoned as a child; but when I became a man, I put away

quisite ode, " Intimations of Immortality from Recollections of Early Childhood." And Tersteegen :—

> " Spirit of childhood ! loved of God,
>   By Jesus' Spirit now bestow'd;
>   How often have I long'd for Thee,
>   O Jesus, form Thyself in me !
>   And help me to become a child,
>   While yet on earth, meek, undefiled,
>   That I may find God always near,
>   And Paradise around me here ! ''

childish things. For now we see through a glass, darkly" (in a riddle) ; " but then face to face : now I know in part; but then shall I know even as also I am known." May we possess this humility which remembers that there are many things which our heavenly Father cannot yet disclose to us, because we should not be able to bear them, that obscurity and apparent contradiction must necessarily accompany our present knowledge of divine things; but that faith and obedience have an all-sufficient basis and motive in the Word of God and in the testimony of His Spirit. Thus our limited knowledge and insight will even strengthen as it tests our trust in God, deepen our humility, and increase our patient yet joyous hope of that future when, with a pure heart, we shall see Him as He is.

The other lesson is one of contrast. We have seen that we are only " little children ; " but we are also exhorted that while children in malice, we are to be men in wisdom and understanding, in courage and perseverance, in self-discipline and usefulness. We are to grow and to be strong, so as to be able to teach others,—nay, to become fathers in Christ. In the conflict with the world we are to quit ourselves as men ; amid the fluctuating and erroneous opinions of the enemies of the Church, as well as the false doctrine arising within her pale, we are to be firm, and not easily moved from the simplicity of the gospel. The sweetness of infancy, the beauty of childhood, the idealism of youth, the wisdom and strength of manhood, and the calm serenity of old age, are all combined in the character of the Christian, according to the Word of God. according to the image of Him who as God's holy Child could say of Himself, I am meek and lowly in heart. And this leads me to speak of the filial spirit:

3. As a spirit of dignity and perfection.

When we viewed the filial spirit as a spirit of reverential confidence and the spirit of childhood, we contemplated the *relation* subsisting now between God and us. But there is not merely a filial relation, there is also a filial *resemblance*. We are the sons of God, not merely because in Christ God regards us as His children, but because by the Holy Ghost we have been born again, begotten of incorruptible seed by the word of truth, created anew in Christ Jesus after the image of the Lord: "Be ye therefore followers," or imitators, "of God, as dear children." This exhortation has its deepest foundation in the mysterious fact, that we are born of God. They that are led (that is, constantly influenced) by the Spirit are the children of God.

The law was contrary to us, and we were opposed to it, because it is spiritual and we were carnal; but now, when God puts His Spirit within us, and gives us a new heart, the law is no longer outside and an enemy, but written on our hearts. Nor do we need it any longer as a schoolmaster and tutor, for it has brought us to Him who has given us power to become the

sons of God, loving and obedient children. "Be ye
holy, for I am holy." This mysterious word has
now its fulfilment in the union between Christ and
believers. "At that day ye shall know that I am in
my Father, and you in me, and I in you."

The filial spirit is the spirit of perfection. "Be ye
perfect, even as your Father which is in heaven is
perfect." To resemble God, to walk worthy of Him,
to be conformed to the image of Christ, the Elder
Brother, to be filled with the Spirit—this is the aim
and the standard of the spiritual life.

It is obvious that such life and walk must harmonise with the law; but equally clear it is that
we are here in a region higher than that of law, and
even that of the sinless condition of Adam in
Paradise. *Here everything is based on the Fatherhood of God, which, through the incarnation and the
atonement, and by the outpouring and indwelling of
the Holy Ghost, is revealed and given unto us.* The
eternal love of God to Christ and the Church
in Him; the self-sacrifice and grace of the Son
and the Spirit, given us through the glorified
humanity of Jesus — these are the sources and
motives of our new obedience, and in them must be
sought not merely the strength, but the very character and tone of the gospel-life. "Walk in love,
as Christ also hath loved us, and hath given Himself
for us." "Blessed are the peacemakers, for they
shall be called the children of God." "Love your
enemies, do good to them that hate you, and pray for

them which despitefully use you and persecute you, that ye may be the children of your Father which is in heaven, for He maketh His sun to rise on the evil and on the good, and sendeth rain on the just and on the unjust." " Let this mind be in you, which was also in Christ Jesus."

While the filial spirit is the spirit of perfection in Christ, it is necessarily a spirit of separation from the world, and hence it is written—" Be ye separate, saith the Lord, and touch not the unclean thing, and I will receive you, and will be a Father unto you, and ye shall be my sons and daughters, saith the Lord Almighty."

It is because we are a chosen *generation* that we are a royal priesthood.　The Sonship of Christ is the basis of His threefold Messianic office.　Because He is the Son of God, He is the perfect Prophet, Priest, and King.　We, as sons of God in Him, are also anointed to be prophets, possessing and imparting the knowledge of God, and to be a kingdom of priests, worshipping and serving the Lord, as well as priestly kings, ruling and subduing our enemies by the spirit of love and patient suffering.　Nor does God call us to such high dignity without supplying us with all needful grace.　He has given us His Spirit. Even to little children, John writes, " Ye are *of God*, and have overcome them, because greater is He that is in you than he that is in the world."

Such is the spirit in which we say, " *Father !*" It is by faith that we can utter so great a word.　It is by faith that we are the children of God, and only by the continued exercise of faith in Christ can we retain the reverential confidence, the childlike disposition, the manly aim at perfection. Faith is simple, even a look unto the Saviour of sinners. Faith is sublime, for the Lord says of it—" He that believeth on me, the works that I do shall he do also." Faith is the characteristic of all God's children ; the babes believe in His name, and their sins are forgiven them ; but faith is the characteristic of fathers, for " He that believeth on me, out of him shall flow rivers of living water." By faith we rest in Christ ; by faith we resemble Christ ; by faith we obtain the position, and by faith we maintain the walk, of children. Faith is our separation from, faith is our victory over, the world. Believe and say, " Father."

II. The spirit of the invocation is the spirit of love.

"Our" is a word of love, its character is Pentecostal, for Pentecost is the birthday of the Church. The new covenant is now established, and God has a people who dwell in Him and He in them.

" Ours" is a word of love, but also of faith. We believe in the holy catholic church, the communion of saints. We believe, though often we fail in realising it in thought and action, that if one member suffers, all are necessarily affected, and that the prosperity, health, and vigour of one portion of the Church are a blessing unto the whole community.

We believe that God, in all His dealings and blessings, has reference to the whole body of Christ; that all gifts and operations of the Spirit, all experiences, works, and sufferings of the saints, all events in Divine Providence have this purpose, that *we all* should come in the unity of faith and of the knowledge of the Son of God, unto a perfect man,* unto the measure of the stature of the fulness of Christ.

"Our" we say, for, belonging unto Christ the Head, we belong unto all, we are debtors to all, and servants of the brethren for Christ's sake. As the apostolic Church had all things in common, and no man lacked anything, so the members of Christ have all spiritual gifts and graces in common; none possesses anything for himself, but for the furtherance of the faith and joy of the brethren. It is by this exercise of love that the body is nourished and strengthened. It is compacted by that which every joint supplieth, according to the effectual working of the measure of every part, and thus is the increase of the body with the edifying of itself in love. We seek to realise this union, and this dependence of the members of the body on each other, when in Christ we call God "Our Father."

And as those who are nearest to God are most humble and most loving, they are most anxious to condescend to men of low estate, to benefit them by

---

* Eph. iv. 1-16. Notice the singular number, Christ and the Church are one.

the communication of their gifts, and to strengthen and encourage them in the faith. Thus an equality is kept up, and what is weak and defective in some is filled up by the generosity and love of the more favoured disciples.

While we regard with a special love the household of faith, and stand to them in a relation which is perfectly unique, the word " our " embraces also those who are still outside the fellowship of grace. The garden of the Lord is separated from the world, and enclosed in a threefold way: First, by the Spirit of God, who makes us fruitful unto every good word and work; secondly, by the blood of the covenant, which delivers us from the wrath to come, and from this present evil world ; and thirdly, by the electing love of the Father, who hath chosen us in Christ, and keeps us in Him by His power through faith unto salvation. But this separation is not a wall which conceals us from our fellow-men, and alienates our affections from those around us. Rather are we to view it as transparent, and as a medium of influence. The world is to see the fruit which is borne in this garden; they are to see our good works, and glorify "our Father which is in heaven." The fragrance of humility, love, purity, kindness, meekness, temperance, joy, is to attract the people who pass by, that they may take knowledge of us as the disciples of Jesus. And we, like the Spirit of God, and as the very voice of the Spirit, are to say, " Come." *

---

* Rev. xxii. 17.

Such is our attitude towards the world, and our feeling towards all men is that of love and hope. "When we call God Father, we know that the title does not lie in the petitioner, but in Christ." * He who saved the chief of sinners—this is the argument of every Christian—is able to save and to renew even those who appear most hardened in sin, most inaccessible to the influence of light. It is the humanity of Christ which gives this breadth to our feeling. The Son of God became *man;* in this is manifested the love of God to the *world*—let *every human being rejoice in it.* The fact that I belong to the human race, entitles me to join the song of praise—" Unto *us* a Child is born, unto *us* a Son is given." Because I am man, I may, like aged Simeon, take the child Jesus into my arms, and praise God in the gratitude of an overflowing peace. Thus though we are separated unto God, we are also debtors of love unto all; a chosen generation, and a peculiar people, yet able to say unto all—" Men and brethren;" secure in the citadel of divine election, and yet continually going forth and seeking the salvation of all men, our heart's desire and prayer for them being that they also may, in Jesus, see and love " Our Father." With a deeper love, and with a more hopeful spirit, does the Christian love mankind, because he loves in Christ, who has brought to light the infinite love of the Father.

Honouring and loving all men, let us cultivate

* Dr M. Dods.

especially fellowship with the saints. Special promises are given to united prayer, and to the meeting of Christ's disciples. How many blessings do we lose when, like Thomas, we isolate ourselves from the company of believers!

And yet, strongly as we feel the need and blessing of fellowship, we cannot disguise the fact that we are often disappointed in our communion with Christians. The society and conversation of Christians has at times proved insipid, and has failed to help and encourage us in our inner life. We have spoken and listened, and though the words have been of divine things, and probably scriptural and true, yet the soul has received neither sustenance nor refreshment. We do not find that we go to the throne of grace with intenser faith and love, or to the performance of our duty with a steadier step and more courageous and hopeful heart. Or we have tried to influence, and failed. Our words made no impression; instead of stimulating a languid believer, we have only offended him; we are active and laborious, and we produce only discontent. It may not be profitable to describe still further the failings of Christian intercourse; it may be more useful to think of the causes of these disappointments and their remedies.

Notice, then, that we must be very near to God if we wish to get near our brother's heart. Natural affection, and attractiveness, and congeniality are not sufficient; Christian communion must be the result of true and deep communings with

God. " The lamp is not nourished by the flame; it is nourished by oil, which has constantly to be renewed; and our intercourse will soon lose all power and blessing unless we dwell much in the presence of the Lord."*

Remember also, that both in giving and receiving benefit from Christian intercourse, it is necessary that we should be humble, willing to accept rebuke and humiliation. As long as we seek our own honour, and are filled with a sense of our own importance, we cannot expect to know much of Christian union and fellowship.

Lastly, bear in mind that love is the soul of communion; and love means self-sacrifice. " A new commandment I give unto you, that ye love one another, as I have loved you."

Christian fellowship without love is but a shadow without the substance, and there can be no true happiness in it. In seasons of affliction, of persecution, and suffering, Christian fellowship prospers. And why? Because private prayer prospers; because then there is more humility and confession of sin, there is more love and sympathy. It is then that Christians, in their intercourse, are enriched and strengthened,—that their words are living, their thoughts varied, their hearts enlarged. Then they build up one another in their most holy faith.

The conversation even of disciples brings no light

---

* Lobstein.

and encouragement, unless Jesus draws near and opens the Scriptures. It is only then that light cheers our fainting souls, and the heart begins to burn in love and joyous hope.

But let us derive benefit even from the defectiveness of our earthly intimacies. Let us seek the more earnestly the countenance of Him to whom we can tell all things, and from whom we receive nothing but blessing, and look forward to that perfect communion which reigns in heaven.

III. The spirit of the invocation is the spirit of hope : " Our Father, which art in Heaven."

The child asks, " *Where* is heaven ?" The thought of riper years asks, " *What* is heaven?" Yet the child's question is true and deep ; unless we view heaven as a locality, our thoughts of heaven as a state will become vague and unreal.

Childhood has no difficulty in thinking of heaven as a locality. It thinks of a place beautiful, yet solemn ; joyous, yet sacred ; where there is rest, and yet varied occupation ; it imagines a temple, which is also a palace.* The descriptions of Scripture and of good hymns find a ready reception in the minds of children. The throne of God, Jesus at the right hand of the Father, the innumerable multitude of angels, the glorified saints—these are pictures which engrave themselves deeply on our minds, when we

---

* In the Theocracy, there was only one word for the Palace and the Temple of the Great King.

are still more incredulous about things seen than about things spiritual and eternal.

Childhood takes also a simpler view of the relation between heaven and earth. It thinks of God as high above, seeing all and ruling over all, angels and men. It conceives Him, a living God, commanding the sun every morning to go forth on his bright journey, and bringing out the moon and stars at night to be lights in the darkness, and though gradually taught about the laws of nature, it finds no difficulty in holding fast the personal living and loving government of God.

Angels, too, we are taught—and the child's heart believes it easily and gladly—are continually sent forth from heaven as messengers of the Most High; they execute God's commands, they guard and help His saints, and their work is done silently and un-obtrusively, as if they did not wish to divert our contemplation and gratitude from God. Yet we know what wonderful preservations we owe to them, and that many great and marvellous acts are attri-buted to them in Scripture.*

And one day—and this also childhood realises, and as a day not very distant—the heavens will be made manifest. Jesus will appear; angels and saints will accompany Him; the Son of man will come with a cloud; the angels will gather the children of God; and then shall we be with Christ the Lord, and be ourselves like unto the angels, and shine forth as the sun in the kingdom of the Father.

---

* See on the Third Petition.

Thus a child believes, and we may add rightly and truly, according to Scripture. For Heaven is a place, and not merely a state. Philosophy may think it more rational and spiritual to suppose that as God is in every place, He is in no place more than another. Scripture maintains most emphatically the omnipresence of God,* and the spiritual character of worship, and yet as distinctly teaches that there is a heavenly sanctuary, a throne of grace, the dwelling-place of the Most High.

Let us at once seek light and revelation where it is to be found clearest and purest, in Christ. He came down from heaven, and He went again to the Father. He who has departed from God may describe his repentance as a return to God; he says, " I will arise and go to my Father." But Jesus never left the Father. He was always with Him. He was in heaven while living on earth. When He said to His disciples, " I go to the Father," He meant nothing else but the locality, the heaven where the Father dwells, the throne of His majesty and glory.

Jesus ascended to heaven. That bodily presence, which the apostles saw, heard, handled, is not here. By His Spirit He is with us, as He assured His disciples when He was leaving them, when He was taken

---

* Omnipresence is an inadequate expression. We have no word which, like Eternal in relation to Time, describes God's infinity above space.

up before their eyes.* But His bodily presence is taken from us. The apostles, who were His family, His household, would feel this absence most at meals, when He was wont to preside over them, when they were most fully conscious of the bond of union and peace which united them with the Lord. And, therefore, till He comes again, we have the supper of remembrance and communion.† We are to "do this," and to show the Lord's death till He come, for He is now in heaven. The eyes which regarded the disciples with love, which filled with tears at the grave of Lazarus, which wept over Jerusalem, which looked down from the cross in sympathy and tenderness on Mary, these eyes are now in heaven. The hands which worked in Nazareth, which fed the multitude and healed the sick, which were pierced on Golgotha, are now in heaven. The Son of man is at the right hand of God. Stephen saw Him standing up to receive His faithful disciple. John, the beloved apostle, who used to lean on His bosom, beheld Him in His heavenly glory.

The apostles saw Him ascending. Whither did He go? We are told there is no Below and Above. Some think it childish to speak of heaven as above. But while science may use its language for its own sphere and purpose, we believe the Word; we know only in part, and the glimpses of the unseen world given us in Scripture, partial

---

* Matt. xxviii. † Comp. Baumgarten, Acts ii.

though they be, are to us full of instruction and comfort. We hold fast, then, that Jesus, when He prayed, lifted up His eyes to heaven, that He ascended from the earth, that He will come in like manner as He went up, that His coming shall be as the lightning, shining from east to west, and that every eye shall behold Him. Faith sees the heaven open, and hope waits to see Him come again from His heavenly throne.

We regard heaven, then, as the place where Christ now lives. It is temple and palace, for He is both King and Priest. Simpler, yet grander, is the name Christ gives it, when He calls it " My Father's house," for Christ's greatest and sweetest name is the Son of God. Hence, we are to pray to God as our Father in heaven, not as our King and Lord. Jesus, even as a child of twelve years, knew the temple of Jerusalem as His Father's house. When, eighteen years later, He visited the temple, He emphatically called it " My Father's house," revealing, at the same time, that His body was the true temple of God, and that, through His death, He would become the tabernacle in which God and man meet.* More simply and directly He said to His disciples before leaving them, " In my Father's house are many mansions." Because He is there now, heaven is our home. His obedience on earth, His death on the cross, all He did and suffered for us, is now presented in His person to the Father. The result of all His experiences

---
* John ii. 16–22 ; 1 Thess. i. 10.

below is continually manifested in His intercession, in which He remembers, and the sympathy, by which He sustains, His people. While He is still the man Christ Jesus, faith beholds him crowned with glory, freed from the limitations of the flesh and earth, delivered from all hostile powers, with which He had to contend during His earthly ministry.

As heaven is our home, all heavenly things, and all the inhabitants of heaven, are near and dear unto us. We know that the angels adore the Son of God in human nature; that, in Christ, God gathers together in one all things, both which are in heaven and which are on earth, and that, as they were created by Him, they adore with us the great mystery of godliness, and are united with us in Him for evermore. We think also of the saints who are asleep in Jesus. For when we come to Mount Zion and to the heavenly Jerusalem, we are also come to the spirits of just men made perfect. We know little as to *where* and *how* they exist; but we know they rest in Jesus; they are with Him in a more blessed and peaceful way than even a favoured apostle like Paul was on earth. Their thoughts are thoughts of adoration and love; they, with us, are waiting for the coming of the Lord, when He shall be glorified in His saints, and admired in them that believe.

When we say, " Our Father, which art in heaven," we remember, also, that all spiritual blessings are treasured up for us in heaven. Above are the things which we, being risen with Christ, now seek. Christ himself, according to the Father's will, dispenses the gifts; they come down from above. No church on earth, no communion, be its assumption ever so high-sounding and pompous, or ever so spiritual and purely biblical, can give the Spirit and the spiritual bless-ings, or secure His presence and the manifestations of His power. We look up to our Father in heaven, and whoever asks will receive the heavenly gift.

Faith is often feeble to say "Father," and love languid to say "our;" therefore hope is added, and courage imparted, in the concluding words, "which art in heaven." From the heavenly throne the Spirit of adoption is sent into our timid and selfish hearts, and while around us there is nothing to deliver us from our enemies, our almighty and merciful King is already enthroned, and in Him, who loved us, we are more than conquerors. Our hope is lively, for it is born of that resurrection of Jesus, which is the fountain of imperishable vitality. It is real, for it is not a feeling a vision of an indefinite future, a dream of the imagination; it is a living fact, even a person, Christ himself. Though unseen, like the anchor of a ship, deep and out of sight, it is fixed and secure. Our hope is sure and steadfast, and entereth into that within the vail.

This hope sanctifies us unto God. It separates us from the love, from the thoughts, the standard, and the aim of the world. Every one that hath this hope in him purifies himself, even as Christ is pure. The treasure we have found in His love makes us strangers and pilgrims below. We are not " of the world," but are partakers of a heavenly calling. Our citizenship is in heaven.

This hope brings with it comfort and peace. Nothing can separate us from the love of God in Christ. There, where our treasure is, no thieves can break through, nor moth and rust corrupt. What we lose on earth for Christ's sake, and in the spirit of childlike submission, we receive a hundredfold above. All our tears have been numbered and treasured up in His bottle. Our sufferings and conflict are seed of a joyous harvest. Believe only, and Christ will say to you—" Said I not unto thee, that if thou wouldest believe, thou shouldest see the glory of God ? "

This hope brings with it animating strength. Our life is hid with Christ in God. Our store-house can never fail. Wisdom and grace, patience and endurance, every needful and good gift, will be sent from above. In Christ every believer can say, " My name is Ithiel, God is with me, and Ucal, I am able." *

This hope is our guiding star while we are waiting for the Saviour ; it is the sound of the trumpet encouraging us in our warfare. Christ will come again ! Wherefore gird up the loins of your mind ; be sober, and hope to the end for the grace that is to be brought unto you at the revelation of Jesus Christ ; as obedient children, not fashioning yourselves according to the former lusts in your ignorance, but as He which

* Prov. xxx. 1.

hath called you is holy, so be ye holy in all manner of conversation.

Thus faith says " Father," love says " our," hope says " which art in heaven."

To Him all angels cry aloud, the heavens and all the powers therein.   To Him cherubim and seraphim continually do cry—" Holy, holy, holy, Lord God of hosts."   But no voice of praise and thanksgiving is so precious to Him as the voice of the blood-bought family, who, in the Spirit, and through Christ, the beloved Son, say unto Him—" Our Father which art in heaven ! "

5

THE FUNDAMENTAL PETITION

"Hallowed be Thy name."

THERE is perfect harmony between true prayer and the will of God. When Augustine said, "Give, Lord, what Thou commandest, and command what Thou wilt," he offered not merely a profound and comprehensive petition, but he uttered words which contain the exposition of all prayer. The soul desires what God commands, and thus attains in prayer that true liberty in which our wills are ours to make them God's.

God spake on Mount Sinai the ten commandments, and Jesus, the Son of God, gave His disciples the seven petitions. Between the commandments uttered by God, and the petitions taught by the Lord Jesus, there must needs subsist harmony. For Christ came to fulfil; and what was written on the tables of stone is written by His Spirit on renewed and loving hearts, and ascends now to the throne of God, as the prayer of His children, whom the Son has made free.

As in the first table of the law, so in the first three petitions, our mind is directed to heavenly relations and blessings. The basis on which the commandments rest is the word of grace: " I am the Lord thy God, which have brought thee out of the land of Egypt, out of the house of bondage;" even as the root and fountain of our petitions is in the invocation, the relation in which God stands to us through His Son Jesus Christ.

No sooner have we uttered by faith the invocation " Our Father which art in heaven," when, in harmony with the blessed angels and the celestial worship, we adore the holiness of God ; for as the seraphim cry, " Holy, holy, holy, Lord God of hosts," we, who are the children of God in Christ Jesus, pray, " Hallowed be Thy name."

The holiness of God fills the heart of man with awe, and his conscience with fear, as long as he dreads the justice which must necessarily accompany it. Guilt cannot bear the thought of a holy God. And as long as the love of sin rules within us, and holiness is known only in contrast with our own desires and thoughts, we are not able to rejoice at the remembrance of His holiness. To angels, we believe, the holiness of God is the divine attribute on which they dwell as the foundation of their safety and the source of their peace and blessedness. Calmly they rest in God, because His omnipotence, His sovereignty, His wisdom are in harmony and inseparable union with His holiness. Thus the law on earth is dreaded by the transgressor, while it is the very protection and peaceful security of the upright. Moreover, the angels rest in the holiness of God, because they themselves love what is good and pure : holiness is the bond of union between them and the Lord, from whom all holiness flows as from its living fountain.

The renewed soul likewise regards the holiness of God in peace and love. The Holy One of Israel is his Redeemer ; the death of Christ on the cross is the greatest manifestation of God's hatred of sin, and the greatest vindication of the honour of His law. And with the clean heart created in us by God, we love Him who is holy, and we love that holiness which He alone can give.

We remember that God's holiness, as it separates Him from all that is sinful and defiled, is most frequently represented in Scripture as connected with His *love*, with His condescending grace, with His reconciling mercy and renewing power. Do the seraphim extol the holiness of God, His separateness from all that is imperfect and impure ?—They immediately add, " the whole earth is full of His glory." It is the good pleasure of His will to manifest His glory and to enrich His creatures with His grace. In the prophet Hosea we read, " I will not execute the fierceness of mine anger, and I will not return to destroy Ephraim, for I am God, and not man, the Holy One in the midst of thee." In the prophet Isaiah, the ideas of God's holiness and Israel's redemption are constantly connected. " Thus saith the High and Lofty One that inhabiteth eternity, whose name is Holy, I dwell in the high and holy place ; with him also that is of a contrite and humble spirit." Thus Mary, when praising the Lord for His wonderful condescension, said, "For He that is mighty hath done to me great things, and Holy is His name."

So numerous and so striking are the passages in which the holiness and the condescending mercy of God are combined, that some have deduced from these scriptures the definition, that the holiness of God means His love, in which He reveals and brings into communion with Himself the children of men as well as the angels.* This is, doubtless, one-sided ; and instead of endeavouring to give an exact definition of that which is best the subject of quiet meditation and prayerful thought, let us hold fast the fact that the

---

* Stier, "Reden Jesu," v. 4–20:—"God is holy in His condescending, merciful, saving *love.* His holiness is revealed not merely in the circle of His angels, in the celestial splendour of His pure creation, but among men, when He draws near to sinners in order to bless them and unite them with himself." He quotes Isaiah xli. 14 ; Ps. xxii. 4–7, lxxxix. 16–19, xcix. Yet Stier acknowledges also the other aspect of holiness, in the anger and wrath of God against all unrighteousness. "Jesus calls God holy when He speaks of His disciples (John xvii. 11) ; righteous, when He speaks of the world (John xvii. 25). The Father is holy when He reveals Himself to His chosen ones; righteous, when He conceals Himself from the unjust. The holiness of God is God's separateness, according to which He remains the same in all relationships which exist within His Deity and into which He enters. . . . But this is only one aspect. God's holiness would not be holiness, but exclusive isolation, unless it pre-supposed God's revelation and communication of Himself. Holiness is the union or impenetration of His separateness, and self-revelation, and communication."—*Schmieder, Hohepriesterliche Gebet.* When we think of God as light and as love, we realise perhaps most fully the idea of holiness, combining separateness and purity with *communion.*

Holy God is our Redeemer, and that the object of redemption is to bring us into fellowship with our Father in heaven, who is holy. Holiness is the beginning as well as the end of all God's manifestations. In His holiness He found a way to save us, and without holiness no man shall see the Lord.

When we think of Christ and the Spirit, the same comforting facts meet our view. Christ is holy, harmless, undefiled, separate from sinners, and for this very reason He can save, He can succour the tempted, He can cleanse by His touch the leper, and give rest by His presence to the weary and heavy-laden.

And is it not remarkable, that the Spirit, who, as it were, comes most directly in contact with our sin, our darkness, the rebelliousness and hardness of our heart—the Spirit who is, as it were, the finger of God touching us, the pure dove brooding over the chaotic waters of the soul, is emphatically called "the *Holy* Spirit?" In Him the Father and the Son have communion with men. With what love and patience does the Spirit watch over sinners, warning, drawing, following us into our paths of disobedience and sin, waiting for opportunities to influence, to rouse, to restore! Surely He is a loving Spirit. "Thy Spirit is good," that is, kind, gracious. Yet is He called the Holy Spirit.

What reason have we to love as well as to reverence the holiness of God—Father, Son, and Spirit! As the God of our salvation God is holy.

To live in the presence of God is the privilege of His children, and no sooner have we lifted up our hearts to our Father who is in heaven, than we think with adoration and peaceful joy of His holiness.

It may be thought strange that our first petition should not be for bread, or pardon, or strength. Creatures, poor and needy, sinful and guilty, weak and helpless, would naturally ask first that their wants may be supplied, their transgressions forgiven, and that protection and strength may be given them amidst their dangers and trials. But remember who it is that offers the petition. As the words " Our Father which art in heaven " are the epitome of the gospel, so they are the first utterance of the regenerate. Here speaks one whose prayer of repentance, " God be merciful to me, the sinner," has been answered ; he is no longer in the far country, but in the Father's house ; he is no longer a sheep gone astray, but in the fold of peace ; he is no longer crying "out of the depths," but he is in Christ ; and, having received the Spirit of sonship, he says "Abba." How natural is it for us to exclaim " Hallowed be Thy name," when we know what manner of love the Father hath bestowed upon us, that we should be called the sons of God ; when we contemplate the glory manifested in our redemption and adoption in Christ Jesus, and rejoice in the lively hope of His inheritance ! We cannot say "Father" without immediately, in the spirit of filial reverence and gratitude, giving Him

His honour.   As in the invocation we are risen together with Christ, so in the first petition we seek
the things which are above.   For it is a petition, and
not merely an ascription of praise.   We ask in it that
God would be our God.   God's children know that
God is the fountain of all life and of all blessedness ;
that to know Him and Christ Jesus, whom He has
sent, is eternal life.*

The Christian understands that idolatry is not
merely a great evil, but, strictly speaking, *the* great
evil from which all evils emanate.†   And there-

---

* "A friend calling on the Rev. Ebenezer Erskine, during his
last illness, said to him, 'Sir, you have given us many good
advices, pray what are you now doing with your own soul ?'   'I
am doing with it,' said he, 'what I did forty years ago ; I am
resting on that word, *I am the Lord thy God ;* and on this I mean
to die.'   To another, he said, 'The covenant is my charter, and if
it had not been for that blessed word, *I am the Lord thy God,* my
hope and strength had perished from the Lord.'   The night on
which he died, his eldest daughter was reading in the room where
he was, to whom he said, 'What book is that you are reading, my
dear ?'   'It is one of your sermons, sir.'   'What one is it ?'   'It
is the sermon on that text, *I am the Lord thy God.*'   'O
woman,' said he, 'that is the best sermon I ever preached.'   And it
was most probably the best to his soul.   A little afterwards, with
his finger and thumb he shut his own eyes, and laying his hand below his cheek, breathed out his soul into the hands of his living
Redeemer."

† Compare the beautiful and weighty words of De Quincey (Works,
vol. viii., p. 306) :—" The true evil of idolatry is this : There is one
sole idea of God, which corresponds adequately to His total nature.
Of this idea, two things may be affirmed : the first being, that it
is at the root of all absolute grandeur, of all truth, and of all moral
perfection ; the second being, that, natural and easy as it seems when
once unfolded, it could only have been unfolded by revelation ; and,
to all eternity, he that started with a false conception of God could

fore He regards as the fundamental petition for himself, for the Church, and for the world, that which Infinite Wisdom and Love have taught us to place in the position of priority, " Hallowed be Thy name."

What is meant by the name of God? And what is meant by hallowing that name?

I. God has revealed His name in creation; He has written it in our heart and conscience. The

---

not, through any effort of his own, exchange it for a true one. All idolaters alike, though not all in equal degrees, by intercepting the idea of God through the prism of some representative creature that *partially* resembles God, refract, splinter, and distort that idea. Even the idea of light, of the pure solar light, the old Persian symbol of God, has that depraving necessity. Light itself, besides being an *imperfect* symbol, is an incarnation for us. However pure itself or in its original divine manifestation for us, it is incarnated in forms and in matter that are not pure, it gravitates towards physical alliances, and therefore towards unspiritual pollutions. And all experience shows that the tendency of man, left to his own imagination, is downwards. . . . God, by a succession of imperfect interceptions, falls more and more under the taint and limitation of the *alien* elements associated with all created things ; and, for the ruin of all moral grandeur in man, every idolatrous nation left to itself will gradually bring round the idea of God into the idea of a powerful demon. Many things check and disturb this tendency for a time ; but finally, and under that intense civilisation to which man intellectually is always hurrying under the eternal evolution of physical knowledge, such a degradation of God's idea, ruinous to the *moral* capacities of man, would undoubtedly perfect itself, were it not for the kindling of a purer standard by revelation. Idolatry, therefore, is not merely *an* evil, and one utterly beyond the power of social institutions to redress, but, in fact, it is the fountain of all other evil that seriously menaces the destiny of the human race."

heavens declare the glory of God, and the firmament showeth His handiwork. The things that are made declare His eternal power and Godhead. The conscience also beareth witness, and thoughts within us could not accuse did they not know justice and purity love and truth. And now, that we possess the light in which we see light, we read the name of God written on all creation and on all relationships of life.* We say with David, " O Lord, our Lord !

---

* Compare my remarks on the parabolic character of Scripture in " Christ and the Scriptures," pp. 118–131.

This thought is expressed by Angelus Silesius :—

> " Nothing fair on earth I see
> But I straightway think on Thee ;
> Thou art fairest in my eyes,
> Source in whom all beauty lies."

Compare also the words of " Jeremiah Horrocks, 1638, a youthful astronomer," quoted by Kelly in " The Eternal Purpose of God," p. 204 :—" Shall we think that He who was content to shadow out these mysteries with the poor blood of bulls and goats, will disdain to have them typified in the more glorious bodies of the stars and motions of the heavens, which David accounted such clear emblems of God's glory, that he goes from speaking of the light of the sun unto God's law, as if the subject were still the same, without any conclusion to the first, or introduction to the latter ? For my part, I must ever think that God created all other things, as well as man, in His own image ; and that the nature of all things is one, as God is one ; and therefore a harmonical agreeing of the causes of all things, if demonstrated, would be the quintessence of most truly natural philosophy. . . . If any one think all this but an idle conceit, I must tell him he doth too rashly deride that book of creatures, that voice of the heavens which is heard in all the world, and wherein, without question, God hath instamped more mysteries than the lazy wits of men, more ready to slight than amend **any** speculation, are ordinarily aware of."

how excellent is Thy name in all the earth ! " God
has lent, as it were, His name to His creatures, that
they may show forth His praise ; that heaven and
earth should be full of His glory. God is the sun,
and Christ is the morning star. The branch, the
rose of Sharon, the apple tree, the vine, the corn of
wheat, the tree of life, the living waters, the consuming fire, are all names, revelations of God. The
worm and the suffering lamb, the lion, the roe, the
young hart upon the mountains of spices, are names
declaring to us Christ in the various aspects of
His person and work. So is the Shepherd, the King,
the Friend, the Bridegroom. All nature and Providence are opened to us as a book of parables of names
or revelations of the Most High.

It is opened to us, for we had lost the power of
seeing. God had become unknown to man. They
had forgotten His name. As the great and distant
Anonymous,* they recognised vaguely and dimly His
existence and power : a great Architect, a wonderful
Artist, a mysterious Influence, incomprehensible, un-
defined, impersonal to all intents and purposes; for
with the name they lost the sense of a personal,
loving God. There is something strange in a name.
" Tell me thy name ? " was the question of Jacob to
the man who wrestled with him. We realise by the
name individual life and relationship. It brings

---

* Compare the celebrated verses of Göthe's Faust, "Wer kann
ihn nennen ?" Significantly enough, this pantheistic Confession of
Faith precedes immediately the transgression of God's Law.

with it love and trust. With it we lose reality.
Abstraction is but the shadow of death. As long as
Israel knew God by name, as Jehovah, they had life.
Since they gave up the name, since they rejected
the last revelation of the divine name " Jesus," they
have lost the knowledge of the Most High and
spiritual vitality. Religious life will be found in this
present age, where God's name is known—Jesus—as
it was of old, where Jehovah was worshipped. When
people speak of heaven, of Providence, of the Creator,
expect no enthusiasm, no victory of faith, no sacrifice of love, no heavenly citizenship.

God revealed His name to Israel. Unto Moses He
spake : " Say unto the children of Israel, I Am hath
sent thee." I Am, the self-subsistent, all-glorious,
living One. I Am ; do not add anything to it—
wisdom, or truth, or love, or power. This only
limits it : All that is good, and true, and strong, and
beautiful, is because He is. It is of Him and in
Him. Jehovah is the name of God in His revelation
to His chosen people ; it is His proper name, which
cannot be given to any beside Him. When He condescends and makes Himself known to sinners, He is
Jehovah. The patriarchs knew and worshipped Him
as Jehovah, though it was only at the commencement
of Israel's redemption, when God called His Son out
of Egypt, that the covenant-name was fully revealed.
The name Jehovah does not merely denote the eternity of God ; rather does it refer to God's revelation
of Himself in history as Saviour, carrying out the

counsel of His love with unchanging faithfulness. " Jesus Christ, the same yesterday, to-day, and for ever," is the true exposition of the mysterious name. He that is to come is Jehovah, and of this coming the first was in humiliation, the second will be in glory. " Behold He cometh. I am Alpha and Omega, the beginning and the ending, saith the Lord, which is, and which was, and which is to come " (Rev. i. 8).* Of Jehovah it is said (and not of Elohim) that He lives,† for the meaning of Jehovah's life is not merely that He is the source as well as the sustainer of all existence, but that He has chosen a people, among whom He manifests His life, and whom He draws into communion with Himself. Hence it is always said of Jehovah, that He speaks, that His word came to the prophets ; Jehovah is the God of revelation.

The Jews knew God as Jehovah-Elohim. Jehovah, their covenant God and King, was the Creator of heaven and earth. This was the wonderful teaching of Genesis, which faith alone receives (Heb. xi. 2), that all things were created by God, and that this Creator was none other but the God who stood in special covenant relationship to His people.‡

---

* Notice in the Gospel of John and the Book of Revelation the frequent occurrence of the title " I Am " ascribed to Jesus.

† Deus est omnium rerum Elohim, omnium actionum Jehovah. —*Oetinger.*

‡ Compare the remark of Delitzsch (Genesis) on Change of the Divine Names. How appropriate is the use of the name Jehovah-Elohim in the section which forms the transition from the creation

God called Himself El Shaddai, the Almighty, when He appeared unto Abraham, unto Isaac, and unto Jacob. The Jews called it " the shuddering name," for it revealed His infinite power, unfathomable, all-comprehensive, irresistible.

God called Himself Jehovah-jireh, when He revealed unto Abraham the mystery of redeeming wisdom and love; and the Father of the faithful beheld in a type, afar off, the Lord providing a ransom even in the person of His Son, His only-begotten and well beloved.

God called Himself Jehovah-rophi, the Physician, the Healer of our diseases, who is able to restore the sick and to bind up tenderly the wounded. In Exodus, the book of redemption, sickness is first mentioned, and, as the evil is disclosed, the Lord unfolds His name in a new aspect.

God revealed Himself as Jehovah-nissi, the Lord is my Banner, when Amalek was conquered through the intercession of Moses, and the Lord delivered His people from their enemies.

God called Himself Jehovah-zidkenu, the Lord our Righteousness; Jehovah-shalom, the Lord-Peace, and thereby reveals to us that He himself will be our righteousness and our peace.

God calls Himself Jehovah-shammah, when He predicts the restoration of Jerusalem; the time when

of the world by Elohim, to the history of salvation, of which history man is the centre and end, and which shows that God the Creator is also God the Redeemer and the guide of history.

Christ the Lord shall be revealed in visible glory, and Jerusalem shall be the joy of the whole earth.

Are not these wonderful and beautiful names?

But, besides these special revelations of the divine name, God manifested His character to His people in many declarations. Thus, when Moses prayed, "Show me Thy glory," God said, "I will proclaim the name of Jehovah before thee." Standing in the cleft of the rock, and covered with the hand of the Lord, who descended in a cloud—the magnificence and awful sublimity of nature forming a fit accompaniment and symbol of the divine revelation—the servant of God heard the name, "The Lord, the Lord God, merciful and gracious, long-suffering, and abundant in goodness and truth, keeping mercy for thousands, forgiving iniquity and transgression and sin, and that will by no means clear the guilty; visiting the iniquity of the fathers upon the children and upon the children's children, unto the third and fourth generation."

God revealed His name to Israel in their history. The dealings of God with His people were one great continued manifestation of His character. And what is the sum and substance of this marvellous and varied history? It is this: "Israel, thou hast destroyed thyself, but in me is thy help." It is a record of the inexhaustible love, wisdom, power, and faithfulness of God; it is a constantly renewed unveiling of that hidden sanctuary of grace, into which God retreats when, according to His justice and the requirement of the law, and the resources of nature, He could only give up His people to the consequences of their sins and their misery. Israel's whole history is the name of God, Jehovah.

God manifested His name in His law. The law is a transcript of the divine will ; and what is His will but a revelation of His nature? Hence the whole law is summed up in this—" Be ye holy, for I am holy."

God wills what He is. All the ordinances and statutes which He gave, even the very minutest, bear as a seal His name, " I am the Lord." " Thou shalt not curse the deaf, nor put a stumbling-block before the blind, but shalt fear God: I am the Lord. Thou shalt not go up and down as a tale-bearer among thy people, neither shalt thou stand against the blood of thy neighbour: I am the Lord."

Every sacrifice was a name of God, showing forth some aspect of His character and of His redemption. So was every festival. The whole law was a revelation of the divine name.

Every servant of God, sent by Him to the nation, was a name of God. Often we find this in the most obvious manner indicated by the very names they bore. Elijah means, Jehovah is my strength; Isaiah, Jehovah is my salvation. But still more important is it to notice that they show forth the name of the Lord in their character, work, and history. For they were types of Him in whom God at last revealed Himself perfectly. We see Abel, the first shepherd, hated and slain by his brother, type of the Good Shepherd,

who was hated without cause, and who laid down
His life for the sheep; we see Enoch ascending into
heaven, and Noah saving the chosen family from
destruction, types of Him who is Abel, Enoch, and
Noah in one person—who died, who ascended, and
who became the Saviour of all who trust in Him.
Isaac, beloved and not spared, reminds us of Jesus,
the gift of the Father; Joseph shadowed forth the
mystery, "through suffering unto glory," as well as
the blessed truth, that He is not ashamed to call us
brethren.   Moses as Mediator, Joshua as bringing
Israel into Canaan, Aaron as high priest, find their
fulfilment in that *one* Lord, who has brought in
everlasting redemption, and, as the true Melchizedek,
the royal priest, brings blessing and joy to all the
faithful.   David, the shepherd-king, and Solomon,
as emblem of wisdom, peace, and wide-spread glory,
typified the true King of Israel, whose meekness and
lowliness in heart, whose obedience and suffering, are
crowned with victory and a glorious inheritance.

God spake thus to the fathers at sundry times and
in divers manners, and the object of all His manifestations and gifts was to make known unto them
His name.   God reveals — *Himself.*   God only
speaks to declare His name.   At last, when the time
was fulfilled, God sent forth His Son, and in Him
the name of God was fully and perfectly revealed.
Now is fulfilled the promise—" My people shall know
my name, therefore they shall know in that day that I
am He that doth speak ; behold, it is I ! "

Christ, the Word of God, is The Name.   Hitherto
we have spoken of names of God; but none of these
names contain the fulness or correspond perfectly
to the idea, "Name of God."   Not even the name
"Father," revealing the new relationship in which
God stands to us, through the only-begotten Son,
can be regarded as absolutely God's name.   The
name of God is not any special word of human
language, in which some aspect of God's character
and will is expressed; but it is He in whom the
fulness of the Godhead dwelleth, who is the brightness of His glory, and the express image of His
person; in whom God reveals Himself to man; in
whom the silent God becomes to us audible, the
invisible God seen, the distant God nigh, the unknown one, known in the spirit. God, from all eternity,
had His "name" in the Word; and hence Christ
is the Messenger in whom is God's name; He is the
countenance of God, or rather (as the word countenance, *panim*, is plural) the perfect manifestation of
all divine features.   It is for this reason that the
name is spoken of with such reverence, that it is
regarded as all-important.   The Lord our God is to
be worshipped; but we cannot worship what we do
not know.   Hence the tendency to make an image
of God, or to give Him a name of our own invention.
But the first commandment is directed against
idolatry; Christ is the only image of the invisible
God; only to Him can we liken God, only in Him
can we see the Invisible.   And having received Christ

the name, the next commandment is to hallow the name.

Jesus revealed the name of God, and Jesus was Himself the name of God. He could say, " Father, I have declared Thy name," and He could also say, " He that hath seen me hath seen the Father." From Bethlehem to Golgotha, from His first testimony of the Father in the temple, to His last invocation of the Father on the cross, His whole life was a revelation of God, a declaration of His name. The whole character of God is revealed to us in Jesus. Behold Jesus, and behold God! The man Christ Jesus is the only Mediator between God and man. This refers not merely to the grace of God, the favour of the Most High, which is ours on account of the obedience and expiatory sacrifice of the Lord ; but it has reference to all mediation. All knowledge of God is mediated by Christ. He is not merely the medium of divine love, but also of divine light. We see the glory of God in the face of Jesus Christ. God had always declared unto Israel that no man had seen Him at any time, and that He could not be likened unto any one, and yet He always promised to come and reveal Himself unto them in a most real manner, and that then it would be said to the cities of Judah, " Behold your God." The promise is fulfilled, and he that hath seen Jesus hath seen the Father. From the least to the greatest, all men may know the Lord, for Jesus is Immanuel, God with us.

All the features of the countenance of Jesus are reflections of the Father's character. Christ's compassion and mercy, His tenderness and pity, His patience and faithfulness, His indignation and zeal— are revelations of what is in God. Thus Jehovah had spoken of Himself before the incarnation, as being grieved and pained ; thus had He complained and mourned over Israel's ingratitude and hardness of heart ; thus had He exclaimed, How can I give thee up, Ephraim ? We see the Father in Jesus ; the whole character of God is manifested in the person of His incarnate Son.*

All the *gifts* of God are in Christ, and thus also is Christ the name of God. Christ is *the* gift of God, which comprehends all divine blessings. The Father hath given Him to be light and life to us, the bread of life, the robe of righteousness.

All the *purposes* of God are revealed in Christ, and thus also is Christ the name of God. In Christ

---

* " God hath on purpose stamped His utmost manifestative glory on the face of Christ, that we might see it in Him (2 Cor. iv. 6). God gives the light of the knowledge of the glory of God in the face ; or, as others read it, the person of Jesus Christ, that as the soul looks out in the face, and you see more of a man's disposition in a look, a cast of his eye, a wink, a blush there, than in all his body; so is the Godhead in Christ Jesus, which is His face. *He is the brightness of His Father's glory*, shining in through a veil of flesh (whereof the shining of Moses' face was but a type and shadow) through the lanthorn of His humanity (if I may so compare it), so to relieve our eyes in beholding the Godhead, which no eye could otherwise have done. There is a sun behind that veil, the glory of which, immediately shining unto Him, put out our eyes." —*Goodwin on the Knowledge of God.*

we see our election unto eternal life. In Christ we see the counsel of God concerning earth, as the scene of the manifestation of His redeeming love; and the counsel of God concerning the Church, who, as the bride, is to be associated with her Divine Lord in His kingdom.

In Jesus is revealed unto us the name of God, *as Father, Son, and Holy Ghost.* This mystery was foreshadowed from the beginning, but it is fully revealed in Christ. As He reveals the Father, so we behold Him as the Lord, who sends the Spirit. One with us, He leads us to the Father; one with the Father, He sends the Spirit into our hearts. Jesus has the pre-eminence as the Mediator; in Him we obtain fellowship with the Father and the Spirit It is He who sends forth the messengers of the new covenant: "All power is given unto me in heaven and in earth. Go ye therefore, and teach all nations, baptizing them in the name of the Father, and of the Son, and of the Holy Ghost."

This name, into which we are baptized, with which God in His loving-kindness meets us at the very commencement of life, is the name of the true and living God, the covenant God of love. Never are the Three blessed Ones mentioned together, except to describe the purpose of eternal love, the grace and peace of redemption, the manifold blessings of the God of salvation. We read of the justice and anger of God; we read the awful words, "The wrath of the Lamb;" we read of the unpardonable sin against the

Holy Ghost; but when Father, Son, and Spirit are mentioned together, it is uniformly in connexion with blessing;* for the revelation of God's name to His own people is to bless them even with Himself. Remember then, before thy life, before thy works, before thy sins, God, who has loved thee with an everlasting love, met thee by declaring His name: a Father of Love, a Redeemer of infinite grace, a Spirit of unspeakable tenderness.

II. Hallowed be Thy name. What is meant by the name of God being hallowed?

All the works of God show forth and glorify His name, but only intelligent and loving beings can hallow it. His name can be sanctified only in and by angels and men, who worship Him in spirit and in truth, who love and serve Him with humility and gladness. It is our prerogative as His children, to know and to show forth His name.

The petition implies, first, the desire to know God's name. The name of God is now simple; the highest, deepest, most comprehensive name, the name above every name, even Jesus. Through Moses and the prophets, God showed His greatness and majesty; our dispensation is characterised by simplicity and sweetness. The emblem of Jehovah, in the days of the law, was the eagle; Jesus compares Himself to a hen gathering her chickens under her wings. Yet no man knoweth the Son but the Father,

---

* Rev. J. Vaughan, Sermon on Trinity Blessings.

" to know Jesus " is the life-long study of the chief apostle. To acquaint ourselves with God is our peace ; to understand the mystery of the Father and His Son, our prayer ; to learn Christ, our constant aim.*

God only can teach us His name. The great promise is, " They shall all be taught of God ; my people shall know my name." The ultimate object of Christ's life and death is to show unto us the Father, to declare His name (John xvii.) This end gives unity to our life. For this purpose we search the Scripture, and give ourselves to meditation ; for this purpose we meet with our fellow-Christians, and let the word of Christ dwell in us richly ; the teaching of Christ's ministers, and the sacraments of the new covenant, are to manifest and seal to us the name of God. All afflictions, all painful experiences of our sin and wayward-ness, all God's dealings with us in Providence, are to lead us to a deeper and more reverential knowledge of His name. Stand in the cleft of the rock, and hear the name of God.

To hallow the name of God is to look unto Christ. In the seven epistles, which the glorified Saviour sent unto the Churches, He invariably commences by revealing His name, by manifesting some aspect of His person, character, and work. The exhortations of each epistle stand in intimate con-nexion with the name, because all our sins and deficiencies arise from our forgetting some aspect of

* Phil. iii. 10; Col. ii. 2.

Christ. If we could see Jesus as He is, we should be like Him, then the name of God would be hallowed in us.

To hallow the name of God is to treat it as a reality—to remember God *is*, what He calls Himself. Hence to trust, reverence, and resemble the Father, is to hallow His name, Father; to rely on Jesus as our Saviour and our strength to overcome sin, is to hallow His name Son; to remember the indwelling, and to use the power of the Spirit, is to hallow the name Spirit.

To hallow the name of God is to rejoice in it. God is our exceeding joy,* and therefore we are commanded to rejoice always. Some rejoice in themselves, their faith, their feelings, their prayers, their works, and hence their rejoicing fluctuates. But we are to joy in God our Lord, we are to be glad in Him, who is our Father in heaven, our Saviour, and our Sanctifier. He is our portion, and knowing that He is our God, our heart is filled with praise. An unknown God brings no joy; for darkness is always associated with gloom. It is pleasant to behold the sun. Light is gladness; and the glory of God is manifested now— the true light shineth. The more we know of God, the more comprehensive is our view of Christ, the more many-sided our conception and experience of God's attributes and works; the greater will be our joy in His name.

To hallow God's name is to keep it separate, dis-

* Psalm xliii.

tinct from our own opinions and the corrupt thoughts and desires of the heart. What a task is this! Our understanding is darkened, our hearts are full of sin; the world around us is in wickedness; in the Church, also, the light is often dim, and love waxing cold. We therefore pray God that He, by His Spirit, may constantly reveal Himself in Christ to our souls, and thus sanctify us through the truth, that we may sanctify or hallow His name. We remember the word of the apostle John: "Little children, keep yourselves from idols." And the warning of Christ, "If the light that is in you be darkness." Feeling the greatness of our danger, we go to God, believing that He, who of His grace has given us His name, will keep us through His own name, according to the Saviour's intercession.*

To hallow God's name means not to divide the name of God, but to regard it as one, sacred and inviolable in its unity. We desire to remember His justice as well as His mercy, His holiness as well as His goodness, that He is Light and Love, a Saviour and a Judge, Redeemer and Sanctifier; we desire to remember His promises as well as His commandments, His work for us and His work in us; to remember Him, who was and is and is to come, that faith may manifest itself in love, and be upheld and guided by hope. And as we know and keep the name of God in the unity of His manifold revelations, our heart, with its manifold tendencies and powers, will

---

* John xvii. 11.

be united (Ps. lxxxvi. 11), our life will gain in variety and in harmony.

To hallow God's name is to live and walk in Christ, as the apostle Paul speaks of his ways, which are in Christ Jesus; and as we read the divine promise in Zech. x. 12, " And I will strengthen them in the Lord; and they shall walk up and down in His name, saith the Lord."

To hallow God's name means, that we ourselves should be manifestations of God, reflecting His image, showing forth His will, resembling His character. Christ was the name of the Father, sent by Him into the world; even thus are we called by Christ's name and sent by Him, that the world may see in us His love and spirit. Our life is to be in the name of Jesus. God has given wonderful names to His people, and what God calls us, is the expression of an eternal reality. One with Jesus, the Church bears many of His names. Thus it is predicted, that when the Branch of righteousness should grow up unto David, *Jerusalem* shall be called the Lord our Righteousness.* And thus it is now that, identified with the Saviour, we are called sons, priests unto God, anointed ones or Christians, light of the world.

God said of old that His name was blasphemed among the heathen, because Israel walked unworthy of his great and high calling. Let us bear in mind that, as Jesus revealed the Father, we are to reveal

---

* Jer. xxxiii. 15, 16.

Jesus. We see Jesus because we have received the Spirit; the world is to see Jesus in His disciples. The Bible is God's Word to us who believe, but we ought to be the Bible to the world, epistles of Christ, seen and read of all men. There ought to be in us something beyond the attractiveness of integrity and kindliness, of honour and benevolence, of affection and self-sacrifice, which we see and admire often in those who are still without the knowledge of Christ; ours ought to be the mind of Christ and the fruits of the Holy Ghost. We are witnesses and representatives of Christ; if we are filled with the Spirit, the name of God, into which we are baptized, is hallowed in and through us.

Bearing the name of God, we pray in this petition for our own consecration, that we may be a peculiar people, separated from the world and conformed to the image of the Son of God. Nor can we truly honour and love the name of God, without seeking to spread the knowledge of His truth. We therefore pledge ourselves to make known God's character and work by earnest effort, by consistent example. And the petition is answered, just in proportion " as we yield ourselves up in deed and truth to the Spirit of God, that we, like our Lord, may glorify His name upon the earth, and may accomplish the work which He has given us to do." *

As the name of God is hallowed by us and in us, we shall discover more fully what is our own name, what

---

* Maurice, Lord's Prayer, 23.

is our individual peculiar position and gift in the
Church of Christ. He who calleth us by name, knows
each of us, and gives to us an individuality of character and work, which remains, even in glory, a secret
beween Him and us; for it is written, that He will
give to him that overcometh a new name, which no
man knoweth save he that receiveth it (Rev. ii. 17).

But the petition is also universal. This fundamental
blessing we ask not only for ourselves individually,
but for all the household of faith, and for all men.
In approaching God, we worship Him as our Father,
and in every petition we are to realise the expansive
power of Christ's love, the union of the saints, and the
priestly character of intercession.

There is no health for the nation or the family
but by the knowledge of God's name. Herein is
life. There can be no rest for our mind, and no
peace in our heart, until we know that name, which
our reason cannot discover, and yet without which it
cannot be satisfied, which hath not entered into the
heart of man, yet without which man's heart is home-
less and weary. It is when there shall be one Lord,
and His name one, that the Lord shall be King over
all the earth ; when God shall sanctify His great
name, which was profaned among the heathen, that
righteousness and peace shall flourish among all
nations.

For this glorious time we pray ; and in the spirit of
the age to come it is our privilege to live even now.
Because we hallow the name of God, our heart's

desire is, " Thy kingdom come."   And in that kingdom the knowledge of His name will be our chief joy.

> Lord, I believe Thou hast prepared,
>   Unworthy though I be,
> For me a blood-bought, free reward,
>   A golden harp for me.
> 'Tis strung and tuned for endless years,
>   And form'd by power divine,
> *To sound, in God the Father's ears.*
>   *No other name than Thine.*

6

THE KINGDOM OF GRACE WITHIN US

"Thy kingdom come."

" THE soul says to God : *

"Our Father, which art in the heavens, we Thy children on earth separated from Thee, and in misery, how great a distance is between us and Thee! How can we ever get home to Thee into our Fatherland?

"God answers:

"A child honours his father, and a servant his master. Am I your Father, where is my honour? Am I your Lord, where is the reverence and fear you owe me? For my holy name is dishonoured and blasphemed among you and by you.

"The soul offers the first petition:

"Alas, O Father, this is true. We acknowledge our guilt. Be to us a gracious Father, and give us of Thy mercy so to live that Thy name is hallowed in us. Let us not think, speak, do, possess, or plan anything in which we seek not first Thy glory and name, and not our vain honour and name. Grant us to love, honour, and fear Thee as children their father.

_____

* Martin Luther, 1518.

" God asks :

"How can my honour and name be sanctified among you, seeing that all your heart and thoughts are inclined to evil, and you are in the captivity of sin, and none can sing my song in a strange land ? (Ps. cxxxvii.)

" The second petition offered by the soul :

" O Father, it is true.   Help us out of our misery ; let Thy kingdom come, that sin may be driven away, and we be made according to Thy pleasure, that Thou alone mayest reign in us, and we be Thy dominion, obeying Thee with all our powers of body and soul."

It is the shortest petition, as the first is the most solemn, and the third the most difficult.   But it is most comprehensive.   It is a summary of the whole Scripture revelation from Genesis to the Apocalypse : it reveals the purpose, the hidden meaning, and the final consummation of all history.   How glorious will yet the answer be on earth to the prayers which from the beginning have ascended to the throne of God to establish His kingdom !

The earth is the very centre of God's kingdom.   It is to the universe what Bethlehem is to the thousands of Judah.   It is here He hath purposed to reveal His glory in the ages to come.   Jesus is to be King over all the earth, and to sit on the throne of His father David.   Jerusalem is to be the centre of the nations who walk in the light of God.   He who is appointed heir of all things, and unto whom the Father hath put into subjection the age to come,* took not upon Him the nature of angels, but the seed of Abraham ; and on this earth, where He was born, where He suffered and died, He shall be manifested in glory, the Son of man, whose is the everlasting kingdom ; and the angels, who never saw in the heavens the glory of God as they beheld it in Bethlehem and on Golgotha, shall behold the manifold wisdom of God when this petition is fulfilled, and Jesus with His transfigured saints shall reign over Israel and the nations. This is the true and ultimate meaning of the prayer: " Thy kingdom come." The bride of Jesus has well understood the Lord's meaning, when she responds, " Even so, come, Lord Jesus, come quickly !"

Who uttered this prayer ? It was the prayer of the apostles and martyrs in the first centuries of the Church, when the hope of Christ's coming was the joy and strength of believers. It has been the prayer of the faithful of all ages and countries (though their knowledge of the mystery varies in clearness). It is the expectation of the saints who are resting in Jesus, and who do not receive the crown until His appearing. It is the desire of the holy angels, who love God, and man for God's sake. It is the day to which the Saviour Himself on His heavenly throne is looking,† and to which He is hastening, for He is coming

---

* " Whereof we speak," adds Paul (Heb. ii. 5). It was a topic of apostolic instruction.

† Heb. x. 13.

quickly. It is the silent prayer of the whole creation, waiting for the manifestation of the sons of God. And can I forget the synagogue, Israel, unto whom blindness has happened in part, but who are praying daily, and every Sabbath and festival, for the kingdom of the Messiah, for the building of the walls of Jerusalem, for the appearing of Him who is to bring light and peace unto them and all nations? I think of them also when I pray, "Thy kingdom come." The Messiah will come, and they shall know that it is Jesus, whom they have pierced. Very solemn indeed is this prayer, when we regard it as the expression of the desire of all saints, living and dead, of the purpose of Christ on His Father's throne, of the mysterious groaning of creation, and of the longing of Joseph's brethren in their dispersion. The answer to this petition must *touch all the circles* from which it ascends: when the kingdom comes, saints will be raised and glorified, the living will be changed, the Lord Jesus will take possession of what He is now waiting for, creation will be delivered from bondage, and Israel converted and reinstated into their central position. Such, I believe, is the meaning of the kingdom. But connected with this final kingdom of glory are the kingdoms of creation or nature, of providence or history, and of grace in the heart. All these are but one kingdom, even as there is only one God,—the Father, the source and end, from whom and for whose glory and self-manifestation are all things; the Son, the Mediator, in and through whom as well as for whom are all things; and the blessed Spirit, who brings all into actual existence, beauty, and perfection.   Let us remember that all the three kingdoms of creation, providence, and grace are imperfect until the kingdom of glory is come.   Nature is imperfect, in bondage, the apostle says, even in sorrow.*   They who have the keenest eye and the most responsive heart to the beauty and voice of nature feel this imperfection most deeply.   It is, indeed, God's kingdom, most beautiful and glorious, showing forth His name, full of symbols of heavenly things: the earth is the Lord's, and the fulness thereof; His works are full of His thoughts.   But the absence of Jesus, the first-born and heir, and the presence of Satan and sin, are manifested even in the external creation; the very earth is waiting for the Lord Jesus.   What a contrast to man, who is indifferent to the return of the Saviour!

The kingdom of providence is not fully revealed; the righteous suffer, while the wicked flourish; the poor lack bread; the cruelty and oppression of man are very grievous; God permits it, and yet it is not according to His will.   When the true Son of David reigns, the poor shall have bread, and be satisfied; justice and equity, truth and mercy, shall rule on earth; in His day shall the righteous flourish.†

---

*There is a quiet crying
As far as the stars are shining
That all parts of nature adhere.

† Psalm lxxii.

Unto Israel, especially, the prosperity of the wicked and the affliction of the saints presented a problem, which they felt as one of the greatest difficulty of faith (Ps. lxxiii.) For the promise was life, health and wealth, and temporal blessings of every kind, unto those that kept the precepts of God. The mystery of the cross was not yet fully revealed. With peculiar joy did the prophets describe the times of the Messiah, when the people of God are to live in peace and in the abundant felicity of God's favour.

The kingdom of grace, also, is not perfected till Christ comes in the kingdom of His glory. It is at His appearing that we shall be presented unblameable in body, soul, and spirit; salvation in the full comprehensive sense will be revealed in the last times; the adoption will then be complete, that is the resurrection, the redemption of the body.* Even in the immediate prospect of death the apostle Paul looks beyond the intermediate state, to that day when the Lord, the righteous Judge, shall give the crown of righteousness to Him, and unto all that love His appearing.

To quote the words of a modern commentator of acknowledged candour and soberness: †—"This is the meaning of the petition: May the kingdom of the Messiah appear. The kingdom of God is in this passage nothing else but the reign of the Messiah,

---

* Rom. v. 23; Col. iii. 4; 2 Tim. iv. 8; Phil. i. 6; 1 Thess. v. 23.

† Meyer, *loc. cit.*

the coming of which was the highest object of the saints' desire (Luke ii. 25 ; xvii. 20 ; Mark xv. 43 ; Luke xxii. 18, 30; 2 Tim. iv. 8).   This eschatological view of the kingdom and its coming, which is also that of the principal ancient fathers, is the only one which harmonises with the historical idea of the kingdom which prevails throughout the New Testament.   The kingdom comes with the coming of the Messiah (Mark xi. 9, 10; Luke xxiii. 42).   The ethical development, which necessarily precedes this manifestation of the kingdom, is presupposed, and in so far included, in the petition, yet not the proper meaning of it ; so that the concrete idea of the coming of the kingdom must neither be given up nor connected with the ethical, more or less spiritualistic one."

This latter expression is scarcely correct, for the kingdom of grace and the kingdom of glory are intimately connected, although they are contrasted.   Unless Christ reigns in our heart by His Spirit, we can never reign with Him ; unless we are one with Him by faith, and in the fellowship of His sufferings, we can never be partakers of His kingdom in power. In like manner, in the kingdom on earth, outward prosperity and peace, righteousness and equity, beauty and harmony will be but the manifestation of the inward reign of love to God and to His Christ.   The gift which precedes Israel's exaltation, is that of repentance and contrition ; the change of heart and the outpouring of the Holy Ghost are inseparable from their external restoration, for the covenant embraces both inward and outward blessings, and the latter as based upon the former.

Remembering this connexion, let us apply the petition to the kingdom of grace as preceding the kingdom of glory.   Notice—

1. If the kingdom has to come to us, we must be by nature outside of it.   This petition reminds us, therefore, of the fall and its consequences.   As an ancient liturgy says, we are the " banished children of Eve."   The world lies in the wicked one, and sin reigns within us.   We are rebels, who obey the usurper.   True, the kingdom of God is around us: for He has surrounded us with a thousand emblems and tokens of His truth and love; the light shineth into the darkness; love seeks the banished ones, even the rebellious : but the place whence the petition now is offered is a province fallen from the King.   It is the longing of the soul that God would *visit and redeem us.*

2. We cannot go to the kingdom; it must come to us.*   When we feel the desire to be restored to God, it is natural that we should think of returning to God, and we hope that, after a long journey, we may reach the kingdom.   We resolve not to be discouraged by the steepness and length of the road, by its rugged

---

* " Come unto us the peace of Thy dominion,
   For unto it we cannot of ourselves,
   If it come not, with all our intellect."
                                        —*Dante, Purgat.* xi.

heights and dangerous paths. Prayer, good works, piety (outward and inward), we imagine to be the road to God. But we cannot thus go to the kingdom; it must come to us.* The door is before the narrow way, and the door is very nigh unto us—even Jesus Christ crucified for sinners. As the merciful Samaritan came to the wounded and helpless man, so Christ comes to us as a Saviour. As in the prophecy of Ezekiel the Lord passed by the infant ready to perish, the great Shepherd seeks and finds the lost. Christ comes to the soul.

Here we see two parallels between the kingdom of grace in the individual soul and the kingdom of glory in the world. As the world will never gradually merge into the kingdom, or reach it by development and effort, so it is with the soul. The kingdom of the earth will become a Christocracy by the direct intervention of God, by the appearing of the Lord: so the soul is born from above, is transplanted by the Spirit into the kingdom of the Son. And as it is Jesus who appears, and afterwards reigns on earth, so it is the personal Saviour who brings the kingdom to the heart, and then dwells in us, our strength and life.

The kingdom of God in the heart consists in this, that we love God as our Father, trust Jesus as our Redeemer, and are guided and comforted by the Spirit. It consists, not so much in our possession of principles as in our being able to say, " O God, thou

---

* But " again " it is written : " I will arise and go to my father."

art my God!" Jesus reveals Himself; the soul believes and loves Him; then He and the Father come
and take up their abode in the soul. And thus the
kingdom of the Father in heaven comes to us when
Christ is received by the power of the Holy Ghost.
It is a personal reign of Christ.

3. Father, Son, and Spirit bring with them
righteousness, peace, and joy. Every kingdom is
based on righteousness: the condition and manifestation of its prosperity is peace; the crown and fulness
of peace is joy. How can God dwell in us who are
sinful, who are full of discord and tumult, who, by
reason of darkness and sin, are without gladness
and the tranquil thanksgiving which God loves, and
with which He has surrounded Himself in heaven?
God brings to us righteousness, even His own, perfect and glorious—the righteousness of Christ, which
is gold tried in the fire: He clothes us with the best
robe, and beautifies us with garments of salvation.
Based on this righteousness is peace. As our salvation in Christ brings glory to God in the highest, it
brings peace to our hearts. Christ at His second
coming will bring peace to earth and make wars to
cease; Christ at His coming into our hearts brings
with Him His peace, the assurance of the Father's
love, and deliverance from the fear of our enemies.
As the Prince of Peace, He continually renews to His
disciples the salutation: Peace be with you. And the
Spirit of God is that oil of gladness which from
Christ descends to us, so that Christ's joy, according

to His own prayer, lives in our hearts, that our joy may be full.

4. In this kingdom there is greatness or dignity and liberty.

The disciples were once disputing among themselves which of them should be greatest in the kingdom. Is not our severity in criticising the apostles out of proportion to the leniency with which we think of ambition and worldliness in ourselves and others ? If they *were* ambitious, if they cherished thoughts of greatness and influence, the honour which they sought was one connected with Christ and with His kingdom, with the glory of God on earth and the accomplishment of His great purposes. Many who criticise the narrow views and ambitious thoughts of the disciples, have not yet understood the very elements of faith, and have not yet taken the very first step of getting themselves out of the land of sight and the present age into the land which God shows unto us.

We can imagine how the disciples would urge their various claims on distinction in the kingdom. John leaned on the Master's bosom ; to Peter, Christ had given a prominent position ; others again were among the first disciples who had followed Jesus as the Messiah, and brought others to see Him while some may have brought sacrifices of peculiar painfulness and self-denial, or have possessed eminent gifts in working miracles. Jesus had noticed their dispute while they were on the way, but He waited till they were at the house at Capernaum, and He asked them what had been the subject of their converse. When they remained silent, rebuked probably by the solemn and meek expression of His countenance, the Saviour sat down and called the twelve, thus giving great emphasis to the teaching He was about to address to them, and said: If any man desire to be first, the same shall be last of all, and servant of all. Then He took a child, set him in the midst of them, and took it into His arms, and said: Whosoever shall receive one of such children in my name, receiveth me; and whosoever shall receive me, receiveth not me, but Him that sent me.* *Humility is the dignity of the kingdom—obedience is its liberty.* The Son of man makes us free; we are no longer in bondage, but we are emancipated from the fetters in which we were held. " Sin has no more dominion over us." We are also no longer under tutors and governors, but in the enjoyment of filial privileges. Christ calls us friends, because He reveals to us what He has received of the Father. Where the Spirit of the Lord is, there is liberty. The more our heart is fixed in God, the greater our liberty; all that is within us breathes and moves freely when Christ reigns.

Yet the apostles, who constantly dwell on our sonship and our liberty, call themselves the *slaves* of Jesus Christ. Joshua was the servant of Moses, but Moses is called the slave of God. We view our-

* Mark ix. 35-37.

selves as God's property, Christ's purchase, the Spirit's temple ; we are not our own ; we owe to our Lord not merely service, but ourselves first of all : "whose I am, and whom I serve." God's slaves have a glorious liberty, while the children of the world are led captive by Satan at his will.

5. Let us think now of the extent and the comprehensiveness of this kingdom. Here, also, there is a parallelism between the macrocosm and the microcosm, the future kingdom on earth and the present kingdom in the heart. The future kingdom is to embrace all nations ; Israel is to have the priority, and all the kingdoms of the earth are to rejoice before God, and serve Him according to their various positions and gifts. And the service of God shall extend to all departments of life, to all institutions of the state, to the minutest detail of daily occupation and rest. "Holiness to the Lord," the prophet says, shall be written on the bells of the horses. The outward creation also shall correspond in beauty and glory to the inward reign of righteousness and truth.

The kingdom of grace in the individual is in like manner to be all-comprehensive. Having its centre in the heart (out of which are the issues of life), it is to extend to all our desires, thoughts, words, and actions. All that we are and have belongs to God, and that always. The only property we can claim is our sin, and that we must give up even by crucifixion. "I beseech you, therefore, by the mercies of God, that you present your bodies a living sacrifice, holy, acceptable unto God."

The connexion between the *body* and sin is very remarkable. Sin, it is true, is a spiritual evil, and has its seat in the soul, in the will, in the mind of man. The body, it is true, is the wonderful work of God, and as such, good : it also is destined for immortality and glory. Yet the Scriptures show us that the flesh, the body, is, as it were, the great medium of sin—its citadel, where it has intrenched itself, and from whence it exerts its baneful influence. " Who shall deliver me from the *body* of this death ?" is the exclamation of the apostle Paul when oppressed with the burden of sin striving within him against God's will. Not until we die do we expect to be delivered from the *presence* of sin, though now we are delivered from its guilt and dominion. The term " flesh " denotes the carnal *mind*, and yet why should this opposition to God be termed " carnal ?"

It is evident that some gross sins, such as drunkenness, are connected with the body. But is not this the case also with more subtle sins also, such as anger, pride, vanity, avarice ? The body is the avenue of the mind, the senses the gateways. Let us make a covenant with our eyes and with our lips ; let nothing enter or proceed therefrom that defiles the heart or is not loyal to our King ; let our hands be hands of diligence and kindness ; let our feet walk in the way of righteousness and truth. Remember that the body also is redeemed by Jesus and inhabited by the Spirit ;

that in the body we have received the water of baptism and the bread and wine of the communion of the body and blood of the Saviour ; that the body also will partake of heavenly glory : in all things that concern the body serve and honour God. " Whether you eat or drink, do all to the glory of God." About dress also Scripture is not silent. Is it worthy of a Christian to spend much thought or money on dress, or to make himself conspicuous by it, or to follow the foolish fashions of the day ? Has dress no influence on the wearer, and does it not say something of your character to the world ?

Our *mind* belongs to the King. Physical health, strength, beauty, are good and great gifts of God ; but mental endowments call for greater gratitude and consecration to His service. And yet how unwilling is man to give glory to God, and to serve Him with His own gifts ! How often have men of intellect, of learning, of genius, been the enemies of God and His gospel ! How often do they, confirmed in this somewhat by public opinion, fancy that their very gifts form a kind of excuse for their disloyalty to God, a kind of exemption from obedience to the Most High ! " In what relation do men of genius stand to the Ten Commandments ?" * is a question to which the answer

---

* Lange (Vermischte, Schriften ii.) " Uber die Freisprechung des Genies von Gesetz." " The Word of Truth says : The law is not given for the righteous. The spirit of our age : There is no law for the man of genius." In looking back on the history of Christendom, it is evident that the highest genius and the loftiest intellect do neither secure the reception of the gospel, nor do these

is—"To whom much is given, from him much will
be required."

In our studies, in our reading, in the cultivation
of art, we ought to remember our allegiance to Christ.
We ought to watch against the reception of any error
in thought, or imagination, or feeling ; to guard
against the spirit of the world.   The society of worldly
men becomes often dangerous in proportion as they
are learned, refined, attractive.   So is it with the society of books, with the influence of poetry, science,
art.   Not that we are to avoid either, but to remember
whose we are, and whither we are going.   It was the
policy of the Emperor Julian to prevent the Christians
from studying the classics, hoping thus to render them
powerless to exert an influence on cultivated minds.
While resisting any such attempt from friend or foe,
we remember that in all things we are bound to seek
God's glory and the health of our soul.   While you
enrich your mind, seek to retain poverty of spirit ;
while you become learned in the wisdom of the
world, remember that the gospel will always necessarily be folly to the Greeks ; and keep your soul
sensitive by constant discipline, that no other beauty
may gain your heart but the beauty of the King and
His kingdom.

---

gifts of God in themselves form an obstacle to simple faith.   While
we find among the disciples of Christ the revered names of Pascal,
Leibnitz, Newton, Haller, Milton, and many others, we know that
the things of the kingdom have often been hidden " from the wise
and prudent."   The world by wisdom knew not God.

All our desires and faculties, our imagination and our will, belong to this kingdom, in which God is Sovereign. Man is like a many-stringed instrument, on which God is to be praised. All within us must be brought into subjection to Him, and thus into harmony. He is the great musician, who, by His Spirit, touches the lyre; for He works in us both to will and to do. And yet is it our work in the truest sense. And this is the beginning as well as the soul of our work, that we ask Him, "Thy kingdom come." Rule Thou in me by the sweet influence of Thy grace, by the power of Thy Spirit, by the love of Christ, by the guidance of Thy providence, by the teaching of Thy word, by the fellowship of Thy saints.

To those that feel discouraged by the comprehensive nature of the kingdom and our service, I say the character of this kingdom is, as long as we are on earth: 6. *Antagonistic.* It is in opposition to sin within and around us. The more we seek to follow and serve God, the more clearly and painfully we become conscious of the evil of our heart, of our unbelief and worldliness. They who swim against the current feel the power of the stream ; they whose citizenship is in heaven, and who seek the things that are above, mourn over the languor of their soul cleaving to the dust, and the attraction which things earthly and temporal exercise over their mind. God insists on the *reality* of a heavenly disposition, not on *the degree* of its strength. It is not yet the time for rest, for exclusive praise and thanksgiving, for unmingled joy; but the time of warfare, of prayer and fasting, of manifold temptations. The Solomonic reign has not yet commenced. It is the period of David, of exile and wandering, of humility and patience, of danger and of struggle.

The weapons of our warfare are not carnal, but spiritual. If we think of gaining the victory in our own strength, by the energy of our will, by the remembrance of our vows and resolutions, by the recollections of past experiences of God's favour and love, we are using carnal weapons. It was by faith that the walls of Jericho fell, that Israel entered the Promised Land, that David slew Goliath; looking off unto the Lord, we run with patience the race set before us; we overcome by the blood of the Lamb. Our whole power to subdue our enemies arises principally from self-distrust and trust in God. We sometimes suppose that we are walking by faith, that our obedience is evangelical and not legal, that we are resisting sin in the strength of Christ by the indwelling Spirit, when we are actually relying on ourselves. "And this will be made clear to thee by the effect produced on thy mind by a fall. If thou art so saddened and disquieted thereby as to be tempted to despair of making progress and doing good, it is a sure sign that thy trust is in self, and not in God; for he who has any large measure of self-distrust and trust in God, feels neither surprise, nor despondency, nor bitterness, when he falls, for he knows this has arisen from his own weakness and want of trust in God. On the contrary, being rendered more distrustful of self, more humbly confident in God,—detesting above all things his fault and the unruly passions which have caused it, and mourning with a quiet, deep, and patient sorrow over his offence against God,—he pursues his enterprise, and follows after his enemies even to the death, with a spirit more resolute than before." *

If we are truly convinced of our own utter weakness, let us hold fast with equal firmness that our sufficiency is of God. All needful strength is in Christ, and we may at all times, by relying on Him, be made strong. As we are made just by simply believing in Jesus, so we are made strong and holy by simply looking to Him. It is faith in the living Saviour which is the beginning and continuation of our life. Sanctification is not an influence exerted subsequent to our acceptance by a remembered and absent Saviour: it is the light and grace, strength and courage, submission and comfort, given by a present loving Christ, and received by the act of faith. As we lean with all the weight of our guilt on Christ for justification, we must lean with all the weight of our weakness on Christ for sanctification. "Only believe," and your enemies are conquered. God is with us, Christ is for us, the Spirit is in us ; why should we fear ? Only be strong and of good courage. And as we receive with humility the word, " without

---

* Lorenzo Scupoli, "Spiritual Combat."

Me ye can do nothing," we can also say, by virtue of our union with the adorable Saviour, "I can do all things through Christ, which strengtheneth me."

And thus every Christian soldier is a victor ; he is more than a conqueror through Him that loved us ; and though our life appears to us a fragment, and to the very last day of our earthly pilgrimage we have to mourn over sin, and to resist it, the kingdom has come to us ; it is ours, and with it the crown which the Lord will give to all who love His appearing.

7

THE MESSIANIC KINGDOM

"Thy Kingdom Come."

THE petition refers primarily and directly to the Messianic kingdom on earth, of which all Scripture testifies.

The King of this kingdom is the Lord Jesus, the Son of David; the subjects of it are Israel and the nations,—the chosen people fulfilling the mission which, according to the election of God, is assigned unto them, of being the medium of blessing unto all the nations of the earth; the centre of the kingdom is Jerusalem, and the means of its establishment is the coming and visible appearing of our Saviour Jesus Christ. When we pray " Thy kingdom come," our true meaning is, Come, Lord Jesus, come quickly!

The Scripture teaching concerning the kingdom is both copious and clear. It is important to notice that the reason why such a variety of opinions exists even among Christians on this point, is not because the declarations of the Bible are either few in number or vague and indefinite in character.

Not few in number, for there is scarcely any book of Scripture which is not prophetic. The Psalms, and even the historical books (such as the Pentateuch, the Books of Samuel, the Gospels), are full of prophecies concerning the Messianic kingdom; while direct prophetic teaching is contained in many of the Epistles, in the Books of the Prophets, and in the Revelation given by God to the Lord Jesus, and communicated to the Church through the apostle John. No doctrine, not even the fundamental doctrine of justification by faith, has assigned to it in the inspired word so large a place as the doctrine of the second coming of Christ and His kingdom. It is not confined to a few-isolated passages, it is not the subject of one or two books of Scripture, but it pervades the whole Bible. When we are asked, Where is it spoken of? we are tempted to reply, Ask, rather, where is it not spoken of ? *

The doctrine of Christ's return, and the kingdom, was an integral part of apostolic preaching to Jews and Gentiles,—it was part of the gospel or glad tidings,—it belonged to the very elements of the faith, even as it was the hope and joy of the experienced believer (Acts ii. 16, &c., iii. 19–21 ; 1 Thess. i. 10).

Nor are the Scripture assertions vague and indefinite. It is true that much obscurity attaches to prophecy as regards detail and the chronological

* Acts iii. 20, 21. "Scripture, though it be never silent, is not always heard."—AUGUSTINE.

sequence of events. It is also conceded that it is very difficult, and sometimes almost impossible, to conceive the manner in which predicted events will be brought about, and that we can only rest by faith in the wisdom and power of God, who will surely fulfil His word, and to whom all things are possible. But that the general outline of prophecy is vague and indistinct must be emphatically denied. The Scriptures give forth no uncertain sound as to the great question, Is Jesus to come before or after the kingdom of righteousness and peace ? No truth is more fully and more clearly taught in Scripture than this, that the promises given to Abraham, Isaac, and Jacob, renewed to David and confirmed by the prophets and finally by the Lord Jesus himself, will yet be fulfilled on earth ; that Israel is not merely a type of the Church, but has a future before it, in which it will have a central position on earth ; and that before the final judgment there will be a glorious kingdom, ushered in by the coming, the parousia, of Christ.*

But if the Scripture teaches prophetic truth so clearly, it may be asked, Whence such variety of conflicting opinions among Christians ? And why has the literal view of Christ's second coming met with so much and so violent opposition in the Churches ?

To give a full answer to this question would require more space than can be afforded here. It

---

* Delitzsch, " Biblisch-Prophetische Theologie," p. 131, ss.

may be said briefly, that the ignorance and error prevalent on this important subject arise chiefly from the deplorable neglect of the study of Moses and the prophets, and from disregard of the warning of the apostle Paul, that the Gentile Church would be tempted to forget the position of Israel and the character of the present dispensation (Rom. xi., 25, 26.)

In the first four centuries the doctrine of Christ's return to establish the kingdom was held almost unanimously by believers. In the apostolic Churches the hope of Christ's coming was the joy and strength of Christians. They realised that they belonged not to this world or age; they waited for their absent Lord; and the martyrs were able to suffer and die with joy unspeakable and full of glory, because they held fast the promise given to all that overcome, and they looked forward to the glory of Christ in His kingdom.* Primitive Christians were unworldly,

---

* The fathers of the first three centuries, whose works have come down to us but only in part, have clearly avowed or implied, that the early Christian faith was premillennial. It is certain that in the second century the opinion that Christ would reign a thousand years on the earth was diffused over a great part of Christendom, and that the most eminent doctors favoured it, and no controversy was moved with them by those who thought otherwise. Tertullian speaks of it as the common doctrine of the Church (Mosheim, " Ecc. Hist.," vol. i., 22, s. Comp. also Gibbon, "Decline and Fall," i. 411). Chillingworth says—" The doctrine of the millenaries was believed and taught by the most eminent fathers of the age next after the apostles, and by none of that age opposed or condemned ; *therefore it was the catholic doctrine of those times*" (Demarest and Gordon, "Christocracy," 113, New York, 1867.) It must, however, be borne in mind that on this doctrine,

because they were other-worldly, citizens of the age to come.

As the Church gained a position of worldly ease and power, she forgot that during this dispensation, the times of the Gentiles, Christians are to be a little flock, whose only mission is to testify, to suffer, and to wait,—whose only weapons are those of the Spirit, whose only protection is the promise of Christ, and whose only glory the hidden glory of the indwelling Saviour. As the pagan element entered the Church, the Jewish scriptural element disappeared. Instead of hoping for the coming of Christ, the Church rejoiced in her outward power, and the recognition and help of the world. Romanism is a false and carnal anticipation of the millennium. The true Church is a widow, poor and helpless, trusting in her Lord, and waiting for His return ; the false Church is a queen, and no widow at all, giving thanks for her prosperous condition, and boasting of her power and splendour. The true Church calls herself an election, a witness for God, separated from the world, shining as a light in darkness ; the false Church boasts of her comprehensiveness, her large numbers, her increasing popularity, embracing all nations and all civilisation. The doctrine of the second coming of Christ and His kingdom could never be held in a Church which is

as well as others, the decline from apostolic clearness and fulness set in at a very early period. The mystery of Israel is very dimly, if at all, seen by the early writers (comp. Dr Brown, " Restoration of the Jews "). A full statement of their views is given by Guers, " Israel's Future," p. 355.

" in its inmost essence a false anticipation of the millennial kingdom—a confusion of Church and kingdom. The rights which Rome as a harlot usurped shall then be exercised in holiness by the bride of the Lamb." *

At the Reformation there was a return to the scriptural and apostolic doctrine of faith, but not to the scriptural and apostolic doctrine of the second coming of Christ. The Reformers did not enter into the *historical* character of Scripture; their whole attention was absorbed by its dogmatic aspect. The question of individual salvation was their great and momentous topic, the false mediations between Christ and the sinner the great object of their attack. But the question of the position of the Church in the history of the world, of the relation of the Church to Israel and to the coming kingdom, scarcely came within their horizon.†

Nor need we be astonished at this. If we review

---

* Auberlen on Daniel, &c., p. 327.

† A full statement of this defect of the Reformation is given by Baumgarten, "Apostelgeschichte," vol. ii. ; also in Auberlen, " Göttliche Offenbarung," 187, and passim. Compare my remarks in " Christ and the Scriptures," chap. v. ; " Israel's Messiah—the Living and the Written Word," p. 69, and Appendix, "Shemitic and Japhetic."

It is interesting to notice, that of the Westminster Assembly of Divines, 1643, who framed the Confession of Faith, Principal Baillie wrote as follows (Letter 117): " The most of the chief divines here, not only Independents but others, such as Twisse (the Moderator), Marshall, Palmer, and many more, are express chiliasts."

the history of the Church, we notice how many important truths, clearly revealed in Scripture, have been allowed to lie dormant for centuries, unknown and unappreciated except by a few isolated Christians, until it pleased God to enlighten the Church by chosen witnesses, and to bestow on His children the knowledge of hidden and forgotten treasures. For centuries the doctrine of salvation by grace through faith only was not known and preached in Christendom. We read but of few, who, in the darkness of prevailing ignorance, knew and declared this great truth. For how long a period, even after the Reformation, was the doctrine of the Holy Ghost and His work in conversion, and His indwelling in the believer, almost unknown ! Christians thought little and vaguely, and spoke still less, on this great doctrine. And thus was it with the doctrine of Christ's second coming. Clearly revealed in Scripture, held with ardour and joy by the apostolic Christians and the primitive Church, it was forgotten and forsaken as the Church became worldly and corrupted by pagan influences ; and only since the labours of the devout and learned Bengel and his school has there been a most extensive and blessed revival of this great and central truth.*

---

* On the great leading questions of eschatology (the restoration of Israel, the kingdom of glory on earth, and the visible appearing of Jesus at the commencement of the kingdom) a very marked agreement prevails among many of the best expositors and theologians of our day—such as Stier, Alford, Hofmann, Delitzsch, Ebrard, &c. Lechler says (" Apost. Zeitalter," 82), " A number of expressions in

The questions which naturally arise in connexion with the kingdom are these:—

I. Who is the King?

II. When will the kingdom be established?

III. What will be its character?

I. *Who is the King?*

In one sense the King is God the Father. It is to "our Father in heaven" that the petition is addressed, " Thy kingdom come." His glory, His self-manifestation is the one great purpose of God, and His is the kingdom, for of Him and to Him are all things.

But the Father has appointed Jesus His Son to be the King, even as Christ is the Vine, while the Father is the Husbandman.

The Lord Jesus is not only the Prophet, the Light of the world, the Wisdom of God, revealing unto us the Father; He is not only the High Priest, who after His sufferings and death on the cross brings us nigh unto God; but He is also the King, upon whose shoulders is the government, and who reigns on earth in the name and to the glory of the Most High. He is never called King of the Church,

the epistles of Paul point to an earthly kingdom of glory, as is clear to every unprejudiced reader, and of all eschatological points this is the one on which his epistles are most unanimous." Delitzsch, in his suggestive essay, " Die Biblisch-Prophetische Theologie," no doubt overstates the fact when he says (p. 7), that " the orthodox Church of the present day has received chiliasm into her inmost life; that there is scarcely a believing Christian who does not partake of this view."

but her Head and Bridegroom. His rule over the Church is the influence which by the Spirit He exercises over all His disciples: it is the reign of life, the manifestation of union, the vital power of the Holy Ghost. As the members of the body are the willing servants of the head, so the Church, as well as the individual believer, can say, "Christ lives in me." The relation thus subsisting between the exalted Saviour and believers is far more vital and profound than that between a king and his subjects. Christ's kingship has therefore no reference to the Church, *who is herself* to *reign with Him*, but to Israel and the nations in the ages to come.

Christ was appointed from eternity to be King—(1.) As the Son of Man; (2.) As the Son of David; (3.) As the Son of Man and of David, after His humiliation, suffering, and death. The Son of God became man, not merely to suffer and to die, but to reign. He took upon Him our nature, that through sufferings He might enter into glory; as Man, even as the Lord, whom they have pierced, He is to reign in righteousness and peace, the glory of Israel, as well as the light to lighten the Gentiles.

(1.) As Son of Man. Our ideas of kingship are limited, and do not come up to the divine conception of man as king. It is the case with all parabolic expressions in Scripture, that the earthly symbol is far less substantial and real than the spiritual truth it illustrates. When God calls himself Father,

King, Shepherd, Husband, He does not borrow these titles from human fathers, kings, shepherds, husbands; but having lent His own titles to them, they are but imperfect symbols of His perfection. The true or real King among men has not appeared yet; the nearest approach to His rule was David. And what are the last words of David, the son of Jesse, the man who was raised up on high, the anointed of the God of Israel, and the sweet psalmist of Israel? His last testimony was, that the Spirit of the Lord had spoken by him, and that he had heard the Rock of Israel, and that the sum and substance of these divine revelations was the coming of the perfect King. " He that ruleth over men must be just, ruling in the fear of God : and he shall be as the light of the morning when the sun riseth, even a morning without clouds, as the tender grass springing out of the earth, by clear shining after rain."

It is from Scripture that we must learn the divine idea of human royalty on earth.

Thus in the beginning God said, " Let us make man in our own image, after our likeness, and let them have dominion over the fish of the sea, and over the fowl of the air, and over the cattle, and over all the earth, and over every creeping thing that creepeth upon the earth."

Hence we find that when Daniel* describes the royalty of Nebuchadnezzar, he says, " Thou, O king, art a king of kings: for the God of heaven hath

* Chap. ii. 37, 38.

given thee a kingdom, power, and strength, and glory. And wheresoever the children of men dwell, the beasts of the field and the fowls of the heaven hath he given into thine hand, and hath made thee ruler over them all. Thou art this head of gold." The reference to Genesis is obvious. The idea of a king is one who derives his authority and strength directly from God, and whose dominion embraces men and the whole earthly creation.

It is to this divine institution of human dominion David refers in the eighth Psalm, the profound meaning of which is opened to us by the inspired commentary of Paul in his Epistle to the Hebrews. The age to come is not put into subjection unto angels, but unto Jesus, and unto Him because He is the Man Christ Jesus, the Son of Man. In Him the original divine order concerning man as king is already realised virtually, but will be realised actually and in manifestation at His coming. Then the kingdom will be given unto the Son of Man.

The reign of Christ as Son of Man appears strange, when, not realising sufficiently the humanity of the Lord, we view His incarnation almost exclusively in connexion with His death on the cross, forgetting His subsequent exaltation, even as the Jews thought of His reign to the exclusion of His suffering. In the immediate prospect of the cross the Saviour testified of His kingdom, when before the high priest He referred to the prophecy of Daniel : " Hereafter shall ye see the Son of Man sitting on the right hand of

power, and coming in the clouds of heaven." For
this purpose He suffered and died, that He might be
heir of all things, and renewing the face of the earth,
reign with His glorified saints over Israel and the
nations.

For Jesus is King, not merely as man, but,

(2.) As the Son of David. He is not merely
the seed of the woman; His genealogy is traced
back not merely to Adam; but He is emphatically
the seed of Abraham, and the Son of David. The
promise of blessing for all the families of the earth
centres in the seed of Abraham, Isaac, and Jacob.
The Messiah, in whom Israel was to possess a
glorious king, whose righteous and peaceful reign
was to extend to all nations of the earth, was
to be David's son, as David was an eminent
type and prophet of Him, who is both his Son
and Lord, his offspring and his root. Of this all
prophets testify, and the angel sent from heaven
before the birth of the Saviour sums up their predictions in words, of which some are already fulfilled, while others yet await their fulfilment. "His
name shall be called Jesus. He shall be great, and
shall be called the Son of the Highest: and the Lord
God shall give unto him the throne of his father
David. And he shall reign over the house of Jacob
for ever; and of his kingdom there shall be no
end."*

Words could not be more explicit. It is impos-

---

* Luke i. 31, 32.

sible to evade their meaning. Mary could only have
understood them literally. No Scripture-taught
Israelite could fail to interpret them in harmony
with the Psalms and Prophets. And can the words
bear any other but the literal interpretation? Did
not Mary conceive and bring forth a son? Did
she not call His name Jesus? Was He not great,
and is He not called the Son of the Highest by
apostles and martyrs, and all the saints of nearly
two thousand years? Have we any reason for
not expecting that God the Lord shall give unto
Him the throne of His father David? That *God*
is His Father is most expressly declared by the
whole message of the angel, but he speaks now of
David, who is His father according to His humanity,
of whom concerning the flesh Christ came. And
did not every Israelite know (and that from Scripture) what was meant by the throne of David? The
throne of David is in Jerusalem, not in heaven.
Christ is now on His heavenly Father's throne. Is
it not irreverent to say that the Lord is *now* on the
throne of David? And His reign over the house of
Jacob, and His endless kingdom, can only mean that
glorious rule of which all prophets witness, that the
Lord himself will establish it, and that then David
will be the shepherd and king of his people.*

But this kingdom is Christ's,

(3.) As Son of Man and Son of David, *by virtue
of His sufferings and death.* This is the great mys-

---

* Ezek. xxxiv. 23, 24; Jer. xxx. 9; Hosea iii. 5.

tery which Israel was slow of heart to understand
and believe. This connexion (not merely contrast)
between sufferings and glory (the two topics of prophecy, 1 Pet. i. 11) Christ explained, after His
resurrection, to the disciples on their way to Emmaus,
even as He spoke of the *kingdom* during the forty
days before His ascension. Gentile Christians, who
now criticise the blindness and unbelief of the Jewish
disciples, sometimes do not even see the difficulty of
the problem which the apostles could not solve. It
is easy to cut the Gordian knot by denying that the
kingdom is to be restored to Israel, that David's Son
is to reign, that on earth the promises given to the
fathers are to be fulfilled. To ignore a large portion
of Scripture, to twist and strain, by a so-called spiritual interpretation, the very passages, the fulfilled
portion of which *sight*, not faith, compels us to take
literally, has been the traditional method, to a large
extent, in Christendom. But this is only a different
manifestation of our slowness of heart to believe *all*
that is written in Moses and the prophets concerning
Christ. These Scriptures already contained the
mystery of the cross as well as that of the reign.
The servant of the Lord is first rejected and despised,
put to grief by God, wounded and bruised for our
transgressions, led as a lamb to the slaughter (Isa. liii.)
The sword awakes against the shepherd ; and He who
comes to deliver Jerusalem from all the nations that
have risen against her, who brings redemption and
glory to His people, and is the King of all the

earth, is none other but the Man whom they have pierced.

But more clearly do we know it now, that there is a connexion, founded from all eternity, between the Lamb slain and the Lion victorious, between the sufferings of Gethsemane and Golgotha and Christ's return in majesty and power. He is King because He died. In Him the 22d Psalm is fulfilled; the Beloved-Forsaken becomes the Lord who gathers all nations, and brings them blessing. The inscription, Jesus Christ, *King* of the Jews, was over His *cross*.

Jesus is the King, and associated with Him in His reign are the glorified saints. Thus the Saviour said unto His disciples, Verily I say unto you, ye that have followed me, in the regeneration when the Son of Man shall sit in the throne of His glory, ye also shall sit upon twelve thrones, judging the twelve tribes of Israel.* They who are redeemed by Christ's blood, and whom He has made kings and priests, shall reign on the earth.† Over whom shall they reign ? Over Israel and the nations. With whom ? With Christ, whom they followed in His humility and in His suffering, having learned, during the dispensation of the Church, wisdom and patience. These are they who attain to the first resurrection, who live again (in the transfigured body) in order to reign with Him a thousand years. For at the coming of the Lord to establish His kingdom, the dead who are

---

* Matt. xix. 28.　　　　　　† Rev. v. 10.

asleep in Jesus, as well as the saints who are then living, will be gathered to receive from their Lord the recompense of the reward.*

Such is the King, surrounded by His saints.

II. *When will this kingdom be established?*

This question is coincident with that concerning the manner of its establishment. It is to be brought about not gradually, but suddenly; not without observation, as is the kingdom of grace in the heart, but with great and mighty signs; not by human efforts and endeavours, but by a direct intervention from above; the stone which smites the image is cut out "without hands." † The world is not gradually changed into the kingdom; but the world is judged. There is a crisis; the unbelief and opposition of men reach a climax, and then God sends forth His Son to judge and to destroy His enemies. As it has been from the beginning, the progress of the world is downward; judgment succeeds judgment. A remnant is left in each, to be the basis of a new dispensation. Thus, we trace the progress of history,—from paradise

---

* One with Christ in glory and reign (συνδοξάζεσθαι, Rom. viii. 17; συμβασιλεύειν, 1 Tim. ii. 12; 1 Cor. iv. 8). The resurrection of the saints at the coming of the Lord, as distinguished from the resurrection after the millennial reign, is clearly taught, Rev. xx. 4–6 (in harmony with the rest of Scripture, Luke xiv. 14; 1 Cor. xv. 23; 1 Thess. iv. 16; Phil. iii. 11, 20, 21). "No one nowadays will still ask whether this resurrection is to be taken literally or figuratively," Hofmann wrote some years ago ("Weissagung und Erfüllung, ii. 373).

† "Without hands." Compare 2 Cor. v. 1; Col. ii. 11.

lost to the flood, when Noah and his sons are saved to form a new commencement; from the flood to the tower of Babel, when the nations, as such, and heathenism commence,* and Abraham is chosen; from Abraham to the destruction of Jerusalem,—Israel, as a nation, is rejected, a remnant is saved, and the Church begins; from the destruction of Jerusalem to the Antichristian reign, when Christ descends and destroys the man of sin and his powers. And this is the final victory. Satan is bound, Israel restored, the nations subdued and brought under the blessings of righteousness and peace. According to Scripture, the last times are perilous, and full of the most subtle and profound ungodliness. When Christ comes, He does not find faith on the earth; the Church does not look with complacency on a world gradually merging into union and harmony with herself, but is sharply defined from the world, and looking up to Heaven, where is her citizenship, for the coming of the absent Bridegroom.

If we bear in mind the characteristics of the kingdom, we shall have no difficulty in seeing what event alone can usher it in. At present Satan is the prince of this world, blinding the minds of men against the light of the gospel, and leading them into sin; then Satan will be bound, and no longer able to tempt man. At present the creature is subject to vanity and travailing in birth; then, in the regeneration of the world the creature itself also shall be delivered

---

* Fabri, "Entstehung des Heidenthums."

from the bondage of corruption into the glorious liberty of the children of God. At present Israel is dispersed, and without the knowledge of Jehovah and their king David; then Israel will know and serve the Lord, and, restored to their own land, and converted by the Spirit of God, they will glorify God and be the centre of light on earth. At present the Church is in humility and weakness, her glory is concealed, her unity is not manifested, tares and wheat grow up together, and the true disciples follow Christ in His sufferings, and are made conformable to His death; then the Church will be manifested in power, glory, and unity, reigning with Christ as the queen, the Lamb's wife. At present the mystery of ungodliness is already manifesting itself, and we know it will sooner or later appear in its culminating embodiment as the Antichrist; then Antichrist will have been conquered and judged by supreme power.

It is evident that these are the essential features of the kingdom—Satan bound, the earth renewed, Israel converted and restored, the Church glorified, and Antichrist judged and vanquished; and the crisis, the turning-point, to bring about these changes, is one,—it is the direct interference of God, the appearing of the great God and Saviour, Jesus Christ. He alone can bind Satan, convert and re-establish Israel, renew the earth, glorify the Church, and destroy that wicked one by the brightness of His coming and the Spirit of His mouth. Think of the great change that must come over Satan, the earth, Israel, the Church, the Antichrist, and you will see at once that no human effort, no exertions of the Church, no missionary labours, can bring it about ; it is, as Scripture teaches, the Lord himself who will bring redemption and glory.

In the prophecy of Daniel we possess a divine revelation of history. The kingdoms of this world are succeeded (after judgment) by the kingdom of righteousness. In the dream of Nebuchadnezzar we have the kingdoms of the world (Babylon, Persia, Greece, and Rome) described in the unity of their character, forming one great image in its power and splendour, and in the deteriorating progress of its development. The last kingdom is destroyed by a stone cut out without hands, that is, as Daniel interprets it, by the God of Heaven setting up a kingdom which can never be destroyed.

In the vision which Daniel beheld he saw the four kingdoms under the symbol of beasts, a description of their moral character, as earthly, material, lacking the element of the divine image, governing by force and cunning, and according to mere selfish principles, and for temporal purposes. After these, a new event is described ; *not a new earthly development, but a new thing from above.* "I saw in the night visions, and behold one like the Son of Man came with the clouds of heaven, and came to the Ancient of Days ; and they brought him near before him, and there was given him dominion and glory, and a kingdom, that all people, nations, and languages, should serve him." " His dominion is an everlasting dominion, which shall not pass away, and his kingdom that which shall not be destroyed." It is the coming of the Son of Man with the clouds of Heaven that ushers in the kingdom.

Most lucid also is the prophecy of Zechariah, after the return of Israel from Babylon. That the prediction of the 14th chapter is yet unfulfilled is abundantly clear ; for in the destruction of Jerusalem it was only the Romans, and not all nations, who came against her in battle. And the Lord did not defend the beloved city, but allowed the enemies to destroy it with a fearful destruction. But the prophet speaks here of all nations uniting and going to Jerusalem to fight against her, and of the Lord going forth to fight against them. Who is the Lord ? It is the MAN who is my equal ; His *feet* shall stand upon the Mount of Olives ; the Lord my God shall come, and all the saints with thee.

This is the crisis to which we look, the great event full of light and blessedness to all who love the Lord and His appearing.*

---

* Parousia means *invariably* the real, personal, visible presence. Compare 2 Cor. x. 10 ; Phil. ii. 12 ; 1 Thess. ii. 19 ; 2 Cor. vii. 6. At the Lord's table we do show Christ's death till He comes ; spiritually He is with us always, especially in the breaking of bread ; but His glorified body is now in heaven, and at His table we look forward to His return. Such was also the promise at His ascension, Acts i. 11. That the parousia of Christ means the death of the believer is an untenable interpretation, rarely maintained.

III. *The character of this kingdom.*

1. In manifested power on earth.

The kingdom is to be on earth. God's will, according to the petition Christ teaches us, is to be done on earth as it is in heaven. It is on earth, where God has been denied and forgotten ; where His honour has been disregarded, and His commandments have been transgressed ; where nations and kingdoms, instead of seeking His glory and showing forth His praise, have not bowed to His authority and reverenced His law: it is on earth that the Lord shall reign ; injustice, cruelty, and war shall be banished, and, instead of idolatry, selfishness, and sin, the fear, and love, and beauty of God will be manifest.*

Christ and the glorified saints reign over Israel and the nations. The appearings of the risen Lord to His disciples during the forty days seem to be a prophetic parallel of the relation of the transfigured Church to the earth. Jerusalem is the centre of the world ; the land of Israel is restored to wonderful fertility and blessedness. We may not be able clearly to conceive the fulfilment of the predictions concerning this earth during the Christocracy, but our danger does not lie in believing too implicitly or too literally what is written.†

* Compare Lecture VIII.

† The literal fulfilment of many prophecies has already taken place. It belongs to history. But the Christian has no more difficulty in believing the future fulfilment of prophecy than in crediting the record of history. He believes, because God has spoken, because it is written. To believe that the Jews are scattered among all

2. It is spiritual. It is a kingdom of grace in which spiritual obedience is offered, and in which men worship God with renewed and sanctified hearts. Israel is converted before it is reinstated ; born again before it receives power ; humbled and filled with true repentance before it is crowned with joy and glory.* The earth shall be filled with the knowledge of the glory of Jehovah. The eternal principles of righteousness and love which were embodied in the Mosaic law will then reign upon earth in the spirit of liberty and power. There will be nations, as such, serving the Lord. Israel will keep the law, which, even in its original form, was so full of mercy and

---

nations, that Jerusalem was destroyed by the Romans, that of the Temple not one stone was left on another, requires no spiritual faith; it requires only common information. But to believe that Israel will be restored, Jerusalem rebuilt, and that all nations shall come up against the beloved city and besiege it, and that the Lord Jehovah shall appear and stand on the Mount of Olives, requires faith, for it is as yet only written in the Bible. But what difference does it make to the child of God whether the prophecy is fulfilled or not ? Can he for a moment doubt it ?

And when we remember how literally prophecy has been fulfilled, we cannot but expect as literal a fulfilment in the future.

How natural would it have been for those who lived before the first advent, to think, that only the spiritual features of the Messiah's coming and kingdom could be the object of inspired prophecy, and that the outward and minute circumstances predicted were either allegorical and figurative, or only the drapery and embellishment of important and essential truths. And yet the fulfilment was minute even in subordinate detail.

Balaam said : " There shall come a star out of Jacob, and a sceptre shall rise out of Israel." He here describes the Messiah

* John iii. 3.

brotherly kindness, and so comprehensive of all human and national relationships, extending to every department of life. Doubtless in a new and free manner, but realising the divine idea of a nation's life and prosperity. The glorified saints will be a new manifestation of God to men on earth, revealing to them what Christ can effect by His mercy and resurrection-power in man, and continually elevating and animating them by their Christ-like beauty and glory. Delivered from the power of Satan, and ruled by the Son of Man and His saints ; influenced by their attractive spiritual power, the nations of the earth will serve God with gladness, and their love and light will manifest itself in all their actions and in all branches of life.

---

under the emblem of a star. But in the fulfilment it was actually a star which appeared to the wise men in the East, and showed them the way to Bethlehem.

Jeremiah prophesies : " A voice was heard in Ramah, lamentation and bitter weeping ; Rachel, weeping for her children, refused to be comforted." In these words the prophet expresses the national grief over the desolations of the land. But it was literally fulfilled, for the lamentation of the mothers of Bethlehem was near the grave of Rachel (Gen. xxxv. 19; 1 Sam. x. 2).

Zechariah writes : "Thy King cometh unto thee, . . . lowly and riding upon an ass, and upon a colt, the foal of an ass." Now this may appear only a poetical statement in parallelism of the fact that the King will come riding upon an ass. But the actual fulfilment was *literal*. The disciples brought the ass *and* the colt (Matt. xxi.), and thus the prediction was fulfilled in its minutest detail.

Ps. xxii. 18 speaks of Christ's garments, and of lots being cast upon His vesture. Thus it happened literally : the soldiers divided the (upper) garments, and cast lots upon his vesture, or coat, which was without seam (John xix. 23). How easy is it for us to believe, with such facts before us, the literal fulfilment of all prophecy.

"Secular" and "spiritual" are distinctions which
will not be known then; even on the bells of the
horses will be written, "Holiness to the Lord."
Science and art will no longer be in opposition to,
or separate from the knowledge of God. Theology
will be the centre of all sciences and the soul of
all art. It will then become manifest that Satan
was a usurper; that man was created in the image
of God, to have dominion over the earth; that the
earth is the Lord's and the fulness thereof. The
ideal will then be real, for it has its source in God,
the only Reality. And this restoration of earth and
triumph of God will have been brought about by
truth, by suffering, by Christ's cross, by the patience
of His saints; carnal weapons, whether of power, or
of learning, or of civilisation, have only retarded the
coming of the kingdom; it is Christ, as the Lamb,
and the saints who followed Him in His meek spirit,
who have gained the victory. Nor can Satan or
the world complain. God had given them ample
time, and ample scope. He allowed them even to do
their utmost to corrupt and poison the Church, after
their persecutions and cruelty had failed. All shall
acknowledge that the Lord is God, righteous, just,
long-suffering, good. Even in hell they shall confess
that Jesus, who, when on earth, lifted not up His
voice in the streets, who resisted Satan only by the
Word of God in the spirit of obedience and humility,
and who finally suffered and was crucified, allowing
all the waves and billows deserved by us to pass

over Him, is rightfully Lord, to the glory of the Father.

Oh, what a manifestation of humility and obedience, of the filial spirit, will then be given to the universe, when the man Christ Jesus, who was obedient unto death, even the death of the cross,—who, when the god of this world offered Him all the kingdoms of the earth and their glory, resisted and overcame him by saying, "Thou shalt worship the Lord thy God, and Him only shalt thou serve,"—when the Son of Man will be seen enthroned as King, whom the Father hath appointed Heir of all things!

Thus Christ and the glorified saints, Israel and the nations on earth, will form the kingdom of which the head is the Father, and the spirit of which is the spirit of filial love and obedience. Our Father in heaven—*Thy* kingdom come.

Consider now the influence this truth exerts on our minds, hearts, and lives.

It endears to us the Scriptures, because it enables us to see unity in the record, and importance in many portions which otherwise seem to possess only a temporary and ephemeral significance. We now behold the book of the kingdom * as the basis, and the book of the Church † as the book of the great parenthesis; and we see that though Israel is set aside for a period, the promises given to the fathers, ratified and confirmed by the Lord himself, await yet their fulfilment.

---

* Commonly called Old Testament.
† Commonly called New Testament.

What Scripture lacks to most people is not authority, but *life and interest;* and for the simple reason that they forget its prophetical character, that they regard it chiefly as a book containing doctrines and practical counsels, and that they view the history which it records as belonging exclusively to the past, and recorded on account of the moral and spiritual lessons it embodies.   Hence many portions are utterly unintelligible, and many appear uninteresting. They do not see that the Scripture contains the history of the kingdom of God upon earth ; that Israel is the divinely-chosen centre, whatever enlargement of the circumference take place ; that the second coming of the Lord is the great point towards which the writings of Moses and the prophets, as well as the books of the evangelists and epistles, converge ; and that then the law, the past history, the land, the prophecies will be fully understood in their permanent importance and significance.

Prophecy, according to popular opinion, is obscure. But the Bible itself announces an opposite view. According to it, we are walking now in a dark place.   It is night.   All around us is covered with darkness.   God graciously gives us a light to guide our footsteps, to show us the real position, the true character of events.   This light is our safety until the Day-star arise, until the Saviour himself returns. And what is this light ?   It is the very word of prophecy, which so many Christians call obscure, and which they neglect.   The prophetic word is given to us that we may know the will of the Lord, and not be like unto the world, upon whom that day shall come unawares. God calls it revelation,—unveiling of what before was hidden. Blessed is he that readeth and he that heareth the word of prophecy. Let us only take Scripture literally, and seek, not merely on the subjects of faith and individual salvation, but on all revealed truths, to have our mind brought into harmony with God's revelation.

The hope of the Lord's personal return enables us to realise Jesus as the Living One,—the same yesterday, to-day, and for ever. We remember His past— this is the object of faith ; we have communion with Him now in love, and we look forward to Himself coming to us—this is our hope. God is the God who was, and is, and is to come ; hence the Scripture must needs be prophetic ; communion with the living God must include the expectation of the future kingdom. Our personal relation to Christ is tested by our attitude to His promised second coming. If we trust in Him, we know that when He comes again without sin, it is to receive us unto Himself. If we love Him, and our life is hid with Him in God, we know that when He shall appear, we also shall appear with Him in glory. If we are faithful and loyal, suffering for His sake, and patiently fulfilling the work assigned to us, we know that at His coming He will give us the crown, and associate us with Himself in His kingdom. The hope of the return of the Lord Jesus illumines and quickens every Christian grace and energy. It gives the right direction and aim ; it supplies the true motive and strength.* And as the author and finisher of faith, Jesus himself endured the cross, and despised the shame for the joy that was set before Him, so the disciple is to be encouraged and animated by the gracious promise: To him that overcometh will I grant to sit with me on my throne. When the God of *glory* appeared unto Abram, the father of the faithful willingly forsook all and obeyed the Lord. If our eye were more steadfastly and believingly fixed on the crown, should we not be more steadfast in our obedience and loyalty to the Saviour ?

The kingdom of heaven is like unto ten virgins, who went forth to meet the bridegroom. Do we go forth from the unbelief, the selfishness, the darkness of the world ; do we forsake the home of our sinfulness and self-love, of our old nature and world-con-

---

* " With regard to the *fourth period of the world,* or the *thousand last years of the world,* there is no book of the Bible which treats of them exclusively ; but the promises referring to that blessed time are scattered throughout the Scriptures, and added as a source of consolation and hope to the prophecies concerning the dangers and afflictions of the Church. And let this suffice. In this order we must speak and write about it. It is revealed, not to satisfy curiosity, but to strengthen our faith and to quicken our hope. It is easy for us to bear good and joyful events whenever they come, though they were not circumstantially foretold, but it consoles a Christian, who is often grieved and distressed in these dark times, and who has a zeal for the honour of Jesus Christ and His kingdom, to look forward to the golden times, when all *pia desideria* will be fulfilled and realised, and to see them even now in the mirror of the divine word."—*Roos.*

formity; denying ourselves and taking up the cross, do we go forth to meet the bridegroom? This also is included in the petition, " Thy kingdom come," that we ask God to give us the spirit of faithful servants, who wait for their Master's return in sincere and diligent obedience, to deliver us from the love of the world, and from the spirit of this present age, to turn us continually from all idolatry, to look heaven-wards to Him who is our Father, and to the Lord Jesus, who has promised to receive us unto Himself.

Above all, this petition reminds us of the union between Christ and His Church. He who will reign as King of Israel and the nations, is Head of the Church; all who in the dispensation of the Spirit believe in Him, are one with Him, and chosen to reign with Him in His kingdom. To abide in Him, to realise His indwelling in our hearts by the Spirit, to live by faith in the Son of Man,—this is our present exceeding great privilege, it is the basis of our future blessedness.

> " Hope of our hearts, O Lord, appear,
>   Thou glorious Star of day!
> Shine forth, and chase the dreary night,
>   With all our tears, away !
>
> " No resting-place we seek on earth,
>   No loveliness we see ;
> Our eye is on the royal crown
>   Prepared for us and Thee.
>
> " But, dearest Lord ! however bright
>   That crown of joy above,
> What is it to the *brighter* hope
>   Of dwelling in Thy love ?

" What to the joy, the *deeper* joy,
    Unmingled, pure, and free,
  Of union with our living Head,
    Of fellowship with Thee?

" This joy e'en now on earth is ours:
    But only, Lord, above,
  Our hearts without a pang shall know
    The fulness of Thy love.

" There, near Thy heart, upon the throne,
    Thy ransom'd Church shall see
  What grace was in the bleeding Lamb,
    Who died to make us free."

8

JACOB'S VISION

"Thy will be done on earth as it is in heaven."

In the kingdom of glory Jesus will reign, and men will obey Him in the spirit of love and liberty. Then there will be no contrast between heaven and earth, but the worship and obedience below will resemble, in purity and fervour, the more exalted service of the angelic host and the transfigured saints. Into this inward depth of blessedness, the third petition descends, thus teaching us both the true spiritual character of the future glory, and the way in which even now we can live in the power of the age to come.

Let us view this petition:—

I. As a Description of the Kingdom of Christ.

II. As a Description of the Angelic Obedience, the Standard and Pattern of Ours.

III. As Pointing to the Lord Jesus, the Ladder between Heaven and Earth, in and by whom this Petition is Fulflled; and,

IV. As Pointing to the Work of the Holy Ghost within us, the Renewal of our Hearts.

I. THE EARTH AS THE SCENE OF OBEDIENCE TO GOD.

In this prayer, as in the Saviour's teaching throughout, we are continually directed to heaven. Our Father is in heaven; there His glory is revealed; from thence all spiritual blessings descend; it is there where we are to set our affections, and to lay up for ourselves treasure. But while heaven is thus described, the earth is always spoken of as the future scene of Christ's reign and man's blessedness.

We have been so long accustomed to see ignorance and sin prevail on earth, that our expectations concerning its future are generally far from the high standard of prophecy. For so many centuries the large majority of human beings have lived without the knowledge and fear of God; Israel and the Church have formed so small a portion of the human race, that the prospect of all nations serving and praising God is little realised by us. We are apt to think only of individuals saved and made meet for heaven; forgetting that God's purpose is, that on earth, and in the forms of our present, physical and national life, His will should be obeyed, and His name glorified. One reason of this view is, that the transfigured Church has not been distinguished from the nations of the earth. The position and the characteristics of the glorified saints, are indeed *heavenly;* but they with Christ are to be the rulers, and under them the earthly nations shall live, obeying the commandments of God. When Christ comes to reign, earth will rejoice. It is true that even at present the Lord reigneth over all; but it is obvious that He does not yet reign in the sense in which Scripture predicts the triumph and glory of His rule. The earth is as yet full of misery, oppression, and bloodshed. God's salvation is not known by humanity. But, "when Christ appears, and is manifested as King, the evil one necessarily ceases to exercise power upon earth; he is confined to the realm of death, and his activity in the formation of communities among the living is at an end. The congregation of the saints (and as the resurrection of the just has then taken place), the *whole* congregation of the faithful, now rule and judge mankind for a thousand years." * The saints will reign with Christ, without abandoning their higher, heavenly sphere. As the angels daily visit the earth, accomplishing their loving ministry, and yet their abode and home is above, so will the glorified saints belong to heaven, and yet fulfil below their ministry as kings and priests. As truly as Moses and Elijah appeared on the Mount of Transfiguration, they will be seen on the earth. Christ himself will have His dwelling in the celestial sanctuary, and yet reveal His glory to the nations. "The Lord hath prepared His throne in the heavens, and His kingdom ruleth over all."

Israel, renewed by the Spirit, and gifted in the richest measure with humility and fervent zeal, will be the first-born among the nations, and then the Saviour's saying, "Salvation is of the Jews," will

---

* Hofmann, Weisssagung & Erfüllung, ii. 373.

find its perfect fulfilment. The worship of Jerusalem will be the centre and model for all the God-fearing nations of the earth. Nowhere but in Israel arose the idea of the union of all people in the worship of God.* Jerusalem † is the only centre of Catholicity. United in the love of God, the nations will at last understand and love one another. They will learn war no more. They will recognise their peculiar gifts and callings, and encourage one another to serve God. Israel will be the great model. In the days of old they kept not the salutary and beautiful ordinances of God, because they were carnal, and had not received the Spirit. They did not fulfil their high destiny of being a holy nation, a kingdom of priests. But when the Holy Ghost shall write the law of God in their hearts, then will be seen the spectacle of a righteous nation, and, imitating them, all kingdoms of the earth shall conform themselves to the will of our Father in heaven.

It is true that the millennial reign is only the beginning of the ultimate, the eternal condition of the world. At the close of the thousand years, Satan is permitted to tempt the nations. This is his last attempt to oppose Christ and the beloved city. Then his ruin will be consummated, and the eternal glory will be revealed in the new earth, to which the New Jerusalem descends.

But while we are taught to look beyond the thousand years to the eternal glory, the millennial

---

* Psalm c.   † Not Rome.

reign forms the great fulfilment of Scripture prophecy, and constitutes the great triumph of divine love and power on that earth which was the battle-field between Christ, the Son, who obeyed the Father, and Satan, the usurper, who exalted himself against God. With the coming of the Lord Jesus begins the "Renovation of nature, the Sabbath of the people of God," the manifestation of divine glory in heaven above and earth below.*

Thus the petition which Christ teaches us to offer will be truly and really answered. It is the teaching of Scripture; and does it not harmonise with our deepest feelings? Is not such a consummation of history a necessary postulate of our thought? Would we not expect such a transition period between the present and the ultimate everlasting condition? As we have seen in the past a succession of developments, of which *man* is the highest, is there not to be the reign of the *Son of Man*, and a sphere in accordance with His character and glory?† Is there to be always the contrast between heaven and earth, the ideal and the actual? Is the history

---

* Nitzsch., System, § 218.

† "Is man the true, perfect, culminating point of rational creation? No being is so impatient and anxious to transcend the limits of his present nature. Creation cannot yet have reached its end, since we have still a craving (*appétence*) for perfection, and dream of a better and higher state, the corresponding organs of which are wanting. I am convinced that the destiny of man is not yet reached, because he is not the end of creation."—*Nodier, Revue de Paris,* 1832. A one-sided spiritualism is not able to comprehend the true meaning of the incarnation. It forgets that

of the world, which began with miracle, and a period of constant manifestation of the higher world unto the children of men, not to terminate in a similar age of heavenly influence and blessedness? Is earth simply a failure, abandoned by God to the power of the enemy, the scene of divine judgment, and not the scene of the vindication and triumph of righteousness? Is not Jesus the Son of Man, the Christ who shall reign on earth?

We believe that He will come, and with Him the kingdom, and with the kingdom the fulfilment of the prayer, "Thy will be done on earth as it is in heaven."

II. The Angelic Obedience.

Scripture reveals, according to the infinite wisdom of God, what is necessary and salutary for us to know concerning the angels of heaven, and the prince of darkness and his servants; not to satisfy a morbid curiosity, or to indulge a sort of luxury of the imagination, but for our comfort and warning, to strengthen and animate our faith, as well as to increase our watchfulness and zeal.

embodiment, outward manifestation, concrete form, is not opposed to the Spirit, but, on the contrary, the "end of all God's ways."— *Œtinger.* The scriptural idea of the kingdom will solve all such problems as are felt by deep and poetic natures:

> *"Oh the heavens above me
> Will never move the earth,
> And the yonder is never here."

> - *Schiller, in his poem "Der Pilgrim."*

Men have fallen into two errors concerning the angels, which may be characterised as the Gnostic and the Roman. The first introduces a speculative, metaphysical element, instead of resting satisfied with the Scripture teaching, in its sober and eminently practical character. The second introduces a superstitious and unscriptural element, by placing the angels in the position of mediators and intercessors.

Contrasted with the Gnostic error, admire the wisdom of Scripture. It is an evidence of its divine inspiration that it contains no elaborate angelology, but only gives us glimpses into the angelic world such as reveal to us those spiritual truths which we need at present, and which stimulate our service as well as our hope. All Scripture disclosures of this unseen world, given at great intervals of time, and interwoven with the history of redemption, are perfectly consistent with each other, from Genesis to the Book of Revelation, and, forming a most striking contrast to the pretended revelations of other books, furnish an important argument for the divine origin and character of the Bible.

To the Roman error, we oppose the truth that the man Christ Jesus is the only Mediator, and that we are nearer the Saviour than the angels. The only invocation of angels mentioned in Scripture is in Psalm ciii., when David calls upon them, asking not their intercession, but, as standing on an equality with them, he encourages and exhorts them, in the fulness of his joy, to praise the Lord.

The Protestants perhaps err by not paying sufficient attention to this topic. Notice the frequent reference to the angels throughout Scripture. The Lord's Prayer daily brings before us the obedience of the angels, and our relation to them as members of the one great family of our Heavenly Father. The awful and dark truth of Satan's power and influence requires the counterbalancing comfort and light of the doctrine of angels, whose sympathy and loving ministry encourage our hearts, while their example raises our standard.*

Scripture teaches us that the angels are the ministering organs of divine government and providence, so that both in nature and history the will of God is done by angelic agency.† The Scriptures recognise the agency of angels in the whole life of nature, even in what we regard as ordinary and regular natural

---

* The following passage occurs in the daily morning service of the Jews:—"Thy name be magnified for ever, our King and Creator of many servants, who stand in the higher worlds, and who proclaim aloud, with reverence, the commands of the living God. They are all of them lovely, chosen, and mighty : they all obey with fear the command of their Creator : they all open their mouths, in holiness and purity, in song and in praise, to bless, and hallow, and magnify, and extol the name of the Omnipotent. . . . All of them, in various gradations, perform the duties of the heavenly kingdom, and encourage one another to praise the Lord with holy delight—in pure language and melody, in harmony and reverence, sounds the ascription of holiness, Holy, holy, holy, Lord God of Hosts, the fulness of all the earth is His majesty. The Wheels (Ezek. i.) and the holy, living beings respond with mighty voices to the Seraphim, and say, ' Blessed be the majesty of the Lord, from Its Place.' "

† John v. 4 ; Heb. i. 7 ; Rev. vii. 1–3, xiv. 8, xvi. 5.

phenomena. The Book of Daniel teaches us that the kingdoms of this world are presided over by individual angels, who take a part in their history.*

We are apt to lose sight of God's personal will, and to dwell exclusively almost on the secondary laws of nature. " Now, here Scripture interposes, and seems to tell us that all this wonderful harmony of nature is the work of angels. Those events which we ascribe to chance, as the weather, or to nature, as the seasons, are duties done to that God who maketh His angels to be winds and His ministers a flame of fire. For example, it was an angel which gave to the pool of Bethesda its medicinal quality, and there is no reason why we should doubt that other health-springs in this and other countries are made such by a like unseen ministry. The fires on Mount Sinai, the thunders and lightnings, were the works of angels ; and in the Apocalypse we read of angels restraining the four winds. Works of vengeance are likewise attributed to them.† *Nature is not inanimate, its daily toil is intelligent, its works are duties."* ‡

There is nothing in this view which for a moment conflicts with our scientific knowledge of natural laws.§ But it enables us to avoid the danger into

---

* Auberlen on Daniel, p. 57.

† Sodom and Gomorrah ; the destruction of the hosts of Sennacherib ; pestilence in Israel under David's reign.

‡ Newman, Sermons, ii. 358.

§ " When it is said that such and such are laws of matter, the real meaning can be no other than this, that some *will* chooses that it *should* be so, and some power secures that it *shall* be so."—*The Mystery, by Dr Young,* 57.

which our increased knowledge of matter and its laws
is apt to lead us, of forgetting the personal, living God,
who even now rules and guides all things by His will,
according to His wisdom and love, through the agency
of spirits, who render Him the obedience of freedom
and intelligence. Instead of fixed laws, self-sustained
and acting of themselves, we behold the will of God,
acting through these laws by the agency of thousands
of His unseen servants. And instead of explaining
the scriptural statements as poetical or allegorical
modes of expressing what we view as merely natural
and regular phenomena, we exercise more wisdom and
humility by viewing these Scripture disclosures as revealing to us the true though unseen government of a
living God in this world.* Thus we believe the past,
thus we realise by faith God in the present, and thus
we expect in the future that the great changes in the
material world will be brought about by the agency
of angels at the coming of the Lord Jesus and at the
end of the millennial reign.

---

* "The centre of natural life and of spiritual life is the same,
but the circumference of the latter is greater, and the radii thereof
transcend continually the boundaries of the visible. Natural
science ends where theology begins. . . . It is thought to be an
interruption of the regular order of the visible world, that it should
be influenced by something spiritual. . . . But what if the rhythm,
the pulsations of the higher and the lower order, the seen and the
unseen, were always the same and simultaneous? What if all things
seen had their life and motion in an unseen element, if *all* laws of
the natural world of phenomena, if all the manifestations of
natural life and its laws, had their root and motive power in some
thing unseen and spiritual?" (*Fabri, Briefe gegen den Materialismus,*
p. 209).

How beautiful is this view of nature! "Every breath of air, and ray of light and heat, every beautiful prospect is as it were the skirts of the angels' garments, the waving of the robes of those whose faces see God in heaven." * But the very poetry of this view will be to some minds a reason for rejecting it as fanciful. So great is the difficulty of our regarding the ideal as the real, and reality as the highest and most beautiful poetry. We have forgotten that true idealism is nothing else but faith which sees substance, truth, that which is spiritual, eternal, and beautiful. The basis and source of poetry is not an imaginary and unreal world, but, on the contrary, the true and substantial world, towards which, among the semblances and shadows of our actual life, the mind of man is longing.†

To do God's will is the delight of angels, and His will is His self-manifestation on earth. Angels are interested in the earth that God may be glorified, even as Satan and his servants are interested in it to retard the progress of God's kingdom and to obscure His glory. Hence we find that, at the first coming of Jesus Christ, angelic manifestations abounded, and at the same time the power of Satan

---

* Newman, l. c., p. 362.

† Compare Schiller's Poem, "Die Götter Griechenlands." The ancient view of nature is indeed more full of poetry and life than that commonly received now, according to which God is banished into inaccessible heights, and abstract laws reign. But the scriptural view reveals a God both above and in the world, and a kingdom of intelligent and loving obedience.

and his legions was exerted on earth as it seems never to have been either before or since. Thus the angels appear to the patriarchs; through them the law is given on Mount Sinai; their guardianship and watchful care is known unto David; the birth of the Saviour is announced by them to the shepherds of Bethlehem, as well as to Mary and Joseph. They ministered to Jesus after the temptation in the wilderness; an angel strengthened Him in Gethsemane; angels announce the resurrection, and explain His ascension and visible return. Jesus Christ is the great centre of their loving interest and service, even as He is the object of their adoration. For apart from those indications of Scripture, according to which Christ's death on the cross is connected with peace and harmony in heaven, it is in Christ crucified that angels behold the manifestation of God, and thus they worship with us the Lamb as it had been slain, they joyfully praise and extol the Son of God in our nature, exalted to be King and Heir of all things.

Loving God and Jesus Christ, they rejoice over the repenting sinner, they minister to the heirs of salvation, they protect us in danger often unseen and unknown; they carry the soul into Abraham's bosom; they accompany Christ at His second advent, when He will be glorified in His saints. Then they shall separate the wheat from the chaff, and doubtless be the agents in the great changes which shall take place in the world. And after we have attained to the resurrection of the just, the Saviour reveals to us that we shall be like unto the angels. Thus God's Word reveals heaven, not as a distant place, separated and isolated from us, but near and in constant communion with earth: we behold clearly what Jacob saw in a dream.

As the angels obey, so on earth God's will is to be done in the age of which we speak; but we desire that *now,* while waiting for Christ, we also may be enabled to render such obedience to our Father. The obedience of angels is in humility and in perfect submission. They obey because God commands. Thus ought we to accustom and train our hearts to reverential obedience. While we experience that God's commandments are not grievous, and that Christ's yoke is easy, the authority of God is the foundation of all service. The Christian seeks to please his Heavenly Father; obedience brings glory to God, and a renewed assurance of our union with Christ.

The angels obey God, because they see His face continually. Their obedience is implicit, but not blind. God's authority is perfect light and love. Thus ought our obedience to be in knowledge and meditation: work is prayer acting.

The obedience of the angels, as we have seen, is very varied and comprehensive. Some watch over little children; some take charge of believers in danger; some seem to have assigned to their care mighty empires, and the various elements of the world. But their motive is always love to God, their object is

God's glory. Thus may we serve the Lord in our daily duties, in our most common occupations, in every ministry of charity, in the conversation of social life.

As God is their centre, the utmost harmony and union prevail among them. Thus they who serve the Lord are to serve Him in brotherly love. In the building of the temple no noise was to be heard. " When the angels are about to enter into the presence of the Most High," says a Jewish father, " they all stand back in modesty; one says to the other, ' Go thou first, thou art more worthy.' " What a commentary on the apostolic words, " Be kindly affectioned one to another in brotherly love, in honour preferring one another."

The angels behold the glory of God in Christ. In Him they see the manifestation as well as the central object of the Father's purpose. As they took the most profound interest in the Saviour's life on earth, so they are now waiting for the marriage of the Lamb. Thus ought we in all our obedience to remember Christ, the Centre, the Alpha and Omega, in whom we are loved, and in whom we are to be raised unto everlasting blessedness.

III. High as is the standard placed before us in the obedience of angels, and manifold as are the lessons to be derived from their example, there is yet a higher standard, another and deeper and more comprehensive obedience, which is our true model, as it is the source of our salvation. By Christ's obedience to God's will we are sanctified through the offering of the body of Jesus Christ once for all. In Jesus the will of God was done on earth; and because He made peace through the blood of His cross, all things will be reconciled unto the Father, whether they be things in earth or things in heaven.*

From all eternity the Son, in the covenant, undertook our salvation. Between the Father and the Son there was concord, concurrence, harmony of will, and co-operation. We may even say that the mind which was in the Son of God from all eternity, was the mind of obedience to His Father.† Thus, before He actually came, He looked forward to do God's will. His incarnation was, of His own free accord, an act of obedience to the Father who sent Him. And throughout His whole life on earth the Son of God, in human nature, learned obedience. He, who is Lord, holy, wise, powerful, eternal, infinite, humbled Himself, took upon Him the form of a servant; He took on Him our nature, and, with a human will, and amid the toil and temptations incident to humanity, He continually submitted Himself to God, His Father.

The obedience of the Lord Jesus Christ was characterised by such continuity, inward delight, and liberty, that we are apt to lose sight of that aspect of it on which the apostle dwells, when he says, that though Christ was a Son, yet *learned* He obedience by the things which He suffered, and which the Lord

* Col. i. 19–21.   † Phil. ii.

himself points out, when He declares, that He did
not His own will, but the will of the Father that
sent Him.   Yet unless we remember this true and
real submission and offering up of His will to the
Father, it is impossible for us to have the full consolation of Christ's sympathy, or to understand the
extent to which He is the example of all who are
renewed after His image, and filled with His Spirit.

From His earliest childhood, knowing that He
came from God, He learned obedience, and fulfilled
the will of God by lowly submission to all His ordinances.   He was subject to Mary and Joseph.   His
life, during the obscure stillness of Nazareth, was no
doubt a life of prayer and faith, a continuous hum-
bling of Himself in meekness to all the statutes of
God, and to all the trials and difficulties of His daily
path.   Of this life we have no record, but we know
it was part of the obedience which was to God a
sweet smelling savour.

After His baptism—itself an act of obedience to
fulfil all righteousness—anointed with the Spirit,
and consecrated anew by the voice of the Father,
He went into the wilderness, led up, not by His
own thought, but by the Holy Ghost, there to be
tempted of the devil.   This was a real conflict; He
suffered being tempted.   After this victory He began
His ministry; and here it is evident that all His
words and acts were spoken and done in prayer, in
faith, in a continual surrender of Himself to the
guidance and will of God.   He shows us, indeed, that

it is His joy to do His Father's will; not a task
or an exertion, but the very nourishment and refreshment of His soul.* In keeping His Father's commandments, He is only abiding in His love.† He
represents His work as easy; whatsoever He seeth
the Father do, He doeth likewise, as if it was the
most natural and simple thing to reflect His Father's
image, to echo His voice, to do His works. He is
anxious to show His disciples and the people that
all His miracles are the answer of God to His
prayer, the never-failing response, in which He
rested with calmest repose. Free also He is, though
He often speaks of a needs be and must, that the
Scripture be fulfilled, and the Father's will accomplished; but His attitude is always that of the
Son, the only possessor and dispenser of liberty.

Yet let us remember that He lived by faith. He
was true man. He came in the likeness of sinful
flesh. There was a real burden on His heart, and
by prayer and supplication He continually obtained
the strength He needed. He lived not merely before
and with the Father, but He lived *by* the Father,
even as Christ is our bread, and we live by Him. ‡
In the Psalms and the latter portion of the prophet
Isaiah, Messiah's life and prayer of faith are revealed.
He said, "I have laboured in vain, I have spent my
strength for nought, and in vain; yet surely my judgment is with the Lord, and my work with my God!"

---

* John iv. 34.   † John xv. 10.
‡ John vi. 57.

Whole nights He spent in prayer, and the Lord heard Him.

But the crown and summit of His obedience was His death on the cross. For this purpose He came into the world, and therefore the Father loved Him, because He laid down His life for the sheep. The account given in the gospels of His agony in Gethsemane reveals unto us the suffering and conflict which this obedience implied. Here the petition, " Thy will be done on earth as it is in heaven," receives its deepest illustration.

The narrative recorded by the first three Evangelists,* and afterwards explained by the apostle Paul,† is one which all Christians have felt to be of the greatest solemnity and importance. What happened in the Garden of Gethsemane is evidently different from any previous sorrow or prayer in the Saviour's life. True, on a former occasion He said that His soul was straitened until His baptism was fulfilled;‡ and when the Greeks came to the feast His soul, in anticipation of His sufferings, was troubled. They had seen Jesus shed tears at the grave of Lazarus, and weep over Jerusalem. But here was something different and so overwhelming that the Evangelists evidently struggle with the inadequacy of language to describe the impression

---

* John, although an eye-witness, does not narrate the agony of Gethsemane, partly because the previous Evangelists contained it, and partly because in his Gospel he views suffering chiefly as the way to Christ's glory—as the lifting up of the Son of Man.

† Heb. v. 7–9.   ‡ Luke xii. 50.

left on the minds of the apostles.* So heavy was this weight on His soul, that in most touching words He seeks the sympathy of His disciples' presence: "My soul is exceeding sorrowful, even unto death; tarry ye here and watch with me." He knelt down, He fell on His face, He fell on the ground. So great was His conflict, that, as Luke (the beloved physician) notices, His sweat was as it were great drops of blood falling to the ground.

Only a few moments before, He had sat down with His disciples in the upper room. They were cast down and troubled, but He comforted them with words of heavenly peace. He spoke of nothing else but of the glory that awaited Him, of His union with the Father and with the Church, of His joy being perfect in His believers. In the prayer which He then offered to the Father there was no sadness, nothing but peace and love, and the calm assurance of His victory. How different do we behold Him now!

The humanity of our blessed Lord, though never for a moment swerving from most implicit submission to the Heavenly Father, was well-nigh overwhelmed by the prospect before Him. The darkness of the approaching sufferings on Golgotha overshadowed Him, and He trembled; the stupendous weight of the burden which He was to bear crushed Him to the ground. His purpose was indom-

---

* He began (says Matthew) to be sorrowful and very heavy (lit., to be in anguish). Mark describes Him as sore amazed and appalled; while Luke writes, He was in an agony—the pangs of death.

itable, His faith unshaken, His love to the Father
unclouded. He had come down from heaven to give
His flesh for the life of the world. But though
willing to die, He loved His life. Now was the hour,
not to form the resolution of dying, but to lift the
burden on His shoulders, and to take up the cross.
Only by the most intense effort of faith in prayer He
gained the victory over the anguish of His soul.

Yet it is not merely the weakness of humanity
which struggles here against the overwhelming sorrow
of the cross. It is Jesus himself, the God-man, who
prays here, and is in an agony. There is only one
explanation, only one key, to unlock this mystery.
He who, adored by martyrs, gave them strength and
even triumphant joy on their way to a cruel and
painful death, was Himself overwhelmed, not by the
prospect of physical pain (excruciating as it was, and
sensitive as was His pure and sinless body) ; not by
the anticipation of the extreme manifestations of the
ingratitude and hatred of the nation whom He loved
even unto the end (deep as His sorrow was over
Jerusalem) ; nor was it the shadow of the valley of
death, in which even David said I will fear no evil,
and from which he knew he would come forth in
resurrection power. The cause of His anguish is, that
He now saw and felt close before Him the curse which
He was to endure as our substitute. He, who knew no
sin, was to be made sin for us. God was to hide His
countenance from Him. It was the anticipation of His
expiatory suffering on the cross, that well-nigh over-

whelmed Him. "Who would have dared to use such strong language—He was made a curse for us—if the apostle had not gone before him ?"* It was not death-sufferings in themselves, but in their penal character, that Christ contemplated. He saw "death in its organic connexion with divine wrath."†

Christ, the sinless One, could not but shrink from this "cup." To take upon Him suffering was simple submission to the Father's will ; to take upon Him *sin*, and the enduring of God's wrath against sin, called forth not merely the greatest sorrow of soul, but the whole *aversion* of His holy will. If it were not for this narrative, and its prayer, we would not have known how grievous sin was to Christ's nature, how abhorrent He was of that iniquity which was about to be laid on Him. He appeals to His Father. He considers Him as the Supreme Judge of all, and His prayer is, that if it be possible according to the divine counsel, to accomplish the object of redemption without this imputation of sin, that this cup may pass from Him ; but immediately He submits even this His will (which showed nothing but His love to the Father, and His dread of being forsaken of Him) to the counsel and will of God. He asks not the protection of God against His enemies. The possibility He speaks of is a moral one, as consistent with God's glory, and the accomplishment of His purpose.

* Bengel. † Beck.

The Father could not spare His beloved Son. It
pleased God to bruise Him; He hath put Him to
grief. Yet was the prayer of Jesus heard. He
gained the victory over the anguish that overwhelmed Him in that hour; He had strength to
rise up and set His face steadfastly to the work before
Him. With meekness He bore the kiss of Judas;
He went forth with calm majesty to meet the soldiers
who were sent to take Him captive; He restrained
the false zeal of Peter, as afterward He remembered
him with forgiving and watchful love; before the
High priest and Pilate He witnessed a good confession, remaining silent, as was becoming, before
Herod; He called the daughters of Jerusalem to
repentance; He prayed for Israel's forgiveness, heard
the petition of the repentant thief, commended
Mary to John's care, and then entered into the
mysterious darkness of His expiatory suffering. One
thought filled his soul—to empty the cup which His
Father gave Him to drink.

We must carefully distinguish between the agony
in Gethsemane and the agony on the cross. In the
one, Christ is in full enjoyment of the Father's
love, in filial confidence He calls Him, Abba; in
the other, Christ exclaims, "My God." In the one,
Christ is overwhelmed by the anticipation of the cup;
in the other, He actually drinks and empties it. In
the one, Christ dreads the moment of His being forsaken by God, of His becoming a curse for us; in
the other, He actually endures the curse, having

been made sin for us according to the Father's
counsel. There was no return on the cross to the
state of mind and conflict in Gethsemane. The
words "My God, my God, why hast thou forsaken
me?" are not a parallel to the words, "Father,
if it be possible let this cup pass from me." No;
He gained the victory in Gethsemane, and now He
endures what He again and finally undertook in the
garden. He now empties the cup. It is the *crucified* Lord who is made a curse for us.*

The Son of God has thus become the author of
eternal salvation unto all believers. By His obedience we are constituted righteous. By His sacrifice
we have gained the position of children. Sin separated heaven and earth, but Jesus, who died on the
cross, is now at the right hand of God, our righteousness and life; in Him we are reconciled and renewed;
one with Him, we receive the Father's love, and the
gift of the Holy Ghost; and thus

IV. GOD'S WILL IS DONE IN US AND BY US.

It is true we have a will. But what is its nature
and tendency? The clearest light was thrown on

---

* Luther, on these two prayers of Christ, says, "The prayer of
Christ in Gethsemane is not to be compared with this cry on the
cross, for in the latter, *God was against Him; the words will not
allow another interpretation*" (Walch, xii. 1926). In that mysterious
moment, when He was forsaken, the adorable Lord atoned for our
sins, and fulfilled the will of God concerning our salvation. This
was *the* obedience. Comp. Steinmeyer, Leidensgeschichte des
Herrn, p. 40 *et seq.*, and 208.

our will by the coming of Jesus. "Jerusalem, Jerusalem, how often would I have gathered thy children, even as a hen gathereth her chickens under her wings, and ye *would* not!" Infinite love and tenderness found the will of man, even of enlightened and religious Israel, in a state of continual opposition and resistance. "Ye will not come unto me," is the language of the Lord, "that ye may have life." *The will of man is invariably opposed to his own salvation, and to God.* The will of man rejects God, even when He approaches us in the most attractive and heart-winning way. So gently and sweetly did He come among us; by the tender mercy of God the Day-spring from on high visited us; meekness and grace were in all His words and steps; the simplicity of light and love were His authority and weapon. And yet men united in rejecting Him; high and low, learned and ignorant, Gentiles and Jews, agreed in putting Him to death. What is the lesson of this event, *the* tragedy of history, but that the carnal mind is enmity against God? Jesus is rejected, because "He is the true God and eternal life." When we stand before the will of God, as revealed in Scripture, as embodied in Christ, we feel not our weakness, but our sin, not our finite littleness, but our departure from holiness. Men were able to resist Christ, and even to crucify Him. It was not a conflict between a powerful will as opposed to a weak will, but between a will of love and holiness and a will of sin and hatred of God.

Nothing can be more certain than this: if we remain in our natural will, and follow it, we reject Jesus and ruin our souls. On this mysterious subject, it is better to dwell in the lowly region of self-examination, and to acknowledge that there is within us a will at enmity with God.* Even from our childhood, there is within us that disposition of insubordination to God which the Saviour describes in the parable (Matt. xxi. 28, 29). "A certain man had two sons, and he came to the first, and said, Son, go work to-day in my vineyard. He answered and said, *I will not.*" Who can change the will? This is the work of the Holy Ghost. Only divine omnipotence can effect it. The gospel is preached; reason is convinced; the feelings are touched; conscience is alarmed; the imagination is gratified. Men admit it is true, it is solemn, it is of the utmost urgency, it is beautiful and lovely. And yet the heart is closed, the citadel does not surrender. It is the will that keeps the gate shut. God only can touch the will. We cannot always trace His method. He does it often gently, almost imperceptibly. The descent of the Holy Ghost is as of a dove. He opens the door so gently, that you think you have done it yourself. He does not annihilate or force the will. He persuades, draws, moves. We yield, and, in yielding, we are for the first time gaining the power of activity; we are constrained, but the will is not

---

* "A separate will is the cause of all the trouble that is to be found in the world."

paralysed ; on the contrary, it is set free from the strange tyranny which held it captive. We are conquered, and yet we feel that we have wrestled with God, and overcome. Love is begotten in the heart— love, which is of all things the most spontaneous and free, and yet, in its liberty, possesses the strongest and most irresistible necessity.

Now we discover that we who chose God are chosen of Him ere time began ; and as we now believe with adoring wonder the doctrine of election, we enter into a new perception of the doctrine of the Trinity. We feel that the two arms with which God embraces us with never-changing love and safety are Christ the Saviour and the Spirit. God's will is done now in earth ; of His own will begat He us by the word of truth, that we might be the first-fruits of His creatures.

Solemn is the thought, that God has taken up His abode in us. Omnipotent wisdom and love are influencing us, and that not merely from without, by the Word and Providence, but from *within*. The Spirit of God is now within us, in depths which we cannot fathom, and speaking with plaints which cannot be uttered, enlightening our thoughts, enkindling our affections, moulding our character, directing our will. The great Lord, with a thousand powerful and delicate instruments or tools, is working in our soul ; and ourself, our eternal individuality, is the work of His hands. The Refiner is within, trying and purifying the soul. Such a thought is, indeed, full of consolation, yet of awful solemnity. When the apostle Paul thinks of it, we see that it rouses him to the greatest energy. It does not soothe him into a passive quietism; it does not establish in him a stationary rest. On the contrary, it excites in him the most lively anxiety; it stimulates him to most intense watchfulness. Because God works in us, we must work out our own salvation with fear and trembling. Most sacred and precious is every good thought, for it is suggested by God; every holy desire, for it is born of Him; every energy, for it is quickened by His breath. "Fear and trembling" is a strong expression, but it is a correct one. It is in harmony with the exhortations of the Saviour; it is the unanimous teaching of the apostles. Narrow is the way, great is the conflict, and the daily putting off of the old man is not easy, as the laying aside of a garment; it implies often the plucking out of a right eye, and cutting off of a right hand. God works in us this great and true will, which manifests itself in life.

The difference between the wise man who builds his house on a rock, and the foolish whose house is built on sand is, that while they both hear Christ's words, the one actually *does* "Christ's sayings." Before grace works in us, we admire humility, but we do not become humble; we admit that faith is the hand which grasps salvation, but we do not trust in Jesus. Nay, we are apt to make our hearing about faith, and our approving of the doctrine, a substitute for the exercise of faith. When God works in us both to will and to do, we actually become poor in spirit, humble and contrite, trusting in the Saviour, and setting our affections on things above.

" To do " means to bring forth fruit,—the fruit of the Spirit, which is described by the apostle.* It includes good works which the world can see and appreciate, as well as sacrifices of gratitude and self-denial which none but God can discern. " To do " denotes activity, zeal, diligence, concentration of energy, such as are illustrated by the faithfulness and perseverance of a devoted servant, the purpose and discipline of one who runs a race to gain a prize, the hardiness and courage of a warrior, the patience and watchfulness of a husbandman, the thoughtfulness and industry of a merchant; while it implies the motive of love and hope of union, such as animates a bride who is waiting for the coming of the bridegroom. " To do " is a comprehensive word; we seek to bring forth all the fruits of the Spirit, to come behind in no gift, to put on the whole armour of God. " To do " is a difficult word. By painful experience we learn that, between feeling and principle, between the clear and admiring vision of the height of duty and our actual ascent, there is a great interval. It is " with fear and trembling," with difficulty and exertion, that we pray in word and life, " Thy will be done." But we know it

---

* Gal. v. 22.

is the Lord who works in us. The slothful servant knew his Master only as a hard man. He had never tasted that the Lord is gracious ; the sunshine of His love had never gladdened him ; the frank forgiveness of his debt had never filled him with gratitude ; the royal spirit of joy and liberty had never taken up his abode in his heart. One solitary dreary thought constituted his religion, which was sufficient to make him miserable, but not happy ; it was his dread of punishment. The high standard of his Master's requirements and the severity of His demands he knew, in a manner ; but the riches of His grace, the power of His love, and the energy of His Spirit, he did not know. He knew fruit was expected, but not what Jehovah means when He says, " Of *Me* is *thy* fruit found." How different is the Christian ! Jesus brings with Him a thousand motives and influences: gratitude, love kindled by His own, joy and elasticity after the removal of our burden and the return of health to our soul, a holy ambition as being partakers of Christ's grace and heirs of His glory, courage and experience as the work prospers and grows, hope of His return and of His approbation of our service,—this, though mingled with salutary lessons to humble and chasten, continually strengthens and cheers us, filling our life with variety and beauty.

Thus we learn to do God's will. But why is it that, when we hear the words, " Thy will be done," we think immediately of sorrow, affliction, and bereavement? The meaning of the petition is very comprehensive, including active obedience, as well as meek resignation ; but it is in suffering especially that we realise the difficulty as well as the blessedness of this prayer. It is then that we find it both hard and sweet to submit to the will of our Father, whose wisdom we cannot fathom, but whose love and faithfulness we cannot doubt. *His will* is our ultimate comfort. All else seems dark ; but we penetrate into the inmost sanctuary of divine love, and by faith we obtain rest. To trust and love God, when He sends sorrow and takes from us what was dear and cherished, is an act of obedience, in which we follow Abraham, whose *faith* was made perfect by works, when he offered Isaac, his son, upon the altar.*

Faith is able to discern one purpose of God—viz., to draw us nearer to Himself, and to fix our thoughts and affections more firmly on His love ; to lead us more into the spirit of Asaph's words, " Whom have I in heaven but Thee, and there is none upon earth whom I desire beside Thee." Knowing the will of God, that chastisement, which is never joyous, but grievous while it lasts, should yield *afterwards* the peaceable fruits of righteousness, the Christian is not anxious to forget affliction ; but while waiting for the time when we shall understand how all things were ordered for our good, he thinks of the more *immediate* future, in which the Heavenly Gardener may see that the purged branch bringeth forth more fruit.

---

* James ii. 21.

It is the privilege of the Church of Christ to know the fellowship of His sufferings. Angels, by their obedience, glorify God, but they do not know affliction; the experience of sorrow is the bond of thrilling tenderness between the Saviour and His people. And in this present dispensation we are called especially to suffer, to follow Christ in His humility and patience, to bear the cross, that we may be conformed to His image, and that we may afterwards share His glory. Such is the union between the Head and the body, that the Saviour regards the sorrows of His people as His own,* while the apostle looks on his sufferings as filling up that which is behind of the afflictions of Christ.† Christ fulfilled the will of God on earth; Christ in the Church is glorifying now the same will, until, after the time of testimony and patience, the kingdom will be given to the Lord and His bride.

When we think of the will of God, our hearts are at peace. The secret will of God is a mystery, into which it is not for us to search; but we know that, while clouds and darkness are round about Him, righteousness and judgment are the habitations of His throne. We see His revealed will in the gift of Christ and the Spirit. We know this is the will of God, that all who believe in Jesus should have eternal life, and that He shall raise them at the last day. This also is His will, even our sanctification, that Christ by the Spirit should dwell and live in us,

---

* Acts ix. 9 † Col. i. 24.

and that, in union with the true Vine, we should bring
forth fruit.   Follow Christ, for this is the sure token
of your predestination to glory.*   Abide in Him, and
then you know that *above* you is the will of the
Father — loving, strong, unchangeable — even as
within you is the will of Christ, by which you delight
in God, and do what is pleasing in His sight. †

> " Something every heart is loving,
>   If not Jesus, none can rest ;
>   Lord, to Thee my heart is given,
>   Take it, for it loves Thee best."

---

* Bourdaloue.

† Within us is the will of Christ. " If I could obey in all things,
yet that would not satisfy me, unless I felt obedience flow from the
birth of His life in me. 'My Father doth all things in Me,' saith
Christ.   This was Christ's comfort, and to feel Christ do all in the
soul is the comfort of every one that truly believeth on Him."—
Isaac Pennington (Society of Friends).

9

THE COMPREHENSIVE SCOPE AND INTERCESSORY CHARACTER OF THE THREE PETITIONS

"Hallowed be thy name; thy kingdom come, thy will be done in earth as it is in heaven."

THE first prayer of the awakened soul is simple. It is the cry of the publican: God be merciful to me the sinner. It is the confession of the prodigal: I have sinned. It is the inquiry of Saul: Lord, what wouldst Thou have me to do? It is the supplication of repentance and faith: Lord, save me, I perish. Simple as such a petition is, it is sufficient. The Lord sends help to all who call upon His name.

But after this first and fundamental prayer, true worship commences; and the prayer of a child of God has a large scope, and is of a most comprehensive as well as exalted character. Personal safety is the starting-point rather than the object of Christian prayer. The great difference between heathen worship and Christian worship is, that in the former the purging of the conscience is the aim of prayer, in the latter the worshipper approaches with a conscience purged from sin. So high is the position of the

Christian, so great and wide is the range of his petitions, that it can be said of him—and what can be more wonderful?—that he prays in the name of Christ; Christ's desires are his.

The Christian is a child of God and an heir of all things. As one has said, the saints shall hereafter judge the world; and shall they be indifferent now to the cause of righteousness and truth on earth? They are represented in Scripture as the confidential servants of God, to whom He communicates the purposes of His will before they are executed. We read of them as " intercessors at the throne of His grace, who plead before Him the cause of great nations, and whom He has chosen as His secret agents, by whom He guides the great movements of the world." And as regards themselves, forgiveness and acceptance, wonderful blessings as these are, form chiefly the foundation on which the majestic structure of their desires and petitions is to be reared; for they are to seek conformity to the image of Christ. And between these two spheres of prayer, prayer for the world and God's kingdom at large, and prayer for our individual souls, there is the intermediate sphere of duty and influence in the narrower circle of our family and our friends, the petitions for wisdom and love, for integrity and kindness, for grace, to walk to edification, and the vast field of intercession for the spiritual and temporal prosperity of all to whom we stand related.

> " Thou art coming to a King,
> Large petitions with thee bring."

The spirit of the Christian, drawing near unto God, is a royal spirit.* He asks great things for himself and for others.

I. FOR HIMSELF.

It is written, " Ye ask, and ye receive not, because ye ask amiss." And one of the errors of our prayer may be, that our aim is not high enough ; that in coming to a King, whose delight is to be bountiful, we do not bring with us a royal spirit and large desires, but a contracted spirit, and limited petitions. The Lord's command and promise are, " Open thy mouth wide ;" and the rule, " Seekest thou great things for thyself ? seek them not," does not apply here. For the great things which we seek are not for ourselves, in any sense separate from the glory of God and the good of the Church, from the joy of our Saviour and the promotion of His kingdom.

A very instructive though elementary illustration of the narrowness of prayer is given us in the case of the prodigal. The petition which he conceived in his mind was, " make me as one of thy servants." He did not rise to the height of the father's forgiving mercy and restoring love. A child's place in the household, the right and privilege of sonship and inheritance, were blessings too great and bright for his thought. And though in one aspect this feature shows us both his humility and his true longing to be under his father's righteous and holy government,

_____
* Ps. li. 12.

under whatever conditions, yet we find that the immediate effect of the father's embrace was to raise at once his expectation and his prayer, to deliver him from the spirit of servantship, which, excellent as it is, engendereth fear, and to give him the royal, courageous, high-soaring spirit of the son.

(1.) High ought to be our thought of acceptance and favour in the sight of God.   The very light of God's countenance is our aim.   That His anger is removed from us, that punishment has been taken away, that our iniquities are blotted out by Him as a thick cloud, is merely the preparation for the great and only satisfying blessing of beholding His countenance in righteousness and peace.   The love of God resting on us can be our only aim ; and the strongest expressions of which human language is capable are used by the Spirit in Scripture to describe the favour of God towards those who believe in Jesus.   God rejoiceth over us, and His delight is in us.   We are dear and accepted children, and He keeps us as the apple of His eye.   The pitifulness of a father, and the ever-watchful tenderness of a mother, are but adumbrations of the intensity and brightness of His love.   The love which He has to His Son Jesus Christ, heightened, to speak after the manner of men, by Christ's obedience unto death, is the love wherewith He loves us.   And as every repentant and believing sinner is at liberty immediately to pass out of the cold, the arctic regions of the law, with its condemnation, into the sunny paradise of this infinite love, those who have believed are still further assured of their perfect blessedness. If He died for us while we were enemies, if we were saved by His death, much more being saved shall we now live by His life. He who loved not His life, but gave it up for our life, shall He not now treasure up with ever-watchful care and never-failing tenderness the objects of His dying love, the very travail of His soul?

(2.) Peace is then ours. How great is the word peace, if we understand it in the royal spirit! The Saviour, even after His resurrection, and to His own favoured disciples, brings no greater benediction than this: Peace be with you. *Only they who know the God of peace know the peace of God.* Only they who know that Christ is our Peace understand fully what He means when He says, My peace I give unto you. That ample, all-capacious, warm, and beautiful robe of peace, which covers Christ after He finished our battle and gained our victory, covers now Christ and all who rose with Him in His resurrection. And therefore it is a peace which passeth all understanding, proceeding from the infinite depths of divine love, secured by the infinite sacrifice of Christ, imparted by the influence of the Holy Spirit; a peace which, divine in its origin and its channel, is beyond the reach of all worldly influences; a peace which is broad as a river, continually renewed in vitality, and flowing on calmly till it ends in the ocean of blessedness.

(3.) And do we seek joy in God? It is written,

" Thou wilt make them joyful in Thy house of prayer."
Christ's joy is to be in us. He is a rejoicing Christ
now. Christ rejoices in the glory of the Father, which
was manifested in the work of salvation. Christ rejoices in the glory given to Him after His obedience.
Christ rejoices in the love of God towards the lost and
saved sheep. Christ rejoices in His union with His
believers. Christ rejoices in every manifestation of
spiritual life, of love, of patience, of self-denial which
He beholds in His people. Christ rejoices in the
prospect of receiving us to Himself. Christ rejoices
even when he is afflicted in our afflictions, for He
knows why He has commanded us to glory in tribulation also. Do we seek the greatest, the highest
joy, to have Christ's joy fulfilled in us ?

Perfect love of God, perfect peace of God, perfect
joy of God, such are *royal* thoughts and petitions.
I have placed these first, because they are the perfect
gifts of God to every believer. These spiritual blessings are yours in heavenly places in Christ. God
expects you to ask them in faith. These petitions
are nothing else but the creed converted into prayer:
I believe in God the Father, the Son, and the Holy
Ghost. But let us look now at the same blessings
in another light—their effects on us. Do we take
a royal view of the power, transforming and elevating, of the love of God, and the grace of the
Lord Jesus Christ ? We are to be *light* in the
Lord. Have we any lofty conceptions of the light
which we may possess ? Children in malice, we are

to be men, strong, mature, many-sided, fully-developed in knowledge and spiritual understanding. Do we realise it that God can and will teach us deep things and to profit, and that He can reveal to us His secret and give us wisdom ? What hopefulness have we in our acquisition of spiritual knowledge ? With God for our teacher, with Scripture for our text-book, with Christ, as the perfect embodiment of all God's thoughts, for our model ; with nature as our picture-book, with Providence as our commentary, with conscience as our monitor, with fellow-Christians as our schoolmates ! You lack wisdom— who among us does not ?—what a solution of the difficulty :—Let him ask of God ! It is written in the prophets, "And they shall all be taught of God." And as regards the effect of God's teaching, do we *seek* to be full of light ? Or are we rather like unto a house, scantily lit up, imperfectly illuminated, in which many chambers are scarcely ever used, in which some are dark and unswept, and others again purposely left untenanted and unvisited ? If our eye is single we shall be *transparent*—the whole body will then be full of light.

And again as to our character and life. We are to be renewed daily after the image of Christ. We mourn over our weakness and sinfulness. Let us start every day with the conviction that we have nothing, that all our resources are spent, all our strength exhausted, yesterday's manna consumed. Be daily *renewed ;* begin the day with a new Christ as it were.

And what is our idea of fruitfulness? Is not Christ
able to make all grace abound toward us, that we become rich and thoroughly furnished unto every good
work? And what is our prayer for victory over
sin? are not " these things written, that we sin
not?" Is not He able to subdue all things within
us and around us, so that we are more than conquerors?

Let us learn from the example of the apostle Paul
the true grandeur of Christian prayer. Starting with
full assurance of the free grace of God in Christ
Jesus, accepted in the Beloved, and clothed with
His righteousness, he seeks and obtains the fulness
of the blessing of the gospel of Christ. He rejoices
in God, though he has no confidence in the flesh.
And he asks for himself and the Church to be filled
with all the fulness of God, to grow in all things into
Christ; that love may abound yet more and more, that
we may be sincere and without offence till the day of
Christ, being filled with the fruits of righteousness,
which are by Jesus Christ unto the glory and praise
of God.

The Church is indebted to the apostle Paul for
his marvellous labours, more still for the Epistles,
which, according to the wisdom given unto him, he
has written; but I hesitate not to add, most of all for
the example of his character, for that singular combination of depth and breadth, of faith and works,
of meditation and activity, of joyousness and fear
and trembling. While his character is the explana-

tion of his works, his prayer is the secret of his character. From him we can learn what is the royal spirit in prayer and life.

II. THE GRANDEUR OF CHRISTIAN PRAYER FOR OTHERS.

A very touching illustration is given by a German writer, who thus speaks of his mother:* "She took such a deep interest in the kingdom of God, that she spent every alternate night in prayer; and when asked to consider her health, she replied, ' I will rest in eternity, at present I have no time. I have to pray so much for the king and his ministers and counsellors, for the universities and schools, for the mission to the Jews and to the heathen, and for my children, relations, and friends.' Her habit was to sit in a corner behind the stove. Sometimes on her knees, sometimes stretched on the floor, she spent numberless nights of her life in prayer. In her last illness she said before her children, pointing with her trembling hand to that little spot behind the stove, ' Lord, Thou knowest how many things I have begun there, have not yet been finished.' "

Prayer in the name of Christ must needs be prayer for the manifestation of God's glory in the good of man. For this is the mind which was and is in

---

* A daughter of the well-known P. M. Hahn, a friend of Bengel and Ötinger, a great student of Scripture and nature. His attainments in astronomy were high, his expositions of Scripture remarkable for their simplicity and depth.—*Paulus, Reden Jesu von Hahn.*

Christ. He lived and died to glorify God in our salvation; He lives now, that in Him and the Church the Father may be glorified.

Even before the full light was manifested in the incarnation of the Son of God, the world-wide character of the affections of the saints was a necessary consequence of their living unto the glory of God. The glory of God is the central idea of Scripture, as well as the culminating point of all revelation; and hence we see the saints men of lofty, fervent, and comprehensive intercession. You remember the intercession of Abraham, in this also the father and pattern of the faithful, when he entreated the Lord so earnestly and boldly on behalf of Sodom. You remember the pleading of self-sacrificing love with which Moses supplicated for his rebellious people. You remember the prayers of Jeremiah and Daniel, and the fervent petitions of David and the prophets, for the manifestation of God's salvation and glory to the ends of the earth. How deep were the longings of these men for the coming of God's kingdom! How absorbed were they in the honour of God's name! When Eli heard that the ark was taken, then he fell to the ground and died; when the children of Israel were by Babel's streams, they mourned in constant remembrance of Jerusalem. And how unfeignedly sincere and jubilant is their joy, anticipating in faith the time when the Lord shall reign upon earth, and when all nations shall serve Him and worship Him in light.

As they possessed in such a wonderful degree the *spirit* of intercession, that unselfish expansiveness of view and affection, which only faith in God can give, they possessed also the *power* of intercession. Thus Job was appointed by the Almighty to be the effectual intercessor for his friends. When God remembered Abraham he delivered Lot. In the battle of Amalek Israel conquered as long as the hands of Moses were lifted up in prayer. In the Book of Jeremiah the power of Moses the lawgiver, and Samuel the great reformer, is spoken of as so great, that only the exceeding weight of Israel's sin was too heavy an obstacle to be removed by them; and in the Book of Ezekiel we read of the potent influence of the prayer of Noah, Daniel, and Job; Daniel, that eminent saint, man greatly beloved, being alive at the very time when God thus spoke of him.

And if such was the spirit and power of intercession before Christ came, and before the spirit of sonship was poured out, how much more ought we, the body of Christ, to be characterised by the spirit and power of intercessory prayer. Intercession is the distinguishing mark of the Christian. The penitent, the inquirer, pray for their own personal safety. The accepted believer prays for others as well as for himself; he prays for the Church and for the world. Nearly all the exhortations given in the Epistles are to intercessory prayer, for all saints and for the spread of the gospel; for all men, for kings, and all that are in authority; for the ministers of the word, and for

all who are in suffering and persecution. Behold the
elevated position of the Christian ! Banished by sin
from Paradise, dead in trespasses, and condemned by
the law, he has, through the grace of Christ and the
power of the Spirit, been brought into the favour and
light of God; he is one with Christ. When he
appears before the Father, he appears not merely as a
creature in humility, as a sinner in contrition, as a
suppliant, full of wants and weakness, but he appears
as one with Christ, possessed of the spirit of the
Son of God, a royal priest, seeking the Father's
glory, longing for the Father's kingdom, and suppli-
cating in Christ's name the fulfilment of God's promises concerning the Church and the world. It is
in intercession that the Christian most fully enters
into his glorious liberty. Then he is not a servant,
but a friend, to whom God has revealed His plans
and purposes; as Jesus intercedes above, he intercedes below; *He fulfils the measure of prayer, for
Christ and the Church are one.* And while his heart
is filled with love, the wings of faith carry him beyond
all difficulties and storms of time, so that, calm, col-
lected, and hopeful, he looks forward to the victory
of God's holy cause upon earth.

Pray especially for the ministers of the gospel, that
they may set forth the love of God to the conversion
of many souls. Pray for them that they may not
shun to declare the whole counsel of God, so that
they may present every man perfect in Christ Jesus·
Remember their difficulties. To be anxious for souls

and yet not impatient, to be patient and yet not in-different, to bear the infirmities of the weak without fostering them, to testify against sin and unfaithful-ness, and the low standard of spiritual life, and yet to keep the stream of love free and full, and open—to have the mind of a faithful shepherd, a hopeful phy-sician, a tender nurse, a skilful teacher—requires the continual renewal of the Lord's grace.

Pray for the mission among Israel and the heathen nations. Christ's command is explicit, God's promise sure. The Church, obeying the divine word, and con-strained by the love of Christ, cannot but send forth evangelists.* Let us regard the missionary spirit as the very spirit of Christian prayer ; and in all our thoughts and prayers and work connected with the missions of the Church of Christ, let us remember how closely we are brought into communion with the Saviour. There is nothing higher and more Christ-like ; there is nothing in which the love of God comes nearer to our hearts. Here all divine truths and gifts meet as it were. You believe the supre-macy of the Father, and that His glory is the end of all things as well as the joy of His chosen ; you believe the universal character of Christ's kingdom, and the promise given to Him, that the heathen are

---

* During the present dispensation the purpose of God, according to Scripture, is to gather *a Church*, an election out of the nations. The gospel is to be preached in the whole world for a witness to all the nations (Matt. xxiv. 14). Wherever it is preached, it bringeth forth fruit ; enough to encourage us, not enough to make us forget that "the kingdom" is only at the coming of the Lord Jesus.

His inheritance, and the uttermost ends of the earth
His possession; you believe that the Spirit alone can
open the eyes of the blind, and turn men from idols
to serve the true and living God; you believe that
the Church of Christ is intrusted with the commission to preach the gospel to all nations; and you
believe that you are members of the body, and that
as at present you stand not alone, so your future life
and blessedness will be in communion with all the
saints, and in an interest in all the kingdom of God.
But what is your faith in all these glorious truths if
you take no interest in missions? Are you not separating yourself from the very love of God, from the
mind and heart of Jesus, from the pure river, which
is to make glad all lands, from the sympathy of the
angels, from the expectation of the saints who have
entered into their rest, from the truest energy of the
Church on earth?

As you worship the Father in heaven, and as you
can find no other safety than in the name of God, no
other home than in His kingdom, no other life than
in the fulfilling of His will; and as this name is
revealed, not for you only, but for all the ends of the
earth, and His kingdom was founded by Christ, not
for you only, but for all nations and kindreds; and
His will is to be done by the Spirit's influence, not in
your heart and walk only, but on earth even as it is
in heaven, I beseech you, by your own personal possession and enjoyment of the Father's love and gifts,
that you cultivate and cherish and manifest the mis-

sionary spirit, which is none other than the spirit of adoption, even of the Son of God, Jesus Christ, the royal spirit of the renewed and sanctified children of the Most High.   And as you pray for the mission of Christ among Jew and Gentile, and give to this work your affection and your contributions, the narrower circle of your immediate duty and work, and the inmost circle of your own spiritual life, will receive the invigorating and fertilising influence of that divine love which never scatters and spreads abroad without increasing the riches and intensifying the strength of the giver; for while we obey the command of Christ, and go forth into the world with the gospel, as far as we can by prayer and help, we realise the promise connected with this very last commission of the ascending Saviour, " I am with you alway, even unto the end of the world."

10

THE DAILY GIFT

"Give us this day our daily bread."

THE child of God seeks first spiritual blessings in
heavenly places. God himself is our portion. His
name is revealed, His kingdom descends, His will is
fulfilled; God, as Father, Son, and Holy Ghost, is
above, and for and within us. Realising thus our
heavenly blessedness, we ask God to descend with
His bounty, grace, guidance, and strength to our
earthly need, our daily sin, danger, and evil. He
who has enriched us with His heavenly gifts, is willing to deliver us from the wants, the trespasses, the
perils, and the evil of the world. In the gift of His
Son, all other good and needful gifts are included.
What would they be to us without Him? If we
seek the kingdom of God and His righteousness, all
other things shall be "added" unto us. Unless God
himself be our portion, and His love the joy of our
heart, earthly possessions will bring us no true blessing and gladness.

We ask God to give us our daily bread. Some

have endeavoured to give this petition a spiritual meaning, either substituting it for the earthly one, or combining it therewith. This arose partly from a morbid feeling that such a spiritual interpretation is more in accordance with the heavenly character of the Christian. But as we depend on God for the life and sustenance of our bodies, it is right that we should seek this blessing by prayer; and of the seven petitions, one has most appropriately been assigned to our earthly wants. Christ himself, the perfect Man, did not exalt Himself above the necessity of food; He entered into all the conditions of our humanity, and He thanked God for earthly bread.

The meaning of the word, which, in our version, is translated " daily," gave rise to considerable controversy.* But there can be little doubt that the primary

---

* Some, as Abälard, following the guidance of several Latin fathers, understood it in the sense of true, substantial, essential, referring it to the bread which sustains our spiritual life. Others, as Jerome, take it to mean bread for subsistence, bread that is sufficient for our need. Others, again, and with much plausible argument, understand the word as referring to the future, the morrow, and render the petition, Give us this day our bread for to-morrow (Meyer). But the spirit of the Lord's teaching, as well as the letter of His injunction, " Take therefore no thought for the morrow," seem to condemn such a view. Another recent expositor is inclined to translate the word " earthly." As in the only other passage in which the word occurs, it means earthly possession (Luke xv. 12, 13); and since the idea of daily is already contained in the words " this day," he thinks it more in accordance with the concise style of the Lord's Prayer to translate the petition, Give us to-day our _earthly_ bread (Steinmeyer, Wunderthaten des Herrn, p. 242).

meaning of the prayer is the supply of our earthly bread. And yet we may find a hundred bridges which lead us from the seen and temporal to that which is unseen and eternal, and no Christian can think of bread, without remembering Him who is the true, the living Bread, which came down from heaven, to be the bread of life to us. Nor ought we to forget, that man, even as regards his body, does not live by bread alone, but by the Word which proceedeth out of the mouth of God. The Word does not sustain us without visible food, but the Word alone confers power upon the earthly bread to sustain the God-given life of our bodies.

Let us consider :—

I. THE GIVER: OUR FATHER IN HEAVEN ;
II. THE GIFT: BREAD ;
III. THE EXPANSION OF THE GIFT: *Our* BREAD ;
IV. THE LIMIT OF THE GIFT: *To-day*.

Notice that both the expansion and limitation of the gift are in opposition to our natural tendency. We are inclined to limit the gift to ourself, and to forget the wants of our fellow-men. Christ expands our narrow thought, and teaches us to pray for *our* bread. And while we are inclined to ask the supply for our future wants, the Lord limits us to the present. Thus do we need the teaching and the influence of the Holy Spirit even in that which is least.

I. THE GIVER IS OUR FATHER IN HEAVEN.

God is the *only* giver. There is none who can give in the true sense of the word but God only. Satan has no gifts. He has only baits. He promises, as he even said to our Lord he would give Him the kingdoms of the world and their glory. In eternity the wicked discover that Satan had no true and good gift to bestow, that his apparent gifts were only snares and fetters. The world also has nothing to give. It can introduce no new element of life, of peace and joy into the soul. It cannot enrich us. It gives only in appearance. Its gifts have a shadowy existence, and are without subtance. They vanish, or they are called back, and we are as poor as before. The world lends and barters; it bestows benefits to receive them again. "Not as the world gives," gives God to us.

God gives because He is the *Creator*. It was a favourite saying of Martin Luther, that all his life he had found the greatest difficulty in learning to believe and realise the first article of the Creed, " I believe in God the Father, Almighty maker of heaven and earth." " We come to Him with our petty good works and promises, and forget that we are not to barter with Him, but to receive gifts from the almighty and rich Creator." In creation the God of love began to give; in providence God is continually giving.

God is the only giver, and yet least recognised. Because He gives *so constantly, so quietly*, we forget to notice and to thank Him. When a gift is withheld, we feel it, and acknowledge the power of God; but when we receive it day by day, and year by year, the very continuity of the blessing renders us oblivious of its great and high source. God gives His gifts so silently, as if He did not wish to be observed and thanked; yet is He not indifferent to our gratitude and affection, but asks, "Were there not ten healed? But where are the nine?" He is so generous and tender, linking His goodness and bounty in a thousand ways with our own thought and work, that only those whom His Spirit teaches think of thanking Him.

God gives constantly; He waits on us the whole day long. God waits on all men, watching over them at night, waking them in the morning, preparing their path before them, protecting and prospering their work. But not all men wait upon God. David, and all God's children, say, "On Thee do I wait all the day."

God gives, for there is none *beside* Him; He cannot receive except of His own; even as He always looks down, for there is none *above* Him; He cannot look up. Go therefore to Him as the Giver, as the Lord, who cannot but condescend and communicate. It is natural for you to ask, for Him to give.

God gives *good gifts*, for He is good, and He is our Father. As an earthly parent would never withhold from his children good and wholesome food when they ask it, and as an earthly parent would never give dangerous and hurtful things, though from their attractive appearance they seem desirable to the child, our Heavenly Father gives only good gifts. If it comes from Him, it must be good. Poverty, sickness, affliction, persecutions, are among the good gifts sent by God. Purple and fine linen and sumptuous fare, Abraham, when speaking to Dives, calls "*thy* good things"—not God's good gifts.

God delights in giving. Love is its own source and explanation. When God gives, if we may so say, all that is in Him is delighted, for God is love. When God rebukes or punishes, His justice requires it, while His wisdom measures. But judgment is His strange work; His delight is in giving; the manifestation of His glory is His love; to bring forth the best robe, to put a ring on his finger, and shoes on his feet, and to kill the fatted calf for the poor returning prodigal, this is the festive joy of heaven.

God gives simply. So James in his profound Epistle tells us, that if any of us lack wisdom, we are to ask of God, that giveth to all men simply ($\dot{\alpha}\pi\lambda\hat{\omega}\varsigma$), and it shall be given him. We have all known generous and loving men who cannot refuse a request, and to whom the fact of being asked is sufficient reason for giving. God gives for the simple asking.

God never takes back His gifts. "The gifts and calling of God are without repentance." This is most strikingly illustrated by Israel. God will fulfil

His promises, though Israel has been guilty of the
greatest ingratitude, and of the most fearful sin.
They rejected Jesus, they resisted the gospel ; and
yet God has not given them up.   He has given them
no bill of divorcement.   He will yet restore them,
convert their hearts, and fulfil the promises given to
the fathers.   Israel is the embodiment of the great
doctrine of election, and the perseverance of the
saints, or rather of divine love and power persevering
with the chosen.

And yet it is written again, " To him that
hath shall be given, but whosoever hath not, from
him shall be taken away even that he hath."
The proclamation of the love of God, and of His
exceeding great, His unspeakable gift is sent to
the world.   It is to be declared, not merely to all
creatures, but to *every* creature ; a message to each
one separately.   Those who are anxious to secure
God's gifts, to receive them, to appropriate them by
faith and love, enter into possession of the blessing,
and they are enriched more and more with the gifts
of God ; while they who feel no need or wish of salvation, and lull their souls to sleep by thinking that
the arms of divine love are always open to welcome
the returning sinner, never run into the Father's
arms, never receive from Him the free gifts of His
pardoning grace, and finally lose even what they
appeared to have.   As we think of God in our
hearts, so we have Him.   He who believes that
God is the Giver, receives from Him, and in grati-

tude and hopeful love, he offers to God of His own :—

> "Love Divine accepteth nought,
> Save what love itself hath wrought."

To understand that God is the Giver, is to understand the sweetness of the gospel, and to possess the Spirit and strength in which alone we can obey His law. That God is the Giver, as Creator, we all grant; that in our redemption and sanctification God is the Giver, we are slow to learn. When the world was lost, God had to come forth with a *gift*. There was nothing in the creature, in the resources of the whole universe, available for the rescue and salvation of sinners. As the things which are seen were not made of things which do appear, the salvation of sinners necessitated the gift of something *new, outside and above the world.* God had to give His own Son. We think of the gift of the Son chiefly as expressing the free and generous love of the Father: it reminds us, however, also of the utter helplessness of the world, and the divine, supernatural, heavenly character of redemption. The gift had to come from *above ;* God had to give up His own Son. The new heart also, the right spirit, the love and zeal of faith, the work of grace within, the fruit of holiness in outward manifestation—all is gift. The gift of God is eternal life.*

* In the world, " God, the Giver, is forgotten, Christ, the Purchaser, is forgotten ; the body that is to be redeemed, and the soul that is to be saved, all are forgotten."—*Howels,* l. c. 103.

II. THE GIFT—BREAD.

It has been remarked, that this petition is the easiest, and offered with the greatest sincerity. If so, it shows that our daily wants are blessed by God, to teach us our dependence on Him, and to bring us to His throne of grace.

We deserve no credit for seeking our present and future hapiness, nor is the dread of misery and punishment a lofty motive. Yet it is a true one,* and everything that causes us to look up to God for help and grace, is sent by Him in love, and with the purpose to bring us into the fellowship of light and blessedness.

The daily necessity for food may well teach us humility. We have no life in ourselves. Here all are equally dependent. This simple fact alone should keep us mindful of our dependence on God, our Creator.† And God wishes us to remember our dependence on Him, that we may constantly rejoice in His loving and bountiful remembrance of us. The son, who abides in his father's house, receives with thankfulness and joy the gifts of paternal love, while the spirit of pride and independence leads us into a far country, where our resources are soon exhausted, and the Great Giver is soon forgotten.

All bread comes from God. " The eyes of all wait upon Thee, and Thou givest them their meat in

---

* Comp. Coleridge's " Aids to Reflection," p. 38.

† As the heathen king said to those who flattered him as a god: "I require sleep every night. I know I am no god."

due season; Thou openest Thine hand, and satisfiest the desire of every living thing."* "He giveth to the beast his food, and to the young ravens which cry." Our Saviour also commands us to look at the fowls of the air; for they sow not, neither do they reap, nor gather into barns; yet our Heavenly Father feedeth them. But lest we, who do sow and reap, toil and work, forget that our bread comes from God, Scripture records so many miracles, in which this constant though hidden truth is manifested, that our perception may be quickened and our eyes opened to recognise the unseen hand of God. Israel fed in the wilderness by manna from heaven; Elijah sustained by the ravens, who brought him meat; the widow's barrel of meal, which did not waste, and the cruse of oil, which never failed; the five loaves and two fishes, by which the multitude was fed, while baskets of fragments remained; all these are but flashes of light from the heavenly regions to illumine our darkness — concentrated lessons, strongly-marked diagrams, as it were, to teach our dull minds that our Heavenly Father gives us our earthly bread.

Yet how slow are we to learn this lesson. How very gross and childish are our thoughts, that, while we can see how David might naturally and most urgently offer such a prayer, as is our text, on the day when he and his soldiers were hungering, and the shew-bread was given them, we do not under-

* Psalm cxlv. 15, 16.

stand how Solomon his son could use it in his reign
of abundance and wealth.   A moment's reflection,
however, ought to convince us that bread, and health,
and skill and energy which earn it, and the sunshine
and rain, the public peace and confidence, and all the
circumstances under which the work of man prospers,
are the gift of divine omnipotence and goodness.   And
as Joseph was enlightened by divine wisdom to fore-
see the years of famine, and to give good counsel, so
that there was corn in Egypt, so now all prudence
and forethought, all wise and beneficent measures,
come from Him who is the fountain of all light.
God concealed gold and silver, iron, and many treasures in the earth, and He gives understanding unto
man to search them out; our bread is His gift.

Bread is the gift of the Creator through Christ.
If we forfeited God's gifts by sin, we can trace the
continuance of them only to Christ's mediation.   For
His sake we receive from God all the good gifts of
His providence.   The blood of Jesus, which has
secured all gifts and blessings to those who believe,
has purchased for all men all the temporal blessings
which they enjoy.   What a blessed thought it is,
that in the bread we eat, and the water we drink,
we may taste that very love which spared not the
only-begotten Son.   The earth would be a wilderness
were it not for that tree on which Christ was made
a curse for us.

Jesus fed the multitude.   They had come to hear
His teaching, and He spoke to them the words of

eternal life. But Christ did not forget the wants
and infirmities of the body, for He loves man. "If
I send them away fasting to their own houses, they
will faint by the way." He had compassion on
them. But first of all, He lifted up His eyes
to heaven, and gave thanks. He is the Son of
Man in His sympathy, and in His dependence
on God. He never cherished an idea of receiving
anything but at the hands of His Heavenly Father.
He thanked God for the disciples that believed in
Him, and He thanked God for the seven loaves and
two fishes. But in His humility, He revealed His
glory. Then followed the miracle, full of lessons
for all ages ; above all, revealing to us how the
gifts of God the Creator come to us, through the
mediation, and through the sympathy and blessing
of our adorable Lord, who is not ashamed to call us
brethren.

Eating and drinking has been degraded by the
folly and sin of man ; instead of invigorating and
refreshing him for his work, excess often weakens
him, and incapacitates him for the duties of life.
Man only, among God's creatures, ruins his body
and soul by the abuse of food and drink. But while
Scripture condemns this sin, it teaches us that man
ate before the fall. In his sinless condition, he was
allowed to eat of all the trees of the garden. Doubtless he ate with gladness and singleness of heart,
rejoicing in the good creatures of God. Remember
how the three men ate with Abraham. Think of

Jesus after His resurrection eating " broiled fish and of an honeycomb." And what is the promise of Jesus, when He sat at supper with His disciples? " For I say unto you, I will not drink of the fruit of the vine,* until the kingdom of God shall come."

There is something festive in eating. We feel that we are more knit together in friendship and confidence with those with whom we have partaken of a meal. Jesus, after His resurrection, we are told, appeareth the third time to His disciples, and taketh bread and giveth them, and fish likewise. And, as Bengel somewhere remarks, *after* they had dined, He asked Peter, " Simon, son of Jonas, lovest thou me? " Let us think of these things, not to bring down heaven to an earthly level, but to infuse a heavenly spirit into earthly things. Very quaint and blessed is the German grace before meat:

" Come, Lord Jesus, be Thou our guest ! "

Bread is the gift of God, and, as all God's gifts, it has a deep and eternal meaning. Since all good gifts come from *above*, from our Father in heaven, is it strange that they should possess a spiritual meaning, and symbolise heavenly truths and realities? As they come from heaven, should we wonder that they have a heavenly inscription, which betokens their royal origin? We call them earthly, but whence come they? There is, after all, only one

---

* If the Lord had said "wine," His word might be taken figuratively in the sense of joy and communion ; but ἀπὸ τοῦ γεννήματος τῆς ἀμπέλου seems to point purposely to a literal meaning.

Fatherland of all things, visible and invisible, material and spiritual, even heaven, where our Father is enthroned. Heaven is above us, but heaven is the birthplace of all things earthly. It is the invisible inner essence of all things which appear.

Scripture teaches us, moreover, that Christ is the beginning of the creation of God, that nothing was made except through the Word. And why should we be astonished that all things are symbols of the truths and realities of redemption, that they manifest in picture, and in the various gradations of their sphere, the laws of the heavenly kingdom of grace? All Bible comparisons and illustrations are the expressions of faith in this hidden harmony, not the mere efflorescence of fancy and poetic imagination. When Christ is compared to a rock, a foundation-stone, to a branch, to the vine, to a lamb; when He is called Shepherd, Friend, Bridegroom; when God is spoken of as our Father; when the Holy Ghost is described as oil, water, fire, wind,—it is because Christ, the Father, and the Spirit are truly and substantially what these creatures are relatively and imperfectly. And likewise all human relationships, such as the parental and the conjugal, are symbols of God's Fatherhood, and of Christ's union with the Church. Human activities also, such as that of the sower and the merchant, are shadows of the husbandry and merchandise of an eternal character. Rest is a shadow of the soul's repose in God, eating and drinking of the soul's living by faith in Christ.

Thus is God the substance, all things visible shadows and types. Christ is the law of all things, the exposition of God's creation, "Nature's God."

The Saviour, who opened His mouth in parables, called Himself the Bread of Life. There is something mysterious in bread, and its relation to man. The ancients called man the bread-eater. The manna explained that bread comes from above. The corn of wheat falls into the ground and dies. Then it brings forth much fruit. Thus Jesus, who came from above, is the Living Bread, and by His death He became the Bread of Life to us. Believers eating the bread, which is His body, are truly one with Him; and thus the Church is His body, the fulness of Him, that filleth all in all. We have eternal life, for Christ, who is Life, is our life. Only God in Christ is life-sustaining food; all else, being dead in itself, can neither give nor sustain life. Thus heaven is a perpetual feast; they hunger no more, nor thirst any more, for God himself feeds them, even by giving Himself unto them; while they who are separated from God hunger and thirst, and there is no bread to satisfy, and no water to refresh. "Eat ye that which is good, and let your soul delight itself in fatness."

III. THE EXPANSION OF THE GIFT—*Our Bread.*

We ask for *our* bread. The spirit of the Lord's Prayer is filial towards God, brotherly towards man. Self is man's idol, for sin has estranged us from the love of God. What the law demands the grace of God bestows through the gospel, love to God and to our neighbour; the law requires it as a duty, the gospel implants it as a life full of blessing.

The little word " our " excludes evidently every calling which is injurious to the interests of our fellow-men. None can offer this petition who are enriched by that which brings misery to others. The word " our " implies also labour. If we eat the bread of idleness and sloth, we enjoy what is not rightfully ours. He that is not willing to work should not eat. Toil is the consequence of sin, but labour belonged to Paradise. Jesus has made labour sweet, and hallowed it by His own example. Some men eat, without praying or working, some men work without praying. The first are the most miserable; most blessed are they who, while not slothful in business, are fervent in spirit.

We are to think of the poor and needy. It is a sad fact that so many of our fellow-men are destitute, suffering from want of food and raiment and shelter. All the ingenuity and energy of men seem unable to remedy this evil. The earth brings forth sufficient food to sustain the children of men, yet pauperism increases. Social problems become more complicated and hopeless. While we look forward to the time when the poor shall have bread and be satisfied, and when all the people of the land shall dwell in peace and prosperity, it is the duty and privilege of the Church of Christ, not merely to offer the words,

but to live in the spirit of this petition, to be like
Jesus, having compassion on the multitude and feed-
ing the hungry.   In the Apostolic Church believers
had all things in common, none were allowed to suffer
want.   And the liberality of the Church, while it
considers with especial thoughtfulness the poor of
the flock, flows over into the world, bringing
gifts of kindness and help of love to the needy.
For God gives that we may become givers; and
we receive in proportion as we disperse, what
is intrusted to our stewardship.   "God is able,"
writes the apostle Paul, when exhorting the Corinthians to liberality, "to make all grace abound
toward you, that ye, always having all sufficiency in
all things, may abound to every good work (as it is
written, He hath dispersed abroad; He hath given to
the poor ; His righteousness remaineth for ever.   Now
he that ministereth seed to the sower, both minister
bread for your food, and multiply your seed sown,
and increase the fruits of your righteousness), being
enriched in everything to all bountifulness which
causeth through us thanksgiving to God." *   And in
this the apostle Paul only carries out the teaching
of our Lord.   "Give and it shall be given unto you;
good measure, pressed down and shaken together,
and running over, shall men give into your bosom."†
The command seems at first sight vague and indefinite.   We ask, to whom am I to give, and what,
and to what extent, and when ?   The Lord simply

* 2 Cor. ix. 8–11.   † Luke vi. 38.

says " Give." There is no limitation. All that you have, whether it be wealth or talent, or knowledge of truth, is to be communicated and to enrich others. Give to all as you have an opportunity. Be always in the loving frame of mind, which delights in giving. Regard nothing as your own, but remember that you are the steward of God, the follower of Jesus. And if we thus live in the spirit of love, as we give we receive. He that spreads light and cheerfulness, kindness and encouragement, gains himself in inward peace and strength, knowledge and wisdom ; in comforting others we are comforted, and in building up the saints our own souls are edified. And as we are liberal in helping the poor, ministering to their wants, God intrusts us with more, and prospers the work of our hands. God in His goodness enables us all to be givers ; and if it were only the cup of cold water, the refreshment of a loving word, a kind look, a symphathetic presence, be givers. It was one of the sayings of the Lord, which none of the Gospels mention, but which is incidentally quoted in the Book of Acts, " It is more blessed to give than to receive." The Gospels do not contain the saying, but in the highest sense they contain nothing else but this word. For what is the life and death of the Lord Jesus, but a commentary on His generous love, rejoicing to give even Himself for the life of the world.

The world, though constantly thinking of it, and very earnestly desiring it, has no clear thought as to what wealth really is, what constitutes the true riches of a nation. For, cleaving to the earth and never lifting up his eyes to heaven, the carnal reason regards the visible and material, and does not appreciate the value of the spiritual. As men progress they see the value of knowledge and of science, the material benefits of abstract laws and exact theory. But this again is material compared with what is moral and spiritual. Hence an intellectual and scientific age is often thoroughly ungodly and earthly in its character. As Pascal has said, no amount of matter can produce thought, no amount of thought love; for it is a higher region. Love to God, faith, self-discipline, heavenly-mindedness, brotherly affection, purity, are the real sources of prosperity—godliness has the promise of this life as well as that which is to come. *Bread on earth depends upon faith in our Heavenly Father.* *

Even the Church of Christ often forgets this truth. She, with a few loaves and fishes, is commanded by Christ to feed the multitude. Spiritually and physically the wants of humanity are to be supplied through her instrumentality. But Christ alone can bless and help, be it by much or little. And Smyrna in her poverty is rich and maketh many rich, while the lukewarm Church, increased with goods, is barren and unfruitful. Faith alone will obtain for home and the whole world daily bread for soul and body.

---

* Contrast the apparently contradictory experience of the Jews in Jer. xliv. 16–19

IV. The Limitation of the Gift.

"Give us *to-day* our daily bread." Christ would have us free from anxious care. The spirit of the world is feverish and restless; men think of the future and of its possible wants and evils, and are burdened with its weight. We all admit that such anxiety is foolish, and that it is painful. We should deem him a benefactor who delivers us from it. But we cannot be delivered from it until we understand that it is not merely foolish but sinful, that it is incompatible with the spirit of adoption, with the attitude of faith. The Saviour devotes a large section of the Sermon on the Mount to this subject. If the evil was not important and deep-seated, He would not have thought it necessary to attack it with so many arguments. Christ's first argument goes to the root of the matter. He says: You are anxious because you are not decided in your love to God. You are serving two masters. If you were entirely on God's side, you would know that your Master would provide for your wants. You cannot serve God and mammon; but if you serve God, then take no thought for the morrow. The divided heart is full of care, the simple-minded is free from anxiety. *As covetousness is idolatry, anxiety is indecision.*

Then the Lord proceeds to show that anxiety is contrary to all God's revelation in nature. God feeds the fowls of the air and clothes the lilies of the field. Analogy should teach you to trust. But as you are of far greater value than the fowls and flowers, nature is but to teach you the deeper truths and the greater love of the Kingdom of Grace.

The Lord then reminds us of the utter folly of care. "Which of you can add one cubit to his stature," or rather, can add the smallest portion of time to the period of his life? God gives us life, and we do not trust Him to supply us with bread and raiment.

The Saviour then refers to the distinction between us and the heathen who are ignorant of God. What difference is there between the world and the Church, between the world and the family of God, if we who profess to believe in our Heavenly Father do not trust in Him with childlike confidence, and do not live in calm and tranquil contentment?

The last argument is the simplest and strongest. "Your Heavenly Father knoweth that ye have need of these things." Our God is not high above us in regions inaccessible. He sees us, and notices all our wants; the very hairs of our head are numbered, and He who created us knoweth our frame. As is His knowledge so is His love. He pities us as a Father. He is neither ignorant of our difficulties nor unsympathising with them. We forget the name of God, we forget His kingdom, we forget His will, if we cherish an anxious and care-burdened frame of mind.

And hence the petition limits itself to the day—the need as well as the duty before us. Our own experience proves the wisdom of Christ's counsel. " Clearness of vision, providence, discovery, are the rewards of the calm and patient spirit. Out of that care for the morrow which the Lord denounces spring the fever of speculation, the hasting to be rich, endless scheming, continual reactions of fantastic hope, and deep depression of individuals, of mad prosperity and intense suffering in nations." * It has been truly remarked, " How many things have frightened us which were exclusively the creatures of our own imagination; but though imaginary, there have been often real and serious things emanating from them; we have weakened our own souls, we give our spiritual adversaries the advantage over us, we suffer them to range themselves in battle-array against us between our covenant God and ourselves."† The Lord does not condemn forethought; He does not command us to spend each day all we possess, dismissing from our minds all thought for the future. The apostle Paul alludes to the practice of parents as laying up for their children, and seems to refer to it as something that is right and sensible. We read, that if any provide not for his own, and especially for those of his own house, he hath denied the

---

* Maurice.

† Howels, p. 110. If we have food and raiment, let us be content. How is it that, while we are so discontented with our outward lot, we are often calm and unconcerned when the soul has neither food nor raiment ? Anxious care cannot procure food and raiment *either for soul or body.* God, who sustains our earthly life, will much more give us the bread and water of life, the best robe of righteousness. But as anxious care is excluded, so indifference and indolence are condemned. Faith receives without working, and yet faith labours for the meat which endureth for ever.

faith, and is worse than an infidel. Yet is it not easy to distinguish prudence, economy, diligence, from the feverish haste to be rich, from the love of money, from the ambitious plans of amassing wealth, from the worldly spirit of avarice. God's children, above all, are not to trust in uncertain riches, they are to exercise faith in a loving God, and they are to bequeath to their children something more precious than gold and silver.

The petition teaches us moderation and contentment. It excludes display, rivalry, waste. It ratifies the prayer of Agur, " Give me neither poverty nor riches; feed me with food convenient for me, lest I be full, and deny Thee, and say, Who is the Lord? or lest I be poor, and steal, and take the name of God in vain."* How few realise that wealth is a burden, and riches a snare ! There are many poor, but not many who love poverty. While there are many hardships and temptations in poverty which none will think lightly of who know something of their variety and bitterness, yet our Saviour never said, How hard is it for those who are poor to enter into the kingdom of heaven. But He often spake of the difficulty of the rich to become poor in spirit, and to set their affections on things above. It may be easier to give away wealth by one great effort of self-denial, than to use it in the spirit of faith, love, and the heavenly hope; but if this petition is offered sincerely and rightly, it includes prayer for grace to

* Prov. xxx. 8, 9.

use this world as not abusing it, to buy as if we possessed not, to be rich as if we were poor. Our Saviour not merely fed the multitude with bread. but at the marriage-feast He changed water into wine. He is able by His presence to bless the poor in their simplicity, and the rich in their superfluity; without Him and the sunshine of His love the life of the world, even in its greatest prosperity, is insipid and without joy, and it can be said of them, even in their most mirthful seasons, " They have no wine." While the child of God, in his utmost destitution, is able to say, " Although the fig-tree shall not blossom, neither shall fruit be in the vines; the labour of the olive shall fail, and the fields shall yield no meat; the flock shall be cut off from the fold, and there shall be no herd in the stalls: yet I will rejoice in the Lord, I will joy in the God of my salvation."*

Sometimes God tries the faith of His people severely, and they are in great difficulties about their daily bread. The Lord delays His help. He did not permit even His mother to fix the time—His hour was not yet come. But God fulfils His promise, and the righteous shall not lack bread.

If we trust in God our wants shall be supplied; yea, we shall have all and abound. Christ will ask us at the end of our journey, " Have ye lacked anything?" and our answer will be, " The Lord was my shepherd, I did not want." We have learned what are the true riches. We have experienced the truth

* Hab. iii. 17, 18.

of the gospel paradox, that we lose what we seek, and that we find and gain for ever what we give up and lose. When we come to die we possess only what we gave away, we must leave what we endeavoured to keep. Whatever gifts of kindness, of sympathy, of brotherly aid, of self-sacrifice we bestowed during our lifetime, remains to us an eternal treasure in heaven, where moth cannot corrupt, nor thieves break through and steal. Whatever sufferings we endured patiently and in the love of Jesus, remains to us an everlasting possession. The rich man, who clothed himself in purple and fine linen, and fared sumptuously every day, is in torment; fire is now his garment, and unquenchable thirst his constant companion : while Lazarus, who on earth knew poverty and sickness, and scarce any other sympathy than that of dogs, is now comforted. Where is now the dance of Herodias' daughter, and the laughter of brilliant wit, and the pomp of Belshazzar's feast? But the tears of the godly have all been numbered ; the death of the martyrs is precious in the sight of God and the saints for ever, and the conflict of faith has gained an unfading crown. The widow's mite is still bearing interest, and enriching the treasury of God ; the cup of cold water given to the least of Christ's disciples is a joy to the heavenly Lord throughout all ages ; the visit of Onesiphorus to Paul the prisoner will never lose its fragrance.

God wants us to be rich ; nay, He wants us to possess all things. But the way to riches is to give up all, even ourselves. He who looks upon himself as his own has nothing, however rich he may appear; but he who looks upon himself as not his own, but bought with a price, the servant of Jesus Christ, can say, All things are ours, whether Paul, or Apollos, or Cephas, or the world, or life, or death, or things present, or things to come, all are ours; for we are Christ's, and Christ is God's. And God is our Father in heaven, who gives—who gives all, who gives Himself, and for evermore!

11

MERCY IN HEAVEN AND ON EARTH

"Forgive us our debts, as we forgive our debtors."

Is there not a depth of sadness in that little word
"and," which connects the prayer for pardon with
the preceding petition for daily bread?* It reminds
us, that as our daily wants return, so do likewise our
sins ; that we need daily forgiveness as much as the
daily supply of our earthly wants. The fourth
petition is one of humility and dependence ; the fifth
one of repentance and contrition. The one reminds
us that we are creatures, the other that we are sinners.
For the first time in this prayer a melancholy chord

---

* Sometimes important thoughts are suggested by the word
"and." For instance, when the Saviour says to the woman of
Samaria, "thou wouldest have asked Him, *and* He would have
given thee living water," He teaches us by this *and* the necessary
and invariable connexion between prayer and His gifts. Again,
what a melancholy force has the word in the history of the rich
man : "he died and was buried, and in hell he lifted up his eyes,
being in torments." Again, how full of rebuke, and what a picture
of our tendency to substitute words, feelings, and intentions for
obedience, when Christ describes the second son, whom the father
asks to work in his vineyard. And he answered and said, " I go,
sir, and (and, not but) went not."

is struck. The first part of the prayer: "Hallowed
be Thy name, Thy kingdom come, Thy will be done on
earth, as it is in heaven," is the voice of children, full
of peace and love, rejoicing in the Father's glory,
loyal and zealous in His service; the petition for
daily bread reminds us of our weakness and poverty,
of the lowliness of our present condition. But when
we say "and forgive us our debts," we come to our true
sorrow, to our most real grief. You must have
noticed it, both when uttering this petition yourself
or listening to others, how our very tone of voice
changes when we come to this "and;" how the
joyous, jubilant, firm tones which characterise the
first petitions, the trustful tone of the petition for
bread, is changed now into one plaintive and pathetic;
sorrow and shame mingle here with faith and hope.
It seems as if a dark cloud had suddenly intercepted
that bright and serene light in which we were rejoicing,
and yet it is only to introduce a still deeper and more
blessed enjoyment of the love of our Father in heaven.
"I, even I, am He that blotteth out thy transgressions
for mine own sake, and will not remember thy sins."
"I have blotted out as a thick cloud thy transgressions, and as a cloud thy sins."

Many receive from God their daily bread, who do
not seek the pardon of their daily sins. But we
know that the very gifts of God, health and wealth,
are no blessings to us, unless we receive also His
pardoning grace. The gifts of God, bestowed by
Him so generously and bountifully, even on those

who thank Him not, only increase the debt of gratitude and love, of obedience and service, and will thus finally be discovered as increasing our guilt and the burden of our punishment. But blessed be God, He is not merely a *Giver,* but a *Forgiver.* He gives us most when He forgives us. David expresses the experience of all believers when he places the pardon of sin as the very first of the gifts of God. In the 103d Psalm he commences the enumeration of divine blessings by saying, "who forgiveth all thine iniquities." This gift includes all others. Sin prevents the true blessings of heaven coming into our lives and souls; and when this obstacle is removed, all things are ours; we are blessed with all spiritual blessings in heavenly places in Christ; we have the assurance that God will not withhold from us anything that is for our good.

And thus we may say that the daily bread for our souls is daily forgiveness. *This* is our daily bread —that we see Jesus our crucified Redeemer, our righteousness in heaven; that we behold the fountain open for sin and uncleanness. As the Saviour himself explains it: "I am the Bread of Life, I am the living Bread which came down from heaven. If any man shall eat of this bread, he shall live for ever, and *the bread that I will give is my flesh, which I will give for the life of the world.*"

It is very strange that some Christians have thought that since God has given us full remission of our sins, it is unbelief to ask Him continually to forgive us our trespasses.* Daily confession of sin and prayer for forgiveness has been the all but universal practice of the Christian Church, so clear is the teaching of our Lord and His apostles on this subject. But we may learn even from the morbid view to which I have referred, and derive from it this benefit, not to lose sight of the connexion which subsists between the acceptance obtained by the first act of faith—between the first cleansing by the blood of Christ, and the subsequent washing of our feet and renewal of our pardon. We fully admit that there is a difference between the first prayer of the awakened, " God be merciful to me the sinner," and the confession of the believer and his prayer for forgiveness. And yet, although we enter into God's presence as forgiven and accepted children, do we not also approach Him exercising the very faith of the publican, casting ourselves entirely on the mercy of God, looking solely to the merit of the Lord Jesus Christ ? It is the *beginning* of our confidence we hold fast to the end ; it is true of us that we have come to Christ, and are always coming unto Him.†

It is necessary and salutary to confess our sin and pray for forgiveness. The melancholy fact that we are constantly sinning, though the object of Christ's death is to deliver us from the power as well as the

---

* Thus, in the south of Germany, a small sect, followers of Pregizer. They rejoice in the merits of Christ. When they meet, their salutation is "Peace." Other Christians they call " Poor sinner-Christians."

† 1 Peter ii. 4; John vi. 37.

guilt of sin, and though the Holy Ghost is given as an indwelling Spirit for our sanctification, may become so familiar to us that we cease to feel its burden and pain. We ought to remember and deplore our sin before God. We ought to feel that it is a bitter thing to sin against Him. We are to keep our hearts with all diligence; and without self-examination and confession can we gain an insight into our condition, or be in a humble and watchful frame of mind?

But is it possible for a believer not to confess his sins unto God and ask His pardon? As some one has said,* " Even if God did not know all, I would tell Him all." Love cannot be silent. Love must acknowledge sin—not to itself merely, but to the Loved One, against whom sin is committed. Love must ask a renewal of God's favour. Love cannot rest on a remembered pardon, on a title-deed as it were, however sure and perfect that may be. Love seeks a present, loving God. We walk with Him from day to day;—and not in unbelief, but because we realise God as our God ; not in doubt, in the spirit of bondage, but in the trustful and loving Spirit of *adoption*, we ask our Heavenly Father to forgive us our debts.

The objection to this petition is an objection against all prayer, for all blessings, temporal and spiritual, are secured to us according to the eternal covenant in Christ Jesus, and, in one sense, actually given unto

---

* Eugénie de Guerin.

us in the Saviour.* God has promised to keep us
from falling, and to perform in us the great work
which He has begun, and to give us the victory
over our enemies; and yet we pray to God to preserve
our souls, to help us in the time of trial, to keep us
from forsaking the Saviour. God has promised us
our daily bread and protection in danger, and yet we
ask Him to supply our need and to defend us in
peril. And this is our confidence, that we convert
God's promises into petitions. When we pray we
realise that God the eternal is also, so to say, cotem-
poraneous with us; that He condescends to live with
us from day to day, to guide us from station to
station. He whom the heavens cannot contain is "to
us as a little sanctuary." †

The question has been asked, why there is no reference in this petition to the atonement? The answer
is obvious. There is only one way of salvation, one
method of forgiveness. From Abel to the last saint
which shall be gathered in, sinners are pardoned for
the sake of that one sacrifice which was offered on
Calvary. Before the incarnation faith looked forward; since the death of Christ faith looks backward.
And hence in Scripture, even where there is no direct
reference to the substitution of Christ, it is always
understood as the only ground of pardon. Very instructive is the commentary of the apostle Paul on
the 32d Psalm. David said: "Blessed is he whose
transgressions is forgiven, whose sin is covered;

---

* Eph. i. 3.   † Ezek. xi. 16.

blessed is the man unto whom the Lord imputeth
not iniquity, and in whose spirit there is no guile."
Paul's comment is : " Even as David also describeth
the blessedness of the man unto whom God imputeth
righteousness without works."   Thus showing that
an imputed righteousness was the *basis* on which
David knew the forgiveness of sin to rest.   So full is
Scripture of the doctrine that salvation is through
sacrifice, that remission of sin is through the shed-
ding of blood, that redemption is secured by the
Paschal Lamb, that this doctrine is regarded as an
axiom ; and when it is not explicitly referred to, the
believing reader cannot possibly fail to supply it in
his own thought and heart.

The doctrine of expiation and substitution is the
very sum and substance of the gospel; without it there
are no glad tidings to the sinner.   It is the very light
and brightness of revelation ; without it there is no
knowledge of Jesus Christ, for Jesus Christ crucified is
Jesus Christ indeed.*   Without it there is no loving
and grateful remembrance of the Saviour ; for to
eat the bread and drink the wine, to discern the
body broken for us and the blood shed for the remission of the sins of many, *this* is to remember Him.
Without it there is no victory over sin, for by the
blood of the Lamb do saints overcome.

The Saviour does not refer here to His own sufferings and death.†   In the parable of the prodigal also

* 1 Cor. ii. 1.

† The time for unfolding the mystery of the cross had not come

He simply represents the Father receiving the returning sinner with overflowing love and tenderness. Luther, referring to this circumstance, says quaintly, Christ did not wish to be praised during His lifetime. It is not an accurate expression, and the thought itself is vague, and, to some extent, false; but Luther probably meant that Jesus manifested in this reticence that meekness and lowliness in heart which so eminently characterise Him, and that passing over His own self-denial and work, He was anxious to glorify the Father and to magnify His wonderful love and abounding mercy. But the generous silence of the Saviour only calls forth our song of adoring gratitude: Unto Him that loved us and washed us from our sin in His own blood, and hath made us a kingdom of priests unto God and His Father, to Him be glory and dominion for ever.

For what would the remission of our debt be to us without the gift of Christ? If we were merely told that God forgives our sin, would this announcement

---

when Jesus taught this prayer. He had come to " His own," to gather the children of Jerusalem ; He was the Son, sent by the Father to see if "they would reverence Him." It was therefore according to the gracious will of God, as well as the wisdom and love of the Saviour, that the sufferings and the death on the cross were not prominently brought forward—not prominently, for we know that from the very first Passover on which He taught in Jerusalem, He did speak to all of His rejection by Israel, but in a veiled manner, and gradually ; more clearly and fully (and this also progressively) to His own disciples. ("*From that time forth* began Jesus to show unto His disciples how He must go unto Jerusalem and suffer," Matt. xvi.)

bring light to our mind, peace to our conscience, love
to our heart, and a new strength to our will?   Only
in Christ pardon becomes the central gift of God, in
which all blessings meet.   Here is light, the revelation of God's character, the manifestation and judgment of sin as enmity against God, the true exposition of the law as perfect, holy, just, and good.   Here
the conscience can rest, for it beholds that, in forgiving us, God is faithful and just, as well as merciful
and generous.   Here the heart learns to love Him who
gave Himself for us.   Pardon is so precious because
it is inseparable from Christ, because, in pardoning us,
God, according to the new covenant, gives Himself to
us.   In no other way can sin be forgiven but by God
himself becoming ours.   Christ is that " forgiveness
of sin " which is with God,* at His right hand,
even as the Word was with God from eternity.
Here we see divine holiness.   He who is of purer
eyes than to behold iniquity must place sin at an
infinite distance from Him.   The ultimate place of
sin was the cross or hell.   But now that Christ was
made a curse for us, and bore the punishment of our
transgression, God accounts us as holy and without
blame before Him ; we are the righteousness of God
in Christ.†

* Psalm cxxx. 3.

† " To be holy and without blame before Him" Eph. i. v. (Comp.
Meyer, Kommentar, viii. 31.) Referring "to that holiness and blame-
lessness which is produced by the expiatory death of Christ through
the 'righteousness of God' obtained thereby " (Rom. iii. 21, v. 1,
viii. 1, 33 ; 1 Cor. vi. 11).   " In love " belongs to ver. 5.   We are *at
present* "holy and without blame " before God, and that *in Christ.*

Here we see the Father's love. All human illustrations must be inadequate; but the Saviour himself, when speaking of the Father's gift,* refers to the offering up of Isaac. God gave up His only Son; and though Jesus was forsaken, yet was He then most beloved; He who was the sin-offering was also the burnt-offering. Infinite love rested on Him against whom the sword had to awake.

God is revealed to us in the method of our forgiveness. Looking back on His past life, Jesus said, " I have declared unto them Thy name; " and looking forward unto His death, He added, " And will declare it." The crucified Saviour becomes, as it were, transparent, that through Him, in His sacrifice, we may behold the Father. We adore the grace of Jesus and His wondrous self-sacrifice; but we know that *God* was in Christ reconciling the world to Himself, that Christ is the Lamb of *God*, upon whom the Father laid our iniquity, and that in Christ's death God commendeth His love to sinners. Christ and the Father are one; we see on the cross, God is love.

Here we see the wisdom of God. Sin was manifested in its true character; it showed its greatest power; it achieved its most marvellous victory. It was the hour and power of darkness. And here sin was judged and conquered. For from this cross flows that pardoning love which renews the heart, filling it with love to God, and with hatred of sin, and imparting to it new strength to obey God.

* John iii. 16.

In the crucified Redeemer we see God and are at peace. All that intervened between God and us is removed, because Christ is now the Mediator, a medium of light, of life, of love.

All this we know and believe when we utter the simple words, " And forgive us our debts." So much, so great things are implied in the word " forgive ; " and according as we know the magnitude of the word " forgive," we feel the weight of the word " debt."

Sin is debt. What do we owe God ? We owe ourselves to Him. All that we are, body, soul, and spirit, is His ; and we ought to be His, and to give all to Him, and that always. And this debt is daily growing, for God is always giving, and we are always misappropriating His gifts. We cannot get rid of our debt except by becoming still more His debtors. He forgives us, and now we owe Him more than ever ; for, as the apostle says, " Owe no man anything except to love one another ; " so Christ expects from the sinner, to whom much is forgiven, that he will love much. Another thought, suggested by the word " debt," as well as the expression " trespass " used by another Evangelist, is to impress on us the character of sin as an offence against God. We take too abstract a view of sin. We think that God is so high in His infinite majesty and glory, that He does not feel sin (if I may say so) as a personal wrong and offence. Christ, therefore, purposely gives the simplest aspect of sin. We know what it is when men owe us a debt, be it of money, or gratitude, or service. We

know what it is when men trespass, step over the
boundary of what is right and just in their relation
to us.   Although we may be independent of them
and their services, yet we feel the wrong.   Sin is as
real a debt and trespass towards God.   " Against
Thee, Thee only, have I sinned." God is displeased
with sin, the abuse of His own gifts, the withholding
of love and obedience from hearts He has created to
love ; and we cannot take too literally, or enter too
deeply, into the pathetic words in which God mourns
over the sins of His people :—" Hear, O heaven ! and
give ear, O earth ! for the Lord hath spoken. I have
nourished and lifted up children (exalted them to
high dignity), and it is they who have rebelled against
me." And as Jesus sighed on earth, so we hear,
as it were, the pent-up grief and sorrow when the
Lord exclaims, " Ah, sinful nation ! "

If sin is a debt and trespass, is it not good for us,
at least once a day (as the Lord evidently intended
and expects us to do), to ask our Heavenly Father
to remit our debt, to disperse the cloud which
intercepts from us the light of His countenance ?
We should lead a happier and a more useful life if
we truly offered up this petition, believing in the
answer which God has already given us in Christ
Jesus. Thus would we receive daily the assurance of
our adoption into the family of God, and our feet
would run the way of God's commandments. Let us
be encouraged to come " boldly " to the throne of
grace. Boldly means with *parrhesia*, that is, saying

all, keeping back nothing.* He who taught us to pray " Forgive us our debts" has Himself paid the debt. He to whom Christ teaches us to offer the petition, is the Father who sent Jesus to bless us, by turning every one of us from our iniquities.

But the Saviour adds, " as we forgive our debtors." The words of our Lord are words of truth and authority,—we dare not ignore them or weaken their force. Some of His words appear hard to those who follow Him only for a season, but those very words which offend the superficial are the words of eternal life which rivet the true disciples so that they cannot leave the Christ, the Son of God.† Sometimes His words appear to contradict other of His sayings ; often they seem in their severity to neutralise the consolation which His gracious declarations bring to the heart. We cling to the announcement of free and unconditional pardon, on the ground of Christ's merit, and received by faith alone. We wonder, when, as it seems, a condition is attached, and our pardon apparently depends on our forgiving those that trespass against us. Perplexing as this may ap-

---

* παρρησια. This word, sometimes translated plainly (as John xi. 14, and xvi. 29, where it is contrasted with proverb or parable), sometimes boldly (Eph. vi. 19, Heb. vi. 16), means that state of perfect trust and confidence when we can "say all," pour out all our heart, keep back nothing, convinced of the affection and good-will of the hearer. Thus, as love and sympathy are necessary to enable the preacher to "say all," so we are encouraged to bring before the throne of grace *all* our need, for the Father himself loveth us, and the Saviour is merciful and compassionate.

† John vi. 66–69.

pear, we cannot possibly overlook it. The Saviour has laid very marked emphasis on this petition; for He singles it out from among all the others, and recapitulates it in a form which gives it, if possible, additional strength, and invests it with greater severity. " For if ye forgive men their trespasses, your Heavenly Father will also forgive you; but if ye forgive not men their trespasses, neither will your Father forgive your trespasses."

The word " as " does not refer to the degree or measure of forgiveness, as if meant to show a kind of proportion between God's forgiveness and ours. It does not mean that our forgiveness is the cause of God's forgiveness, that it must precede His, or that it is the measure of it, determining the kind and degree of divine mercy. It means simply "since." It does not seek to establish an equality between divine mercy and human, but to express the fact that we also forgive. For who among us, however tender-hearted and forbearing, could have peace if God's mercy to us was measured and limited by our mercy? We find it difficult to forgive—still more difficult to forget. Our patience is soon exhausted, our pardon often more extended as a necessary tribute of obedience than an overflowing of affection. And how rarely do we take the initiative, and go to the offending brother or neighbour, drawing and melting him by our generosity and kindness! Whereas God forgives fully and from the heart, rejoicing and delighting in mercy; He forgives not merely, but He forgets; He forgives daily, and always with the same sweetness and tenderness ; He hastens to tell of His pardon, and by His own love, and the drawing of His Spirit, melts the soul to confess and return to the path of righteousness.

God forgives in heaven ; we forgive on earth. God forgives to manifest His glory in the salvation of sinners, thus establishing His kingdom in the renewed hearts of believers, who are conformed to the image of Christ. The object of God's showing mercy to us is, that we may be not merely forgiven, but that the mind of Christ may be in us ; we obtain mercy in order that we may be merciful. Hence this petition is intimately connected with the third. *In both we have a parallelism between heaven and earth.* The angels in heaven do the will of God. Earth is to resemble heaven. Sin frustrates apparently God's purpose, but forgiving mercy intervenes and restores. In no other way can earth be brought into harmony with heaven than through mercy, accepted not merely, but becoming to him who received it, a fountain of mercy, forgiving, forbearing, going forth to heal and to bless. God's will is done on earth as in heaven, when mercy reigns below in our hearts and lives, as it reigns on the throne above. God forgives in heaven, His dwelling place, that we, in the spirit of Christ, and not in the spirit of mere justice and equity, may bring peace and love to all around us. Then are we indeed the children of God, the disciples of Christ, and prove ourselves the elect of God, putting on bowels of mercy, kindness, long-suffering, forbearing one another, forgiving one another.   Even as Christ forgave you, so also do ye.

Let us not put asunder what God hath joined together : love to God and the other commandment, which is both *second* and *yet equal* to the first, love to our neighbour, mercy received and mercy bestowed, drinking of the water of life, and rivers of living water flowing from our inmost heart.*   Look not upon this petition as limiting the forgiveness of God, but rather regard it as explaining the true object, the vital power, the blessed influence of this pardon.†   God forgives us that we may abide in Christ and be like Him ; and, on the other hand, no holiness can be ours but that which we derive from Christ, as the Forgiver of all transgressions and Healer of all diseases.

The deepest comment on this petition, and especially on that little word " as," we find in the Epistle of the Apostle John.   The thought so constantly

---

* John vii. 38.

† " We must thoroughly believe and understand that what seems to be a limiting condition of the request is really an enlargement of its scope and power. . . . We should pray, not for a momentary sense of forgiveness, but for the spirit of forgiveness ; not merely that we may know what God is, and is to us, but what He can accomplish in us ; that we may understand in Him, and show forth in ourselves, that mercy which is a fire to consume the evil of all in whom it dwells, of all to whom it reaches.   Forgiveness is not forgiveness when it is turned to our ease and comfort.   It is, in its nature expansive, diffusive ; it cannot be cooped up in the heart of any creature ; it must go forth into the open air or it dies."—*F. D. Maurice, Lord's Prayer,* 87, 88.

recurring there is the union of the love of God *towards* us, and the love of God *in* us; of our love to the Father and to the brethren ; of our love to Him who is unseen, and our love to those who visibly represent Him.   Sometimes the apostle places the love of God and our love to Him first, and then infers from this our love to man.   At other times, to show the inseparable connexion between the two, he reverses the order, and asserts, if any man love not his brother whom he hath seen, how can he love God whom he hath not seen ?   And " we know we have passed from death unto life, because we love the brethren."

The Saviour himself has clearly explained that he who has not received the spirit of forgiveness has not truly received the gift of pardon.   He enforces this in the most impressive and solemn manner in the parable of the unmerciful servant.   From this parable we are not to infer that any of God's children may, after having received the grace of God, lose His favour and the indwelling of His Spirit.   Christ only shows us that the love of God cannot truly rest on us if it does not also dwell in us.   In a narrative it is not possible to illustrate this principle, except by representing the consequences which will necessarily flow from such a false reliance on divine favour.   Just as the apostle Paul says to Christians, " If ye live after the flesh ye shall die."   But we must in nowise seek to blunt the keen edge of the Saviour's teaching. Unless we forgive, we are not forgiven.

And without this loving spirit we cannot truly

worship and serve God. "If thou bring thy gift to the altar, and there rememberest that thy brother hath aught against thee, leave there thy gift before the altar, and go thy way ; first be reconciled to thy brother, and then come and offer thy gift." How can we approach without love the throne of eternal love ? The Saviour has given these words, " as we forgive our debtors," to be like a net, in which He takes us captive, and from which we cannot escape. They are like a flame of fire, consuming all anger, wrath, malice and bitterness. They remove all obstacles which prevent the inflowing of divine love, and the outflowing of brotherly kindness.

He who does not forgive, forsakes the spirit of the gospel, and returns to the spirit of legalism. He does not know the power of forgiveness to melt the heart, to convert the desert into a garden, the barren wilderness into a fruitful field. He forgets that it was not by severity, and by exacting the claims of justice, but by the manifestation of love that his own heart was gained to God, else would he seek to become an imitator of God, and a follower of Jesus.

He who does not forgive will soon lose the sense and enjoyment of God's pardon. Here also we see the divine law exemplified, " Give and it shall be given you." Live in the atmosphere of love and forbearance, cultivate the spirit of humble and brotherly meekness and endurance, and you will enjoy the assurance of God's favour, you will taste the blessedness of walking in the love of God, you will have the perennial sunshine of that grace which in Christ Jesus brought salvation unto us.

He who does not forgive lacks one of the great evidences and confirmations of faith. There is no surer test of our having truly received the grace of God, than the indwelling of love in our hearts. It is the inseparable companion of faith in the Lord Jesus; it is the mark of regeneration, for every one that loveth is born of God. We are of God because we love, for love is of God.

How beautifully is this twofold love and forgiveness set before us in the Lord's Supper. There we receive the assurance of God's mercy in Christ Jesus. The love of the Saviour is set before us, even His love unto death. We rest in this perfect love, we rejoice in this perfect pardon. But as we rest in it, so we live by it. Christ's love becomes ours, the Father's gift of remission becomes within us the spirit of forgiveness. We now love with Christ's love, and we anticipate at the Lord's Table that blessed consummation of our union with Christ, when we shall be like Him, when we, to whom so much has been forgiven, will love much, when we shall be perfect, even as our Father in heaven is perfect.

12

SIN AND SALVATION

"And forgive us our debts."

Sin and salvation are the two great subjects of divine revelation.

The more we feel the burden and guilt, the pollution and bondage of sin, the deeper is our knowledge of the Lord Jesus, and the greater our joy in His blessed person and work. And again, the more we know of Christ, of His perfect obedience, of His sufferings, of His death, the more we see the exceeding sinfulness of sin, the better we understand its character and power. The knowledge of sin is to drive us to the Saviour, the love of Jesus is to deliver us from sin.

Sin and salvation are the two topics of Scripture. There must, therefore, be much in the Bible that is sad, gloomy, awful. Sin and guilt, misery and sorrow, curse and death, judgment and wrath, are subjects grave, solemn, and appalling. And yet the Bible itself is nothing but light and joy. For it is the message of pardon and life. It *finds* man a child of wrath and an heir of death, but it *brings* to him redemption. The messenger of pardon, entering the cell of the condemned prisoner, sheds light on the dismal chamber, on the fear-stricken countenance, on the fetters and emblems of bondage and degradation; yet who would call him a herald of gloom, and regard his advent as the approach of sadness? Thus Scripture *brings* with it nothing but liberty, peace, and glory. The evil and the sadness are all our own, the actual condition in which we are, the fruit and result of our own departure from God. Yet, while vindicating the joyous character of Scripture, the truth must be acknowledged, that, like God from whom it comes, the Word kills as well as quickens, and wounds before it exerts its healing power. Nor is it necessary to deny that men dread the Scriptures, because of the true disclosures it contains of their sinful, wretched, and dangerous condition.

Even without the announcements of Scripture, we notice the existence, and we feel, to some extent, the evil of sin.

Sin is a great mystery.

The origin and future of sin are alike hid in darkness impenetrable. We are lost in thought when we ask whence came it? And equal is our amazement when we contemplate the future of sin in the ages to come. Sin is a great enigma, it is irrational, and defies explanation, and yet most problems of human character and conduct are explained by it.

In every sin there is a dark and almost infinite vista. It is like an opening into a mysterious cavern. Imagination dreads dangers and evils, serpents hidden in the cave, pestilential, poisonous atmosphere, concealed dungeons or pit-falls. It is like the entrance into a dense wood ; we hesitate whether we should venture, we dread the attack of fierce beasts or cruel men. And yet men are so little afraid of entering into sin, though they know not what it leads to, fancying they can retrace their steps at any moment.

Sin prevails everywhere, yet few know it. They who are most familiar with it, and most obedient to its sway, are least acquainted with its true character, and feel least its tyranny. Sin is myriad-shaped. It wears a thousand masks, speaks with a thousand voices, and pursues a thousand methods. It can be childish and ambitious ; now it is heroic and laborious, now frivolous and effeminate ; now it is gross and revolting, now polished and beautiful ; yet it is ever the same : life without God, enmity against the Most High.

Sin has a wide dominion and many servants. On the broad road there are so many paths which never intersect and interfere with each other. Men of lofty intellect, of noble purpose, of philanthropic activity, never dream that they are ruled by the same despot who leads the vicious and degraded, captive at his will. Yet sin connects them all ; it is one way, and it leadeth to destruction.

Sin is courageous and defies Heaven ; it rebels against the will of Omnipotence ; it attacks the immovable pillars of God's throne : yet sin is a coward ; when the voice of the Lord is heard at even-time it flees in horror, and when the Lord shall appear in judgment it will cry in despair to the hills and rocks to fall upon it and cover it.

Sin has a hundred eyes. Quicksighted as an eagle in discovering its prey, no opportunity escapes its watchful gaze, no opening, however minute, evades its piercing glance; but like an owl in the midday sun, it sees not the light of a merciful and loving God; and like the ostrich, with its head buried in the sand, perceives not the awful death of eternity which is pursuing it.

Look at sin in the individual. Where does it dwell? It has poisoned every faculty, polluted the imagination, darkened the understanding, enslaved the will, estranged the affections, blunted the conscience; it has taken possession of speech and of action; it has entrenched itself in the very members of the body, and established itself as a law and habit. Work and rest, toil and pleasure, solitude and the world, are alike the spheres of its activity; yet the strength of sin is not in its breadth, but in its depth—out of the *heart* come the issues of life. Sin is in man, he carries it with him, but never can cleanse himself from its defilement, or destroy its power. No water can rid us of this spot, not even the burning tears of self-reproach and bitter grief. No axe can fell this tree; branches may be lopped off, but *within* is the energy continually renewing itself, which no human power can eradicate.

Sin does not purpose to remember or to be remembered, and yet it registers itself with perfect and unfailing regularity and faithfulness in two books —the book of God, which shall be opened on that day, and on our own character, mind, and imagination. Only the blood of Christ can blot out sin from the one book, only the Spirit of God from the other.

Sin aims to depart from God into a far country, and to break every tie that binds man to his Creator; yet every step it takes is but another link in that heavy chain of debt by which the transgressor is bound to the throne of Divine Justice.

Sin is in man; alas! it is our only property; it is ours, inseparable from our person, our act, and our guilt; and yet the foundations of it are in hell beneath; it belongs to a kingdom of vast extent and power; it is the reign of the adversary, serpent, and lion, subtle, bold, and undaunted.

How fearful is sin!

Yet who can say what sin is? He alone, who died for us, knows the greatness of sin; He alone, who is of purer eyes than to behold iniquity, has seen it in its depths. None know how much they hated Him, this is known only to Him who died for His enemies.

But the most marvellous fact about sin is this: Sin obscures God, hides Him from our view, like a dark cloud intercepting the light, like a huge mountain separating us from God. And yet sin alone *reveals God,* manifests the depths of His love, brings out the hidden recesses of His grace, the great purpose of His will.   Angels did not know *God* until they beheld our redemption.   They did not see the true, the full glory of God—not when they first sang together in holy harmony, and shouted for joy ; not when they beheld the marvels of creation, not when they watched the outgoings of divine power, wisdom, and justice,—" Glory to God in the highest " was their song,—a *new* song we may call it,—when *Jesus* was born at Bethlehem, the Saviour of sinners.   They beheld God when sin nailed Christ to the cross, and when the sinner's substitute and friend ascended and sat down at the Father's right hand. Who is a God like unto Thee, angels and saints exclaim, who pardoneth iniquity, transgression, and sin ?

Oh that we may make this *only* use of sin, and learn the divine alchemy which caused grace and glory to abound where sin abounded ! that we understood the truth in Augustine's dangerously-expressed paradox, Oh, blessed guilt ! which procured me such a Saviour ! Only your *sin* brings out Christ.   Produce your righteousness, Christ retreats.   Produce your sin, Christ reveals Himself.   Come to Jesus, as to a prophet ; He will teach you.   Come to Him as to a righteous man ; His life will be a perfect model.   But this is not Jesus himself.   Invite Him as Simon the Pharisee invited Him, and you will not see His heart.   Come to Him as the woman came who fell down at His feet as a *sinner*, and you will behold Jesus, the Saviour, the glory of the Only-begotten of the Father, full of grace and truth.

Sin forgiven is sin known and hated. Only in Christ we gain a point from which we can both see and conquer sin. We are now willing to see the depth of our disease and guilt, for we are delivered from fear. We stand now on God's side, not on the debtor's side, anxious to diminish and explain away our debt. There is now no guile in our spirit. And Christ lives in us ; so that, if we would only wield it, ours is a supernatural strength to resist and overcome sin.

The true gospel method is, to combine a deep sense of sin, a joyous assurance of forgiveness, and a resolute and entire departure from all iniquity. The method of the world is, to take forgiveness of sin for granted, and to forget God. The child of God seeks and obtains pardon, and fears the Lord. The unenlightened religionist feels the burden of sin and struggles against sin, but he does not rejoice in the Saviour, and his fight is not the fight of faith. The dead formalist acknowledges his sin to be great, and Christ's salvation to be complete, but his faith is quiescent and stagnant, he does not resist and overcome evil. *There must be the union of the three elements—humility, faith, life,—a contrite heart, a heart rejoicing in Christ, and a heart determined to obey God.*

The whole Scripture is now seen to move round

these two points, sin and salvation. In the law sin is in the foreground, and the longing after the Saviour is the result which God aimed at when He gave the revelation of His character and will condemning the sinner. In the gospel salvation is in the foreground, and the object aimed at in the gospel is, as John expresses it, "These things are written that ye sin not." The grace of God, which bringeth salvation, hath appeared, disciplining us to deny ungodliness and worldly lusts, and to live righteously, soberly, and godly in this present world.

In the old dispensation the test of sincerity was, Do you need a Saviour? In the new, the test of sincerity is, Do you hate sin? In the old dispensation God said, " I am holy and you are sinful; " the true children responded, " Oh that the Saviour would appear, and the new covenant, with the Spirit implanted renewing the heart." In the new dispensation God says, " Here is Jesus, and with Him the gift of the Holy Ghost; " and the response of the believer is, " I reckon myself to have died to sin that I may live unto God."

In the old dispensation sin was represented as loathsome, even as leprosy and adultery. In the new dispensation, *union with Christ* is represented as the only source of obedience, the only antidote even to the lowest sin. Lie not one to another, for ye are members one of another. Abstain from fleshly lusts, for your members are the members of Christ, your body is the temple of the Holy Ghost.

The holiness of Jesus, the purity and loveliness
of His character, the perfection of His obedience,
reveals to us clearly and strikingly our sin and transgression ; His death on the cross explains to us more
fully than aught else the holiness and justice of God,
the nature of sin and guilt, the honour and power of
the law, the bitterness and awfulness of God's wrath.

And yet the previous revelation is also necessary.
Some think, now that Christ's cross is revealed, we
need not study the Books which precede the gospel ;
we may at once begin with the culminating point.
Is it so ?

God sent the law to Israel as a schoolmaster to bring
them to Christ ; for by the law cometh the knowledge
of sin.   But we cannot enter on the labour of our
predecessors.   We must begin from the same point.
The teaching which God saw to be necessary for the
Jews is equally needed by us; and for this reason
the five Books of Moses retain their fundamental
position, even during the present dispensation.   In
Genesis, we learn the origin of our present fallen
condition ; in Exodus and Leviticus, we see our
image in the mirror of God's perfect law ; while in
Numbers, we read a description of the sins of God's
people during their earthly pilgrimage.

To understand our present sinfulness, we must go
back to the Garden of Eden.   There we fell, and in
this history of our fall we must learn what is our
ruin.   Our very hearts are sinful, our nature corrupt.
We all admit readily that we are not perfect ; we

are ready to acknowledge isolated faults, even sins; but we do not fully admit that we are members of a degenerate race.   We still cherish secretly the flattering hope, that if we only earnestly willed it, and with energetic exertion set ourselves to the task, we could elevate and ennoble our character, and bring forth good fruit.   We forget that the very fountain is poisoned, and that from the heart proceed evil thoughts and an evil life.   " Ye, who are evil," is the incidental expression of the Lord Jesus, and the very circumstance that it is incidental reveals to us the profound conviction the Son of Man had of man's depravity.   " Thy first father hath sinned," is an inscription written legibly on our persons and characters, if we were only willing to read the awful truth.

The fall of our first parents does not hold as important a place in our minds as it ought.   Hence so many fail to see their lost and guilty condition in the sight of God.   They judge themselves by isolated acts, and not by the whole spirit of their life, and the dispositions of the heart.   They judge themselves by comparative merit, taking for their standard the average of a fallen and God-estranged race; they forget that God created man in His own image, and they forget that standard of perfection, of which conscience still witnesses.

We are apt to forget the momentous issue of that trial in paradise.   First we weaken the force of the Scripture narrative, and then we fail to see our immediate connexion with it, on the childish ground that six thousand years have elapsed since that event —as if, in the spiritual world, a thousand years are not as a day, and a sinner as near the fall as if it happened only this moment, and a believer as near the cross as if Jesus, to use Luther's expression, had died only yesterday. Some look upon our first parents as if they had been only undeveloped, innocent beings when they fell; they take a low view of man's original condition, and the fall seems to them rather a progress and development, than a fatal step, an apostasy from God. But when man fell, God was forsaken as the centre of his life and self substituted. God was forsaken as the guide of his life, and Satan gained an entrance into the soul and a tyrannical influence over the will.

The education which God gave to Israel is in all ages the education of His children. The law is the schoolmaster to bring us to Christ. It fulfils now as ever its original purpose of convincing us of our great guilt and utter weakness. Think not of the law as simply a scaffolding, which is thrown away as useless now that the edifice stands complete. Think not of the law merely as a diagram, a shadow and type, which becomes superfluous, now that the fulfilment is evidently set before us. Think not that only the predictions and types of the Saviour are profitable for our study. The whole law is full of vitality and instruction. The sacrifices and purifications have ceased, but they still testify of our corruption. The ceremonial of the Levitical law presents us with a picture of our daily life. It shows us that we are daily sinning, that we are constantly touching the unclean thing, and require cleansing; that our thoughts and deeds are full of defilement; that our birth and our death, our sickness and our infirmities, are connected with sin. Sacrifice is needed also for sins of ignorance; for we have gone so far astray from God, and our darkness is so dense, and our corruption so great, that, even without knowing it, we commit that which is hateful to God and horrible for angels to behold. Thank-offerings also require cleansing. Our holy things are full of sin; selfishness insinuates itself even in the offering of praise and gratitude. What great and awful lessons are contained in Leviticus, to show us our condition in the sight of God!

As an old German divine (Roos) says: " See here that God has concluded all under sin. He sees sin everywhere, and requires cleansing and expiation throughout. Man's body and soul, from his birth to his death, his words and works, his prayers and offerings, his house, and his food, and his garments; his days, and months, and years; his field with its harvest, his vine and his olive tree; his earthen, wooden, and brazen vessels; the cattle, birds, fishes, and creeping things with which he has to do—*all* stood under law, under sin, under atonement and purification. How clearly did God teach the Jews that flesh and blood could not enter the kingdom of God on account of sin. The first-born had to be redeemed; every mother had to offer a sacrifice of purification; to touch a dead body, even the nearest relative, was defiling, and the water of sprinkling was needed for cleansing."

We must combine the lessons of the fall and of the law. Man was changed by transgressing God's commandment; but God cannot change, His holiness remains immutable. Man is carnal and sold under sin, but the law is holy, just, and good. *The law reveals the depths of our fall*—it shows us the length and breadth of sin; and thus it convinces us of the need of a Saviour to atone, and of the Holy Spirit to renew.

How precious is now the gospel! Forgiveness of sin is connected with the deepest sorrow and the greatest joy. Here is both Mara and Elim.

Thus we see it in the prayer of Moses, the man of God (Ps. xc.) How dark are the clouds with which it opens—man's sin and death, the anger and wrath of God! The light of God's countenance is mentioned, but only as revealing clearly our hidden sins. But how glorious is the sunshine with which it closes—the mercy of God filling us with joy and gladness, the beauty of the Lord shining on us, so that we are irradiated with the glory and light of divine love!

Thus we see it in that great Psalm of repentance, (Ps. li.) The broken and contrite heart which has confessed sin desires to hear joy and gladness, and prays for the restoration of the joy of salvation,—a joy so strong, and pure, and overflowing, that it communicates itself to others; the penitent is forgiven, the pardoned one rejoices, the rejoicing saint becomes an evangelist. And as he goes forth with peace and joy to sinners around, he returns with a royal spirit to God's Zion and Jerusalem his beloved city.

> " God to the contrite can dispense
> The princely heart of innocence."

Thus we see it in the words in which the spirit of prophecy has described the mission of the Anointed. He comes unto them that mourn ; He gives unto them beauty for ashes, the oil of joy for mourning, the garment of praise for the spirit of heaviness (Isa. lxi.)

Thus we see it—and this is the most striking, even as it is the highest, illustration of this great truth— thus we see it in the Lord's Supper. It is a feast, and yet here the soul is most deeply humbled by a sense of sin and unworthiness. It is a season of rejoicing, for the Bridegroom is with us, and yet a time when we confess our guilt, and mourn over our hardness of heart ; we eat the Paschal Lamb, but with it bitter herbs of repentance and contrition. How different the joy of the Christian is from that of the world, is most clearly seen in the feast of love. The world, in its festivity and mirth, banishes from the mind the remembrance of sin and the thought of death. And sin and death are indeed the two elements and roots of all sorrow. But at the Lord's Table sin and death are the two prominent ideas: sin

—but it is forgiven; death—but it is the death of Christ, who has brought unto us life eternal, victory over the grave, and everlasting glory.

Let us consider the joy which arises out of the forgiveness of sin.

1. The Triune God rejoices over the sinner saved. Who is the shepherd that left the ninety-nine sheep in the wilderness, and went to seek the lost sheep until he found it, and carried it home on his shoulders rejoicing, but Jesus the Good Shepherd, who laid down His life for us, and who now is filled with joy over His disciples, who are in perfect safety, inseparable from Him who is now in heaven, in the Father's house? Who is meant by the woman who lights the candle, and sweeps the house, and seeks diligently till she finds the lost piece of silver, but the Holy Ghost, who, by the testimony of the Church (" the Spirit and the Bride say, Come "), brings light into the dark heart, a light penetrating and searching, convincing and rebuking, and who then restores the helpless soul, filling it with joy and peace in believing? The Spirit rejoices over the believer added to the treasury of Christ. Who is the father who commands the festival to be prepared, and says, " It is meet for us to make merry and be glad, for this my son was lost and is found, he was dead and is alive again," but the Heavenly Father, who has no pleasure in the death of the sinner, but whose delight is in His mercy, whose joy is in the life of the soul which repents and believes? Joy is in God, the

Father, Son, and Holy Ghost, over the pardoned sinner.

And with God all angels rejoice, while they behold the mystery of godliness, and adore the Lamb that was slain. All creation is commanded to rejoice: " Be ye glad and rejoice for ever in that which I create; for, behold, I create Jerusalem a rejoicing, and her people a joy."

Sin, the mother of all sorrow, has become the occasion of the greatest joy. *God has introduced a new joy into the universe*, higher and deeper than the primeval joy of angels, and the short-lived joy of our parents in the state of innocence,—a joy based on the new revelation of the love of God which the Lord Jesus Christ brought unto us sinners. In the ages to come, the ransomed children of God, whose name is " Hephzi-bah," will be the centre of the kingdom of glory, even as now the manifold wisdom of God is made known, by the Church, unto the principalities and powers in heavenly places. Christ, as the Lamb of God, will be the light and the joy of that city, which shall come down from God out of heaven, prepared as a bride adorned for her husband.

2. The incarnation of the Son of God, His life on earth, His spotless and perfect obedience, filled the Father with joy. Christ fulfilled the commandment which He received of the Father. His body was broken for us. This obedience is our salvation—it was, and ever is, a source of joy unto God.

3. The expiation of the cross by His blood is a

source of joy. The cup of salvation, even the cup of the New Testament in His blood, is taken by us as a cup of joy, though to Him it was a bitter cup—how bitter none can know. But here was more than punishment transferred. The punishment of the wicked is necessary, but it cannot please God. But here was satisfaction, here was something of infinite value to God,—love and faith, which were to the Father infinitely precious. He who was a sin-offering, and was made a curse, *was in this very substitution an offering and a sacrifice to God for a sweet-smelling savour.* Hence His blood speaketh better things than that of Abel. He is the Mediator of the better covenant, and His death is ever precious in the sight of God. It has gained not merely the acquittal of the Judge, but the unspeakable favour and abundant love of the Father. By the blood of Christ sin is not merely removed, but we are brought nigh ; God's anger is not merely turned away, but infinite love rests upon Christ as our substitute, and upon us in Him.

4. For God, by redeeming us, has betrothed Himself to us. Christ is our Saviour, but by His death on the cross He has also become our Bridegroom. By His broken body and His shed blood, we become members of His body, of His flesh, and of His bones. He gave Himself for us, that He might sanctify and cleanse us to be His bride, beloved and glorified throughout eternity. A judge may acquit a criminal ; a substitute may satisfy the

demands of justice, so that the guilty go free.   But
here is this marvellous combination of stupendous
mercies.   He dies for us, and through this very death
becomes one with us.   We are free, because His
righteousness is ours, as our sins were His.   God acquits us, but not to leave us to ourselves, at a distance
from Him ; He acquits us by uniting us with His own
Son, and making us, by His Spirit, partakers of the
divine nature.   He *gives* us His Son to be ours for
ever, when He gives Him up unto death.   Christ for
us, to become Christ in us.

Greater joy there cannot be than to be ever with
Christ.   Well may we stand in awe before so great
a mystery.   We cannot comprehend it, but it is
ours to rest in it with humble faith.   We believe
the mystery of the holy and blessed Trinity—the
Father, the Son, and the Holy Ghost, three, and
yet one God.   We believe the mystery of the union
of the divine and human natures in one person—
Christ Jesus.

We believe these unions, though we cannot comprehend them, but we have experienced in our hearts
and lives what we shall afterwards also behold in
clear vision.   The Father's love, the Saviour's grace,
the Spirit's power,—these three, one and undivided,
are to us the threefold cord which cannot be broken.
Likewise, we rejoice that Jesus is the Son of God ;
that the Child born and the Son given is the Mighty
God, that the man Christ Jesus is the Word made
flesh.   And thus we hold fast the third, the mystical

union, that Christ and the Church are one. Believe it because it is revealed. Take hold of this mystery by faith; measure it not by your feeling. More really and truly than we can understand it, Christ and we are one. He is the vine, and we are the branches. Not, as at first sight we explain it, Christ the root, or the stem, but Christ the (whole) vine; and yet *we*, not losing our individuality, and not losing our finite and dependent creature nature, are the branches; for Christ lives in us. He is the head, and we are the members: Christ and the believers are one man, even as Paul says, " Till we all come in the unity of the faith, and of the knowledge of the Son of God, *unto a perfect man*" (Eph. iv. 13).

Of this, as of all truth in Christ, the Lord's Supper is the sign, the seal, the pledge. Blessed ordinance! no frequency can lessen its solemnity or its sweetness; the fulness of its meaning is inexhaustible; it speaks the simplest form of speech, which babes in Christ can understand—it sets forth the highest mysteries, in which experienced saints delight with awe and adoration. It shows forth *joy through the forgiveness of sin.*

13

KNOWLEDGE AND CONFESSION OF SIN

*"Forgive Us Our Debts, as We
Forgive Our Debtors."*

THE apostle John writes to believers, " If we say we have no sin, we deceive ourselves, and the truth is not in us." He describes here, not an imaginary, but a real danger. None of us deny the general fact of our sinfulness ; but we are apt to neglect self-examination and the confession of our present sins. The reason of this neglect, we are here taught, is twofold: self-deception, and the weakness of the light of Christ within us. Again, the apostle Paul says, " If we would judge ourselves, we should not be judged." We, however, rest satisfied with vague impressions concerning our state ; we are satisfied with the light which accidental circumstances cast on our character; we do not assume the position of a judge, who summons the transgressor, addresses to him searching questions, confronts him with disinterested and well-informed witnesses, and arrives at a knowledge of his guilt by an exact and systematic process.

Such self-examination may become morbid, and produce nothing but torture and despondency. It will necessarily have only such results, unless it is in

God's sight, before our Heavenly Father, in faith of the Son of God, who loved us and gave Himself for us. And it will be unprofitable, without any practical result, unless it is accompanied with the prayer, " Search me, O God, and know my heart; try me, and know my thoughts: and see if there be any wicked way in me, and lead me in the way everlasting."

Let us not, however, overlook the necessity of systematic or rather active self-examination, as the condition of thoughtful confession.

It is evident that the commencement of Christian life is absolutely impossible without some knowledge of self. To seek pardon, we must know our sin; to pray for renewal, we must know the evil of our heart. And is not the Christian's progress, that repentance and faith become deeper and stronger ? Christ becomes more precious to us as our righteousness and sanctification, as we acknowledge and feel more deeply our sin and corruption. And how can we follow Christ, and yield ourselves to the influences of the Holy Ghost—how can we fight the good fight of faith, and keep ourselves unspotted from the world, except by constantly taking heed to our ways, and by submitting to the separating and dividing power of the word, the sharp, two-edged sword, which reveals the conflict between flesh and spirit, nature and grace, Adam and Christ ?

It is true David exclaims, " Who can understand his errors ? " He appeals to God to search him, even as Peter, in reply to the Saviour's words, " Lovest

thou Me?" refers the question to the Lord's omniscience. But the meaning of such passages is not
to exonerate us from the duty of self-knowledge, but
rather is this the purport and object of such declarations: " Even my most careful and diligent search
can never be exhaustive, so numerous and subtle are
my sins: yet is it so necessary that I should know
myself; I therefore beseech God, who searcheth the
heart, to enlighten me, to show me my secret faults,
which offend Him, and are obstacles retarding my
progress and diminishing my happiness."

Why is self-knowledge so difficult? It seems
as if we took almost too great and absorbing interest
in ourselves. People like to have their character
described from their handwriting, the formation of
their head, their physiognomy. And yet a little
reflection shows us that this rarely arises from a
desire to obtain a true knowledge of their character;
for not merely are they not inclined to credit any un-
favourable statements, but they neglect the infallible
methods which the hand of God gives us by which
we may see our true image. The great difficulty in
this work is, that we do not like our vanity to be
wounded, our pride to be brought low; the more
skill we obtain in examining our heart and life, the
deeper will our humiliation be.

Another circumstance seems at first sight to render
this work easy—the constant opportunity which we
have of engaging in it, and the abundant and ready
material at our disposal. A sudden, quicker beating

of our pulse shows us what has been our cherished idol, where our treasure lies, what we dread most. A momentary feeling of disappointment when we hear of our neighbour's success,—a feeling so transitory that none could notice it in the tone of our voice or the play of our features,—reveals to us the existence of envy and jealousy in our heart. We see our want of brotherly love and considerateness when, hearing of some one's kindness and help, we say to ourselves, " I never thought of his need, and what I could do for him." And without even taxing our memory with a recollection of our thoughts (which, like busy and acute pleaders, go accusing and excusing in the inner court of justice), sufficient data register themselves on our memory to render our knowledge of self true and clear, and our confession of sin definite and real, if we only applied our mind to the work. But, as a rule, we know little of our heart, and are not much at home with ourselves.

Others we can judge, sometimes so keenly and minutely that we notice even a mote in our brother's eye. We have sometimes even seen what had no existence except in our uncharitable suspicion. Turn this badly-employed power to good. Learn from your observations and criticism of others. We know that other people deceive themselves, that they are not conscious of sins and faults which are obvious to others. Let us bear in mind that we also are ignorant of what all others see often in us, and that if we occasionally suspect it, we do not sufficiently distrust ourselves, and bring our heart and life into the light of a rigorous self-examination.

But even if we saw ourselves as others see us, and even if men could find in us nothing to censure and blame, we must say with the apostle, "It is a small thing with me that I should be judged of you or of man's judgment. He that judgeth me is the Lord." We ought to avoid the very appearance of evil, and to value the good opinion of our fellow-Christians; but God alone sees our hidden motives, and the stirring of evil thoughts and desires; and because we are to know ourselves in God's sight, self-examination is difficult.

Consider, again, the facts of Scripture, which show how little even the best men know their sin and weakness. Failure in trial reveals to them what forethought ought to have pointed out. Prometheus is rarer than Epimetheus. David's fall and the relapse of Hezekiah, after very special mercies, are sad but instructive lessons. Nor do we know the weakness of our strong points. The gentle Moses, meekest of all men, utters passionate words; Elijah, most intrepid in the hour of danger, yields to abject despondency; Solomon's wisdom yields to the folly of idols; Peter's courage and self-forgetful devotedness is changed into ignoble denial of his Master, and cowardice; Barnabas, the son of consolation, has a sharp contention with Paul. It is difficult to know ourselves.

Notice the constant forgetfulness, ingratitude, and

failure of Israel. " In tracing the progress of Israel in the wilderness, I read the history of my own heart and life." * And notice how most of the seven churches to whom the Lord, " who knoweth our works," sends epistles, deceived themselves on some great point. A striking exception is poor, persecuted, and suffering Smyrna ; from which we may gather this lesson, that prosperity is not favourable to a true estimate of ourselves ; that we are never in greater danger than when our course is smooth, that health and ease and the constant occupations of life may lull us to sleep, and that we may mistake our very sloth and apathy for peace of conscience. Laodicea was the deepest sunk in self-deception, and most fully convinced that she was rich and endowed with goods, and had need of nothing.

Remember, then, the difficulties of the work ; bear in mind that self-love always blinds us, and sin itself brings with it the darkening atmosphere to hide it from our eye. We deceive ourselves ; and Christ, the truth, not being allowed to reign in us, we say we have no sin.

The recollection of these difficulties may incline us to give greater heed to the Scripture counsels on this subject.

True, candid, and full confession depends chiefly on our realising the divine presence—the presence of a forgiving and loving God.

However much we may deceive ourselves, we

_____

* Hamann.

cannot deceive God. He not only knows all things, but He actually searches and tries the hearts of men ; it is His purpose and will to examine us; He looks down from heaven to behold. And as there is a most special providence guiding our every step, and numbering the very hairs of our head, so we believe that the words, " Thou God seest me," apply to each individually, and that if he was the only person existing in the universe, God's knowledge of his thoughts, words, and actions could not be more minute and accurate.

The vivid realisation of this truth is usually the turning-point in our spiritual experience. The soul sees God face to face. Christ and the sinner meet. " Behold a man who told me all things which ever I did !" is the exclamation of the heart. For the divine omniscience is felt as that of a loving, forgiving, healing Saviour. Jesus knows all our sins, and yet His presence brings comfort. We feel ashamed before Him, and yet we have courage to remain ; we feel sorrow, but it is not the dull sorrow of the world, which leads unto death. We feel that Jesus forgives, renews, strengthens ; He does not merely soothe, but He restores the soul ; the waves are calmed, and it is peace.

Let us connect self-examination and confession with our study of the divine Lord and with meditation. *We do not need a human confessor to probe us and to direct to, us searching questions.* That would be not without serious danger both to him and to us.

Christ asks the question, Lovest thou me? Take the word of God, and convert it into a confessor. Here is a precept,—do I obey it? Here is a statement concerning man's heart and life,—do I believe it? Here is a promise,—am I resting in it, am I acting on it? Here is a warning,—am I dreading this danger?

Let us not be led astray by the opinions of the world, or even of Christians. Many things the Bible speaks of in terms much more severe than we think necessary. Many statements, such as " covetousness is idolatry," appear exaggerated. Why should the lukewarm believer be so repulsive in the Saviour's estimation? Why should we have to give an account for every unprofitable word? Why does Christ so often accuse us of hypocrisy, when we appear to ourselves only uncharitable, hasty, and ignorant? * Here are subjects for thought and self-probing.

Scripture history also is given for the very purpose that we should apply it to ourselves. It is not of private, or merely local and temporary application; it is written for our instruction and guidance. Believers ought to consider especially the sins of God's people. There are sins outside the kingdom of God or the visible Church, and sins within the congregation of professing (genuine and false) believers. The former are generally more revolting and degrading, the latter perhaps deeper and more subtle and hateful in their character. Scripture describes chiefly the

---

* Matt. vii. 5 ; xvi. 3, &c.

sins of Israel and the Church. The sins of the Jews
in the wilderness, and after their entrance into the land
of promise, are narrated with great faithfulness. How
much self-knowledge may we gain from considering
their ingratitude and murmuring! What lessons
may we derive from their want of faith alternating
with false zeal and mere carnal courage ; their formal-
ism and hypocrisy ; their idolatry and conformity to
the nations around them! And while their history
humbles us, the thought that "nevertheless He saved
them for His great name's sake," is our consolation.

We ought also to study the variety of character
among God's own children. Some bring forth sixty-
fold, some only twenty, some a hundred. We ought
to compare Abraham with Lot, Mary with Martha,
that thus we may gain an insight, not merely into
the contrast between faith and unbelief, but into the
various phases and dangers of the spiritual life.

Let us especially study the life of Christ. "Follow
Me," is the Saviour's command. "Learn of Me, for I
am meek and lowly in heart." "We learn Christ,"
saith the apostle. Let us arm ourselves with the
mind of Christ. The world may admire Christ, but
only the regenerate can imitate Him. The evil in
Christendom is, that men who do not believe in
Christ profess to imitate Him, and men who do not
imitate Christ profess to be believers! Let us remember that to follow Christ is our calling, and by
this model let us search and examine ourselves. If
Christ stands before our eye,—if Christ, the truth,

dwells within us, we shall not deceive ourselves, but know and confess our sin.

This very petition which we are now considering, is the greatest help to self-examination. The same may be said of the whole prayer. If we have uttered the preceding petitions thoughtfully and sincerely, we must feel abased before God, and with a contrite heart we ask for His pardon. For does not every word of this prayer reveal to us our sin? When we say Father, can we forget our want of gratitude and love, and how little we resemble Him whose children we are? When we call God *our* Father, does not that little word reveal to us, as in a bright mirror, our sins against the second table of God's commandments? We speak of heaven as the Father's house, whither we are going, and we are ashamed on account of our worldliness and apathy. We pray that His name be hallowed, that His kingdom may come, and His will be done, and we remember how little we have lived in the contemplation of Jesus, in loyal service to Him as our King, and in diligent and meek obedience, bringing forth the fruits of the Spirit. Even in offering up the prayer for daily bread, our covetousness, our selfishness, our unbelieving anxiety stare us in the face. Thus, by the time we arrive at the fifth petition, conscience is enlightened, and the heart burdened with a knowledge of sin.

But our relation to our fellow-men, and to those that trespass against us, is the chief test of our actual condition before God.

If our hearts are loving and humble towards God, our attitude to our neighbour will be kind and forgiving. He who feels his sin and unworthiness is able to bear the unjust opinion and the severe criticism of men ; without bitterness he will endeavour to profit by every humiliating experience. He who rejoices in God, and praises Him for His goodness and patience, will be cheerful, long-suffering, and hopeful in his dealings with others. If we know God, and if the countenance of Christ is our study, we shall be able not merely to praise the dead and to build the graves of the prophets, as the Pharisees were wont to do, but to help and comfort the disciples as we have opportunity.

Trespasses we must expect ; and here is a test of our true condition : whether we are self-righteous, or debtors of mercy ; whether we know and hate all sin, our own included, or feel indignant only with sins to which we are not tempted, or when their injury falls on ourselves ; whether we live according to the standard of justice merely, or in the power of the love of Christ and of the Holy Ghost.

Even if we have no enemies, the question is : Are our hearts so full of humility and of love, so entirely trusting in God, from whom all things come, that we would be ready and willing to forgive, nay, even to love, when we are hated ? Have we the *disposition* described in the Word of God : " Love your enemies, bless them that curse you, do good to them that hate you, and pray for them which despitefully use you,

and persecute you." " If thine enemy hunger, feed
him ; if he thirst, give him drink ?"* Are we peacemakers, as we are called by our very adoption—peacemakers in heart, prayer, word, and life ?

And what if, instead of having to forgive, we need
forgiveness ? " Solomon was one who knew human
nature probably as well as any man that ever lived ;
he had an opportunity of reading himself as well as
others.   When we hear any one speak ill of us, we
should remember what he says : ' Take no heed unto
all words that are spoken ; for oftentimes also thine
own heart knoweth that thou likewise hast cursed
others.' † Here we are sent into the recesses of our
own bosoms, and duties omitted and evil done to our
neighbour will be remembered."‡

How low is often our standard of love to our
neighbour !   In how many different ways do we not
say, " Am I my brother's keeper ?"   Even in relation to our most loved children, relatives, and friends,
how many are our sins of omission !

When we utter this petition, with its comparison and
vow, we think of the Lord Jesus Christ, the perfect
embodiment of love, in whom the mercy of God visited
earth.   We can only adore Him, that contemplating
His beauty we may be conformed to His image.

Praying *daily* for pardon implies a daily survey.
This is sufficient, though there are times which call
for a more general and more extensive self-examina-

---

* Matt. v. 44 ; Rom. xii. 20.   † Eccles. vii. 21, 22.
‡ Howels, 130.

tion,—in seasons of affliction, before partaking of the Lord's Supper, at turning-points in our history, and whenever God's providence and His Spirit point it out. This to a large extent must be left to the individual Christian.

Our past sins are forgiven, and faith rests in the assurance of God's love. Yet the same David, who could bless the Lord who forgiveth all thine iniquities, prayed also, " Lord, remember not the sins of my youth." God forgets our sins, but sometimes we cannot forget them ; let us guard against unbelief, let not the enemy fill us with doubt and despondency, but let the remembrance of past sin deepen our humble faith in Jesus, as Paul, when he remembered that he was once a persecutor and injurious, added, " I have obtained mercy."

Lastly, Let us not merely remember the experience of God's saints, but expect it to become our own. When God gave unto Job a fuller revelation of His power and wisdom, and a deeper insight into the divine sovereignty, the effect was a deeper knowledge of sin, and a more intense consciousness of his guilt. John the Baptist confesses, " Christ must increase, I must decrease." Paul explains the true Christian to be one who has no confidence in the flesh, but rejoices in Christ Jesus. Experience such as this will be ours also if we do not deceive ourselves, and if the truth dwell in us ; if we learn to confess sin, and to confess Christ ; if we are sorrowful, yet alway rejoicing. As we have sinned much, it is our joy to love much.

14

TEMPTATION: FROM GOD AND FROM SATAN

"And lead us not into temptation."

WE need daily forgiveness as much as we need daily bread. We go with all our wants to our Father, who is the Giver, and to Him who is the Forgiver we bring all our sins, that He may deliver us from their guilt and pollution.

But the daily pardon of sin is not to diminish our dread of sin. God's forgiveness is to deepen our repentance, and to increase our hatred of evil. No sooner have we asked and received forgiveness than we look forward with fear and anxiety to the power and subtlety of temptation; having washed our garments, and made them white in the blood of the Lamb, we are anxious to keep ourselves unspotted from the world; we therefore pray, "And lead us not into temptation."

The forgiven soul fears God and dreads sin.

We may view the word "and" in this light: The believer has wants in the *present*,—he asks God to supply them; he feels the burden of *past* sins,—he asks God to remove it; he looks forward to the *future*, and his great fear is, that in this world of sin and temptation he will yield and fall into transgression,—he asks God to lead him and guide him safely.

But why think of the future ? Because Jesus says not merely, Come unto Me and rest, but also, I have ordained you, that you *go* and bring forth fruit ; because He who says, Be of good cheer, thy sins are forgiven, says also, Go and sin no more. We must go forth unto our daily duties and trials, and there glorify God. In prayer we find repose ; but prayer is also the starting-point of our race and fight of faith.

But has not God promised to keep us by His power through faith unto salvation ? Has not Jesus assured us, that none shall pluck us out of His hands ? Why then be afraid of temptation ?

The promise of God is our safety and our strength ; but what is this promise ? He will keep us, but through faith, not *without* faith ; Jesus will keep us if we abide in Him and His words abide in us. Clinging to Christ is our safety ; and in clinging to Christ we dread sin, and all that tends to it.

It is the petition of humility which looks unto our Heavenly Father for help. It is the petition of wisdom which has learned not to trust in self. Ignorant of danger, ignorant of our weakness, the young believer, like a young sailor or soldier, is anxious to meet the storm and rush into the battle. The more we know, the more we dread sin and the precincts of sin— temptation.

Temptation is sometimes spoken of in Scripture as coming from God, sometimes as coming from Satan. God tempts no man to evil, but for good; He tries and tests, as He tempted Abraham and the children of Israel in the wilderness. Satan tempts unto evil; he tries to infuse evil into the human mind.

Many of God's providential dealings are probations —such as prosperity, health, talent; or sickness, poverty, affliction. Satan converts them into temptations; and our sinful hearts give him abundant facility in this. Are we rich, then we are apt to forget God; are we poor, then are we apt to murmur; are we neither poor nor rich, we are apt to forget both generosity and liberality on the one hand, and our dependence on God and humility on the other. And thus with all God's providential dealings.

Again, God can turn Satan's temptations into beneficent probations. Thus in the case of Job. Job was tempted by Satan, but through God's grace he came out pure as gold, and elevated to a higher experience.

Or again, God can overrule Satan's temptation yielded to, and bring good out of it. Thus in the case of Peter. Satan tempted, Peter yielded; Christ, by His intercession through His look, brought blessing to His disciple, a broken heart, self-reliance destroyed, humility and love deepened.

God leads. Satan cannot tempt without nor beyond God's permission. He is a thief and a robber, but the road on which he walks belongs to the King. And Satan must obey the Lord. Even the deeps, hail and storm, serpents and dragons, praise the Lord.

The child of God distrusts himself, dreads sin, and says to God, Lead me not where there are snares and pitfalls—I am shortsighted ; where there are strong enemies, for I am weak ; keep Satan, keep sinful allurements, from me ; keep my heart, so that probation may not become temptation to me ; lead me, that I may not fall, but abide in Christ. We deprecate temptation in this sense. But if God allows circumstances to try our faith, and Satan to sift us, while we thus cling to Him in humility, we can count it all joy when we fall into divers trials—that our faith may be purified.

The Lord Jesus, in teaching us this petition, implies that we ought to dread and to shun temptation.

To dread it. Jesus knew the nature of temptation. He was tempted in all things as we are, yet without sin. Jesus the Son of Man counsels us to dread temptation. His perfect purity, His strength of faith, give additional force to His warning. How much more ought we poor sinful creatures to dread the assaults of the wicked one.

And while we dread it, let us avoid it. Draw a margin and a hedge round sin. Go not close to the precipice. As Solomon, in speaking of the evil woman, says, " Remove thy way *far* from her ; come not nigh unto the door of her house." When Jesus warns His disciples against false Christs, He advises them not even to go near them : " Do not go forth to see." How can we offer up this petition sincerely if we do not avoid the dangerous border-line, if we are not careful not to pitch our tent towards Sodom?

In considering this subject, it may be useful to view it, first, with reference to Satan's temptations; secondly, with reference to God's probations, and God's overruling of Satan's temptations.

I. Speaking of Satan's temptations, is in itself a temptation, unless in humble dependence upon God our object is practical, to guard against the enemy, and to be prepared and strengthened for the conflict.

The world does not know or remember Satan's existence and his aim. This is one of his stratagems. The young Christian does not sufficiently think of Satan's strength and subtlety. He is a serpent, and an old serpent,—skilful, experienced, insinuating; he is a lion,—strong, bold; a roaring lion,—his energies roused; he is full of devices, resolute, and indefatigable. But while a remembrance of Satan's history, character, power, resources, alarms us, is this alarm in itself salutary? I think it is in danger of not producing any lasting and good result, unless we learn at the same time not to be afraid of Satan. He is conquered. The prince of the world is judged. His head is bruised. Christ is our Saviour, and in Him we are more than conquerors. Look to Jesus, and this faith is your victory. None can separate you from the love of God. "Satan trembles when he sees the weakest saint upon his knees." He cannot harm you if you look to your loving Father and your faithful High Priest.

We have every reason to be watchful, to be on our guard, to concentrate our energy, to dread temptation, to distrust ourselves; but not as into a battle of doubtful issue go we forth, but as the followers of one who was once a soldier like us, but who is now a crowned victor at the right hand of God. Think then of the love of God, of the Saviour's constant intercession, of the indwelling of the Holy Ghost; think of the ministry, unseen, but most certain, of the blessed angels, and of the efficacy of prayer, thine own and that of Christian friends, and that of the whole Catholic Church, united in this petition, " And lead us not into temptation."

How ample is Scripture's teaching on Satan!— ample for guidance and instruction, though not to satisfy curiosity. The origin of evil we may not know, but our chief anxiety ought to be to know its *destruction*—the victory over evil—as far as we are concerned. The first temptation in Paradise, and the temptation of the Lord in the wilderness, contain the most important and fundamental lessons. Let us try and gather a few.

1. It is of the utmost importance in our conflict with Satan to know what is his real and ultimate aim. Bear in mind that the object of Satan is not your destruction. This is only the means to his end. Satan's object is to diminish, to obscure, if possible to take away God's glory; and this object he wishes

to effect through the fall and ruin of man. He can never attain his end. God's glory is manifested even more brightly in consequence of sin, through the redemption of Christ. But Satan succeeded in man's fall. Here, from the very first, see your safety in God. God is *glorified* in man's faith, obedience, and blessedness. It is not *your* enemy so much as the enemy of God whom you are called to resist. Identify then your welfare with God's glory. Say, when Satan tempts to sin, It is my Father's honour he attacks, my Father's joy he wishes to cloud. But I will say, Glory be to God, and glory be to God in me, in my salvation, and in my faith and obedience, leading to salvation. Here is the ultimate position of safety, and it is impregnable, for already, though the warfare may be raging, the joy-bells of the Lamb's marriage are ringing, " Thine is the kingdom, and the power, and the glory."

2. Satan's method is to alter your attitude towards God. It ought to be under God; so that all that comes from Him descends from the height of authority and love, and is received with humility and gratitude. Satan suggests to Eve to examine God's word, as standing on a level with God, or rather for the time being surveying and criticising God's command. The moment Eve follows the suggestion of Satan, and considers the word of God *objectively*, without the conscious feeling of reverence and submission, she has fallen from the true attitude of the creature.

Christ answers, " It is written."   There is no argument, but an echo of the divine voice, authoritative and safe.

3. Satan suggests that God's threatenings will not come true, and that His love is not great. "God threatens punishment, but you need not fear it; He forbids pleasure: does He truly love you?" All Satan's temptations have this aim, to make you doubt God's truth, and not rest satisfied in His love.

Jesus says, all God's arrangements are for good, for life; though He surrounds me with stones, man liveth not by bread alone; I doubt not His love. I rejoice in walking after Him, following Him; I dare not go before Him.

4. Satan says: As you are God's child, God's favourite, God's chosen one, assert your own will, seek your own pleasure, achieve your own exaltation. Christ said: Because I am God's Son, I honour, I obey Him. In obedience and love I became a servant, and as a servant I am learning obedience.

5. Satan promises glory apart from God, and in rebellion against God. This is his last attack, but the essence of all his temptations. Here nothing avails, and nothing is appropriate but *worship of God.* Satan must be commanded to flee; God must be adored and praised.

The deepest and most fundamental point, then, is humility, or worship, or the spirit of sonship.

Christ heard the Father say: Thou art my beloved Son; after this He was led into the wilderness. "If thou art the Son of God," was the basis of Satan's temptation; it was the basis of Christ's victory. Christ is the only-begotten of the Father; but it was as man, as servant, by the sword of the Spirit, that Christ overcame, to show us an example. Then learn to be forearmed, as Christ was; to be prepared we must hear the Father's voice: " Thou art my Son." Believe in Jesus, and, through Him, rest in the Father's love. When Satan tempts you, let him find in you one who is a child of God by faith in Christ, and who has received the spirit of adoption.

Learn from Christ what sonship means, what election means, what liberty means.

Sonship means humility. Election means separateness or holiness unto God. Liberty means service.

Learn from Christ to use the Scripture. It is the sword of the Spirit. God's word is a final authority. It is possessed of power. It brings its own light with it. But how are we to find the right scripture? The Holy Ghost teaches us. Satan's quotations are refuted by the quotations of an enlightened conscience. There is a holy instinct which makes you cast your weight on the heavenly, self-denial, obedience side, when Satan's sophistry attacks the bias of vanity, pride, ease, and worldliness. Let the Scripture be in the memory, in the heart, cherished by the affections, revered by the conscience.

Above all, never lose sight of a living, present God. Instead of answering Satan, speak to God; pray, worship, praise. All temptations centre in this, to forget or doubt the love of God in Christ.

Believe this, and you are strong. Believing the love of God is the source of all holiness. Presuming on the love of God is the very opposite of believing it. It is forgetting and forsaking the Father, the Redeemer, the Spirit. A man who sins, and thinks he is trusting in the love of God, has been deceived by Satan, who has substituted an idol of indulgence for the true and living God.

Look unto God, and you are safe, for the way of life is above to the wise, that he may depart from hell beneath. Look unto Jesus Christ, and you will run the race set before you.

While the fundamental lessons are clearly given us in Scripture, we ought also to attend to instructions referring to secondary points.

Remember, then, the occasions and channels of temptation, —God alone is our safety. For Satan regards not the sanctity of place. He enters the garden of Eden, and he stands on the pinnacle of the Temple. He is not deterred by the influence of holy companionship: he tempts Achan in the camp of Israel, Judas among the disciples of Christ, Ananias and Sapphira among the first Christians in Jerusalem. He is not afraid to attack the most favoured saint: David, the man after the heart of God; Peter, the first of the apostles; the three disciples in the garden of Gethsemane; he tempted even Jesus, the Lord of glory. He is not moved to pity by the helplessness and innocence of childhood; he will not relinquish hope, even when the aged pilgrim is on his death-bed.   Everywhere and always he tempts.   And what are the channels of temptation? He tempted David to number the people, by presenting to his imagination a picture of gratified ambition; he tempted David on another occasion, at a time when the king was free from any great and good pursuit.   We must guard the imagination; we must exclude idleness; we must avoid evil companions; above all, we must keep the heart with diligence. Satan disdains not to use the basest instruments—the allurement of Delilah, the dance of Herodias' daughter, the thirty pieces of silver.   He is able to use the thoughts of the loftiest intellect, the feelings of the most tender heart, the plans of the highest ambition, as channels of his influence.   Thoughts and words of divine truth and holiness he can quote for his own purpose.   Great is his subtlety, and manifold are his methods.

Dreading temptation, shunning temptation, praying to be delivered from and in temptation, our comfort is, God leads.

If we are God's children, the Lord is our guide. But if we have not come through Christ to the Father, who is our leader?   Man thinks he guides himself, and that it is in him that walketh to direct his steps.   It is not so; man must have one to lead him.   In Paradise it was God; when man fell he did not obtain independence and self-government, but he permitted Satan to become his leader.   Since then, the human race has been led captive at his will.

There is no alternative for us but to be led by God or by Satan. The way of life is above, even Christ at the right hand of God; hell is beneath; earth is either connected by faith with the home of blessedness, or unbelief links us to the region of death.

And as there is no middle region, so there is no possibility to stand still without reaching the final end. The younger son first sought independence, then left his father's house and went into a far country. But the further progress was inevitable; he joined himself to a citizen in that country, whose service was hard and degrading. The broad road leads— and all who walk on it must turn or walk to the end —to destruction.

Satan blinds our minds against the peaceful light of the gospel. We are prejudiced against God's truth, unwilling to learn, proud and vain, in love with our own thoughts and imaginations, and we are led on and on until the darkness becomes very dense, and our opposition to God's invitation very bitter. Satan hardens our heart against the love of God in Christ; he leads us into the far land of doubt, and carnal security, and worldliness. We go on following him. The blessed Jesus says, " I am the way;" but the great Antichrist is followed by the world. The world lieth in the wicked one, resting in him in peace and safety, as if reposing on a soft luxurious couch, to awake in the flames of hell.

We who believe in Jesus have been rescued by the omnipotent hand of love, translated from the kingdom of Satan into the kingdom of God's dear Son. The obedience and righteousness of the Second Adam has separated us from the sin of our first parent; through the death of Jesus on the cross we are delivered from death. With Christ's resurrection dates our new life; in the risen Saviour is our safety. The Head is in perennial sunshine, and we are His.

II. *God tempts.*

When James writes, "Let no man say, when he is tempted, I am tempted of God," he expresses a thought which is hidden in our hearts, although it may not always be uttered distinctly. It is only grace which enables a man to say truthfully, "*I* have sinned." From the very commencement, men have laid the blame on the peculiar circumstances of their life, on their nature and temperament, on Satan and his temptations. Thus Adam laid the blame on "the woman which Thou gavest me," and Eve on the serpent which beguiled her.

But let us bear in mind that whatever temptation may surround us, sin is ours, conceived by our lust, originated by our will. Satan beguiles, but he cannot force. "*Why* hath Satan filled your heart?" This question of Peter implies that Satan cannot fill the heart without our consent. Sin is our own; the responsibility and the guilt are ours individually.

Evil may be God's instrument, and in this sense

the prophet says, "If evil be in the city, the Lord hath done it." Equally true is it, as our conscience testifies, that it is we, and we only, who will and who do the evil.

As it is our sinful heart which receives the suggestion of Satan, so it is our sinful heart which turns the dealings of God in His providence and in His grace into temptations. The very blessings which He sends are turned into channels of curse. He sends light, and men are blinded because they are evil. He reveals His love, and men, resisting His mercy, are hardened in their hatred of God. He accepted Abel's sacrifice, and His thoughts of peace became the occasion of the thought of malice; Cain killed his brother. He revealed His power to Pharaoh, and showed him mighty signs, and Pharaoh hardened his heart, and became an example of pride and resistance. He gave His good and holy law to Israel, and the law worketh wrath. He sent Christ, the light of the world, and this light becomes a judgment to the self-righteous and ungodly; Christ, the message of peace, and rebellion reached its culminating point; Christ, the way, and men stumbled and fell.*

And if God, giving up the sinner who thus resists Him, makes of him the only use that can be made of him—viz., a beacon, a vessel of wrath, to "show His power in him, and to declare His name throughout all the earth"—we must acknowledge both the patience and long-suffering with which He endured

---

* Hosea xiv. 9.

the resistance of evil men, and the justice of His punishment.

Recognising the evil of our hearts, which changes the very blessings of God into dangers, we beseech God to change—not His ways, but to change *us,* for He is God, perfect in light, love, and holiness. His paths are justice and truth—they need not to be changed ; but we need to be renewed, that we may walk, and not fall, in God's most blessed way.

The way of the Lord must be prepared within our souls : rough places have to be made even, and crooked ways to be made straight.   Christ is a foundation-stone; it is we who make Him a rock of offence and stumbling-block.   Christ is "the sun of righteousness, with healing in its wings ;" it is we who, resisting the light, increase our blindness.   Christ was the greatest temptation that God ever sent into the world.   " Behold this child is set for the fall and rising again of many in Israel, that the thoughts of many hearts may be revealed." If you accept Christ, you stand on the safe side·of temptation.

Let Christ reign within, and prosperity and adversity cease to be dangerous.   If covetousness is rooted up, gold will not tempt us ; if humility reigns, ambition will not consume us with feverish heat.   If we trust God, the fear of man will not bring a snare; if the joy of heaven be our melody, the sorrow of the world will not enslave us.

Here, indeed, is the test, and all temptations go

back to this fundamental question, " What is God to us ? "

God is a sun to them that fear Him; but to the ungodly the sun is not joyous, beneficent, health-bringing. God is good—but to Israel, to such as are of a clean heart. Jesus came to bless; but the demons cry out, " Art thou come to *torment* us? " The presence of the holy angels and the presence of the Lamb will be torment to those who have rejected God. God above us is a crushing weight unless God dwells within us.

Hence, is not this implied in our petition, " Lord, dwell Thou in me, and even darkness shall be light ? "

God tempts. His motive is love; His object is our good. Even during the temptation, He weighs with fatherly pity the burden and our strength, and with the temptation He makes a way to escape. The trial of our faith will be found unto praise, and honour, and glory at the appearing of Jesus Christ.

Temptations sent by God bring to light hidden sins and infirmities; they are meant to deepen our humility, that, sinking deep in self-abasement, we may rise higher in simplicity and strength of faith. Such temptations bring us into closer fellowship with God, they prepare us for greater usefulness in the world, and they manifest unto angels and devils the power of divine grace in human hearts. On a subject so difficult and obscure, we are safest in limiting our view to the Scripture statements.

God tempted Abraham. He commanded him to give up his son, his only son, the son whom he loved. Isaac was, moreover, the son of the promise. Abraham's faith was tested. And we may suppose that it needed testing ; that Abraham, who, before Isaac's birth, was hoping against hope, was now in danger of looking at the things seen, and not exclusively relying on the word of God. He obeyed; his faith gained the victory ; he believed that God would fulfil His promise, even by raising up Isaac from the dead.

This is a temptation in which most of us are called to follow the father of the faithful. God hears prayer, and then He apparently takes away the very gift He bestowed, and we receive the blessing again, after having given it up in faith unto death.*

Take the case of Job. He was a man of deep and consistent piety ; but he was in danger of falling into self-righteousness. Severe trials are sent. Job learns humility ; he sees, as he never saw before, the majesty, holiness, sovereignty of God ; he abhors himself in dust and ashes. God, in the case of Job, manifested unto angels and devils the power of divine grace in the frail earthen vessel. He delivers Job from a great and hidden evil ; He prepares him for greater prosperity and blessing. Therefore James says, " Ye have heard of the patience of Job, and have seen the end of the Lord. The Lord is very pitiful, and of tender mercy." Forgetting the end of

---

* Compare Bridges' exquisite little Treatise (edited by the Countess of Huntingdon) on Faith.

the Lord (which sometimes is not seen on this side
of the grave), we feel as if the Lord were severe and
cruel; but even in trials as great and fearful as were
Job's, "the end of the Lord" explains that He is of
tender mercy.

As in Abraham's case the object of the temptation
was to purify faith, and in Job's case to eradicate
self-righteousness, so in the case of Joseph the object
of temptation probably was with reference to his
future. Joseph had dreamed of his exaltation, but
not of his sufferings! He savoured not the things
of God, and had to learn the mystery of the cross.
He was cast into prison, his feet were made fast in
the stocks. He had resisted and overcome Satan's
temptation, but now the *word of the Lord* tried him.
What a contrast between God's promise and the condition of a prisoner ; between the reward annexed to
obedience and the actual consequence of Joseph's
faithfulness! But it was the experience and victory
gained in this temptation which appeared afterwards
in Joseph's exaltation, and in his forgiving love to
his brethren.

Another and most instructive aspect of temptation
is taught us by the history of the Jews in the wilderness. Forty years God tempted them, to prove them,
and to know what was in their heart, and to humble
them, and to make them know "that man liveth not
by bread only, but by every word that proceedeth out
of the mouth of the Lord." Here God explains very
fully and clearly why He tempts us. There is a ne-

cessity, but it is not the necessity of fate (we believe not in an absolute fate, but in a sovereign God and Father) ; the necessity is our pride and self-sufficiency on the one hand, and the love of God, which must draw us to Himself. " To humble us," these constant temptations are needed. To reveal to us the folly, sinfulness, and weakness of our own hearts. To show us that principles, motives, remembrances of past mercies, are easily overcome—that God only is our strength. And then to teach us that we must live by God's word. As Christ lived by the Father, so we must eat the word, feed on Christ, seek in all God's dealings *Christ*, God's message and bread for our souls. Be humble and feed in your hearts on Christ ; distrust yourself and rely on the Lord ; thus you will avoid temptation.

Lastly, let me mention the case of the apostle Paul. God gave to His servant wonderful revelations ; and there was danger lest Paul should be exalted beyond measure. God then sent the thorn in the flesh. It is well, that Scripture does not specify what that thorn was. As it stands now, the idea is general, and, therefore, the application very wide. God sends something which is a constant difficulty, and trial, and hindrance. But the assurance is given, " My grace is sufficient for thee." The object of God then is to show that we depend entirely and to the very end on Him alone, that we live by grace, that our strength is our weakness, but that our weakness is our strength.

We cannot ask God never to send to us trials and tests. But we ask God that He will not suffer us to be tempted above what we are able to bear; that He will carry us through temptation, if we needs must have it, and that He will keep us humble and rejoicing in Christ, that we may not enter into temptation.

Let me point out a mistake arising from a wrong use made of religious biography. Some men of God have to pass through very bitter experience. They have sharp, piercing convictions of sin. They have great and long-continued difficulty in accepting God's message of peace. Do not desire similar experience. Do not fancy that it is necessary, or that it would be safe for you. God leads. God leads us one by one, and each a different path. And not the state of your heart, but the word of the Lord, is your warrant to come to Him.

Again, God is simple to the simple, complicated to the complicated. Many believers have a most peaceful, quiet pilgrimage, and why? They take God in all simplicity as a living, forgiving, and bountiful Father. They are so childlike that God takes very easy, small steps with them on a lowly and plain path.*

Again, ordinary Christians have chiefly to fight against inward enemies—the sins of their heart. The

---

* Bengel says, "all his life his great aim was to think chiefly of the loving Father-heart of God (das liebreiche Vaterherz Gottes), which, in Christ Jesus, He has revealed to us."—WACHTER, *Leben Bengel*, 434.

temptations which come directly from Satan are mostly experienced by Christians who have reached a high eminence, or are called to some great work in the world—as Luther.

But let us all watch and pray that we enter not into temptation. Watching is necessary, but it only convinces us that our help is from above. Watching will not keep out and overcome temptation; but it will lead to prayer, and prayer leads to God, and then God leads either not into temptation, or through it to victory.

15

BELIEVERS TEMPTED, YET SAFE

"Lead us not into temptation."

THERE is one little word in this petition which we have not yet noticed. It is the word *us*. It seems to suggest three important thoughts.

1. It reminds us of the universality of temptation. All children of God are taught to offer this petition, because they are all in danger of temptation. No age is exempt. From the earliest dawn of life to the very last breath we draw on earth, temptation is near us. The temptations of childhood, youth, manhood, and old age vary, but in entering on a new phase of life we do not leave temptation behind us. Again, no condition of life, no occupation, no temperament, renders us safe from this danger. There has been no period of the world's history in which there were not manifold temptations. It is true, some places seem especially exposed to the assaults and allurements of the great adversary. The Lord Jesus writes to the church of Pergamos: " I know where thou dwellest, even where Satan's seat is." In like manner, there are periods in history which are especially perilous when sin abounds in the world

and lukewarmness prevails in the Church. But there is no place and no age in which this petition is not needed. There is no pause in the battle. The enemy never relents. The road never loses its narrowness and steepness. Until Jesus comes, the Church must beseech God to guide and help her in temptation.

2. Whenever you notice the sins and failings of your fellow-Christians and of others, remember they were tempted. Think not so much of their guilt as of their actual condition, and come to their rescue. They have yielded to temptation, the strength of which you are not able to measure. Think rather of the cruelty and subtlety of the enemy, than of the sin of his victims. Regard them with sympathy, as wounded men lying on the battle-field. It is our common foe who has injured them. Thus will you be kept both from the spirit of the world, which ignores or excuses sin, and from the spirit of the Pharisee, who thanks God that he is not as other men are. If we stand, it is owing to God's grace, to the intercession of loving friends, to the encouraging and invigorating influences of Christian communion. Let the strong help, in love and tenderness, those who have been overtaken with sin and faults, and thus they will fulfil Christ's mind.

3. If we say, " Lead us not into temptation," we profess to be concerned about the safety of others as well as our own. Our first anxiety must be, that we ourselves become not a temptation to our neighbour.

Our want of faith and love, our inconsistent life, our unedifying conversation, may prove hurtful to those around us, may retard the progress of some fellow-believer, chilling his ardour and restraining his zeal. Let us endeavour not to offend one of Christ's little ones. See that you do nothing whereby your brother stumbleth or is made to err. Walk in wisdom towards them that are without, adorning the doctrine of God our Saviour in all things.

As we dread infection, let us beware lest we become mediums of the noisome pestilence. Let us be a savour of Christ, bringing the fragrance of heaven to our friends and neighbours. Let us be lights like Paul, not beacons as Demas. Let us edify one another. If we walk closely with God, all our garments shall smell of myrrh, and aloes, and cassia, out of the ivory palaces. Workers together with God, we shall spread the knowledge of His name, and refresh the hearts and strengthen the hands of His people. We also shall become leaders in the narrow way, under-shepherds of Christ; as Paul says, " Be ye followers of me, even as I am of Christ."

Let us consider now the special temptations of the believer.

Properly speaking, the Christian is the only subject of temptation. God cannot be tempted with evil. He dwells in pure light; He is full of glory. Satan and his servants cannot be tempted unto evil, for there seems in them no conflict against sin; all their antagonism is against God above, not against His

influence within them.   Angels also, who see the
face of God and rejoice in Him, have an abhorrence
of evil; and as far as we know, there is no temptation which tests their obedience to God, or suggests
to them thoughts of impurity or selfishness.   The
world is rather instigated than tempted by Satan;
for the carnal mind itself loves and pursues the
things which are contrary to the will of God.
Temptation is peculiarly directed against God's
children.

It is in the nature of things that the presence of
God should rouse the opposition of evil.   I did not
know sin until the law came.   The advent of God's
holy and good law causes sin to revive.   When
Jesus draws near the soul, temptation immediately
arises, and we are kept from the Saviour either
through the love of our sin, or through the love of
our righteousness.   When Jesus enters the heart,
the conflict is decided, but only to begin in a new
form.

Sin is present, but sin has no dominion over us.
Satan may accuse us, but the conscience is purged
by the blood of Christ, and at the right hand of God
is He in whom we are justified.   The prince of the
world is judged; his head is bruised, and though he
may assail us, we have an almighty friend to protect
and to deliver us.   Yet the temptations of Satan are
exceedingly subtle and strong, and the flesh continually warreth against the spirit, while the world around
us is constantly presenting difficulties and trials.

Even in the most sacred moments, and on the loftiest height of communion with God, in the festival of love, we have need to remember our danger and our foe. " Thou preparest a table before me in the presence of my enemies." God gives joy and triumph even during the warfare; but even the table of the Lord does not banish the enemy, and our tendency to yield to his influence.

The most gifted are perhaps the most tempted.

The Corinthians were enriched in all utterance and in all knowledge; they came behind in no gift; and see into what grievous sin they fell: discord, and impurity, and desecration of the Lord's Supper, and disorder and pride in their assemblies. The apostle tells them, " Knowledge puffeth up, but love edifieth." He was afraid lest Satan should beguile them from the simplicity that is in Christ Jesus. Do we think more of the various *gifts* of grace than of the great *gift* of grace?

The Galatians rejoiced in the gospel; they received Paul as a messenger of God, and would have plucked out their own eyes and have given them unto him; they did run well; but false teachers came and tempted them to add works to grace, law to gospel, their own glory to the cross of Christ, by which we are crucified to the world, and the world to us. Have any of you erred from the truth, and returned again to Mount Agar and bondage? The minister of the gospel travails in birth again until Christ be formed in you.

Unto the Ephesians Paul writes of the mystery of

our election, and of the Church, chosen, quickened together, raised and exalted with Christ; but, having shown them their heavenly calling and position, he exhorts them to lead a heavenly life on earth, to flee from carnal lusts, from covetousness, from dishonesty, from drunkenness, from falsehood; he exhorts husbands and wives, parents and children, servants and masters; and he admonishes them to put on the whole armour of God, and resist the evil one. Are you an Ephesian, enjoying deep and high views of divine truth, beholding the position of the Church as the Lamb's bride? There is the temptation of forgetting that though the Head is in heaven, the feet are on earth. Beware lest you fall into the very sins which you think so much beneath you; beware lest, in the ordinary relations of life, fixed by the Father, you do not dishonour Christ, by forgetting that He came to sanctify and to fulfil all that God has ordered.

Like a beautiful, peaceful, well-watered garden, the Church of the Philippians lies before our delighted eye in Paul's epistle. Faithful, loving, full of gratitude and liberality, suffering for Christ's sake. Yet even them the apostle exhorts: "Let nothing be done through strife or vainglory, but, in lowliness of mind, let each esteem other better than themselves;" and again, "I beseech Euodias and Syntyche that they be of the same mind in the Lord."

Look at the Colossians. They were in danger of being led astray by false wisdom and false service.

Christ is wisdom; let us study Him. Christ is the way; let us walk in Him, and not invent little paths and methods of will-worship, service, and work which do not raise and strengthen us to put off the "old man," and to be conformed unto Christ.

Timothy was a very godly and devoted Christian, brought up in the blessed enclosure of family piety, a warm-hearted and fervent disciple of Paul, and follower of the Lord Jesus. Yet Paul does not hesitate to exhort him to flee youthful lusts and covetousness.

See, again, how we must guard against depression, anxiety, too much sorrow. In all the epistles, believers are exhorted to rejoice, to look forward to the appearing of the Lord, to remember that God will supply all their wants, that He will perform in them the good work which He has begun.

In the Epistle to the Ephesians we see heavenly privilege and humble obedience combined; in the Epistle to the Thessalonians we see how the most precious doctrine of the Lord's second coming was misunderstood. While we wait for the return of our Lord, we must wait with patience; we must watch the signs of the times; and, above all, we must do the will of God in all soberness and diligence, like the good and faithful servant, who yields not to feverish excitement and dreamy indolence, but who feels strengthened and encouraged by the prospect of his master's return, to go on steadily and vigorously in his appointed work.

The Hebrews, to whom Paul writes, were most sorely tried, and stood in the greatest danger of apostasy. Notwithstanding their first faith, and their many sufferings for Christ's sake, they needed the most earnest exhortations, warning them against their fearful peril. And what is the apostle's great remedy ? He unfolds to them the glory of Christ ; he speaks to them of the Lord, the height of His divinity, the depth of His humanity, His exaltation above angels, above Moses, above Joshua, above Aaron, the exceeding great mystery of His priesthood ; he speaks to them of *faith* as the great victory by which all saints overcome. No church was ever lower and nearer defection ; no epistle is more profound than that addressed to them. What are we to learn from it ? Dwell much on the glory of Christ ; drink deeply of the well of revelation ; go on to perfection ; consider the great High Priest of our profession. We need the strong meat if we are to stand in the hour of temptation !

Temptations of a more subtle and fierce character than the Church has yet seen are before us, according to the warning of the divine Word.* God has given us a chart, in which perilous and deceptive places are described. While we acknowledge with gratitude and joy the progress of truth and the activities of love in our day, are we to resemble the world, who say, Peace and safety ? are we to expect a calm, when Scripture bids us prepare for a storm ?

* Epistles of Peter and Jude, and Book of Revelation.

The deceptive stillness fills the thoughtful soul with more earnest foreboding.

Notwithstanding the clear and copious teaching of Scripture, we learn but slowly to recognise and to overcome temptation, its approaches and methods are so various. Sometimes slow and insinuating, sometimes sudden and violent, so that we are now gradually and imperceptibly moved from our steadfastness, now overcome by the unexpected and forcible nature of the assault. Some temptations are pleasant to us, in others we feel pain; some are in darkness, others in the glare of much high knowledge, and the fever of much excited feeling. The example and opinions of our fellow-men are used by Satan as a net, while isolation and eccentric peculiarity may confirm us in selfish and vain actions. An experienced apostle like Paul could say that he was not ignorant of Satan's devices. An earnest and many-sided Christian like Luther is able to instruct us from the treasury of his own experience. And what is their frequent testimony? It is, that Satan's great aim is to divert our faith from the love of God, to beguile us from the simplicity of the gospel, to make us doubt the grace of God, sufficient to pardon and to sanctify our hearts. To look unto Jesus only is our safety. " The last device of our adversary, when he cannot make us look elsewhere, is to turn off our eyes from our Saviour to our faith, and thus to discourage us if it is weak, and to fill us with pride if it is strong, and, both in the one case and in the other, to enfeeble us; for it is not from faith that strength comes, but it is from the Saviour, by faith; it is not by looking unto our own look, but by looking unto Jesus." *

Let us consider, more fully, the safety of the believer. The believer may fall, but he cannot fall away. This doctrine, like all Scripture truths, is salutary and comforting to earnest, prayerful, God-loving souls; misleading and dangerous to the formalist and prayerless. When you are struggling against sin, mourning over your transgressions, discouraged by your constant failures, perplexed and alarmed by the injury you have done and the opportunities you have wasted—when you are sorrowful, God comforts and upholds you. He assures you that He will help and strengthen you, that He will heal your diseases and restore you to the way of righteousness, that you will yet praise and serve Him among His saints in glory everlasting. For all who love and follow Christ this cordial is prepared, to revive and cheer them in their steep ascent: " I have loved thee with an everlasting love."

Christians cannot fall away, but they may fall. And is this not a great evil? Our life may be embittered, and our usefulness impaired. Lot was finally saved, for the Lord, in His mercy and power, knoweth how to deliver His people, even when, through their own sin, they are in the midst of evil and woe. But when we think of Lot's sojourn in Sodom, what a sad picture opens to our view! Years, during which

_____

* A. Monod.

his soul was vexed daily on account of the wickedness
of the people among whom he dwelt; the desolating
and degrading influence on his family; the gradual
decay of his own piety—at least, of his joyous faith and
service; and, finally, the appalling sight of the vengeance of God! Let none of us, therefore, think of the
safety of the believer in a manner which would be at
once foolish and ungenerous, without true love to ourselves and to our most merciful God. We are safe in
Him if " near the cross abiding."

Christ is our High Priest, and we are safe. As the
names of the children ot Israel were engraven on the
shoulders and breastplates of Aaron, even thus are
we represented in Heaven by the Lord, who died for
us. We are protected by His power, and blessed in
His love. Golden chains secure the precious stones,
so that none can ever be lost. Christ will present us
unblamable unto the Father, and the Lord will perfect that which concerneth us, for we are the work of
His hands.

As Christ keeps us in His loving heart and hand,
He sustains us during our time of temptation by His
sympathy. But let us remember when we speak of
Christ's sympathy, that we are speaking of the holy
and perfect One. Sympathy is not indulgence; it is
not a secret tendency towards the sinner's feeling,
that God's law is too strict, and that His trials are
too severe. The High Priest, who can be touched
with a feeling of our infirmities, was tempted in all
points as we are, yet without sin. His sinlessness is

the basis of His perfect sympathy. He sympathises with us against sin, not with sin against our true self. He desires for us a complete victory, that we may pass unscathed and uninjured out of Satan's assaults. When temptation appears pleasant, Christ cannot sympathise; but when we loathe it, and when we offer to it our strong resistance. Temptation, when felt as a burden, secures to us immediately the sympathy and aid of our Saviour. When you say, Sin is hateful to me, then you are following in the experience of Christ; and when struggling against the world, Satan, and evil, you feel the difficulty and the hardship of the conflict, Christ's unbounded and tender sympathy is with you. Christ can have no sympathy with mortified pride and wounded vanity, with impatience and irritated restlessness, with doubt and waywardness, with sorrow that seeks not consolation in God, with the temper which waits not on divine guidance. Christ was without sin, always honouring, trusting, and obeying the Father.

But the Saviour suffered when He was tempted. He felt the weakness of the flesh, the pangs of hunger, the sorrows of ingratitude and evil, the burden of all human infirmities and sicknesses. His temptations were so exquisitely keen, because He never yielded, but stood erect, bearing the whole burden. In all His weariness, in all His painful disappointments, in all heart-rending experiences of His life; when He wept over Jerusalem, when He agonised in the garden, and during the long six hours of the cross

—Jesus suffered and was tempted as we are. None as He suffered and endured temptation, because He yielded not.

When He was tempted by Satan, when the adversary exhausted all the resources of his might and cunning, when he had appealed to Christ's deepest affection — His Sonship; to His firmest faith, the written word; to His most ardent desire, the possession of the world; when afterwards he tempted Him through Israel, now welcoming, now threatening Him; when he attacked Him even through His trusted apostle Peter, and that in the most solemn and blessed hour of his confession; and when, finally, he tested the Son of Man with all the dread and awful power and darkness of his hour — Jesus suffered. Only Christ's purity, fervour, devotedness to God, could evoke such malice and strength of the enemy. In that He yielded not, His suffering was perfect.

This is Jesus, the Lord, whose sympathy is with us, to cleanse us from all sin, and to deliver us from all evil. As His tenderness is infinite, so His standard of our victory over temptation is perfect.

As Jesus died for our safety and protects us by His loving sympathy and faithful intercession, so He effects His gracious purpose by the Holy Spirit. Unless Christ was constantly praying for us, our faith would fail. By the constant supply of the Spirit we are kept abiding in the living vine. The Holy Ghost seals and preserves us unto the purchased redemption. The Spirit of Him that raised up Christ from the dead dwells in us, and by this indwelling Spirit shall our mortal bodies be quickened. Body, soul, and spirit are preserved unto that day in Christ by the Holy Ghost.

Christ and the Spirit are the Father's gift. Of Him are we in Christ, and He sent the Spirit of His Son into our hearts. Our safety is thus in the ever-blessed triune God; in that Name, revealed and sealed unto us in our baptism; in that kingdom of which Christ in the Spirit is king, to the glory of the Father; in that will, which through the cross of Jesus is revealed a will of love, holiness, and power. God only is our rock and defence.

Fear not the subtle serpent, dread not the mighty foe; "one little word," as Luther says, "can fell him." *Look to Jesus!*

16

THE LAST PETITION

"But deliver us from evil."

WHAT wonderful pictures are presented in the Lord's Prayer to the eye of an enlightened understanding ! Here we behold infinite heights, bright as glory, peaceful as love, immovable in strength, from which cometh down every good and perfect gift: Our Father which art in Heaven. Here we see a sanctuary of true and spiritual worship, filled with the revelation of God: Hallowed be Thy name. Here we see the Son of Man crowned with many crowns, the citadel and bulwarks of Zion, the throne of David : Thy kingdom come. Here we behold the hosts of angels and glorified saints above; Israel and the nations below united in loving obedience of God : Thy will be done on earth as it is in heaven. Here we see corn-fields and vineyards, the open hand of God satisfying the desire of His children, manna from heaven, the barrel of meal and cruse of oil, never exhausted: Give us this day our daily bread. Here we see a fountain cleansing the defiled, and springing up within them as a fountain of mercy and forbearance: Forgive us our trespasses as we forgive them that trespass against us. Here we see labyrinthine mazes, pitfalls, snares, precipices; a subtle fowler, an angry lion, and a people blind and weak, carried through by an Invisible Hand: And lead us not into temptation. And here we see at last, death, sorrow, and crying pass away, Satan bruised under our feet, and eternal glory brought in: But deliver us from evil.

The last petition is not least as to importance and extent of meaning. At first sight it seems as if every one was prepared to ask for deliverance from evil; but a little reflection will show that only the believer knows and hates evil, even as he alone knows and desires what is good; for evil is everything that disturbs our communion with God, and nothing is evil that is compatible with peace and joy in Christ.

The petition stands last, because all previous petitions are summed up in it. We appear before God, and call Him our Father in Heaven; in a child-like and reverential spirit we ask God to give us Himself, to enrich us on earth with divine blessings, to reveal to us His name, to bring to us His kingdom, to work within us His will, to be to us Father, Son, and Holy Ghost. We then ask God to look on our earthly condition, to supply our want and to forgive our sin, and to guard us from danger. But though delivered from care in the present, from the burden of the past and from fear for the future, there remains still evil around us, and evil within us, and we desire to be delivered from it, and long after the glorious liberty of the children of God. Bread, pardon, security, are not sufficient ; we long after perfection, after holiness and glory. We ask to be delivered from all that interrupts and clouds our fellowship with God. And we long for that inheritance which is incorruptible and undefiled and which fadeth not away, where all things around us and within us will be in harmony with truth and love.

We may learn also another lesson from the position assigned by Christ to this petition. The whole Lord's Prayer teaches us to begin from above, to descend from the summit of divine holiness and love to the valley of our need and weakness, and to the depth of sin, temptation, and evil. And this method of the Lord's Prayer is most characteristic of the gospel. The kingdom of Heaven has come nigh unto us. The Son of God has come down to us, bringing with Him the Father's love and the blessings which we need, but which we could never obtain by our own exertion. The gospel is "not a gradual process of working our way upwards by stairs, winding, broken, endless," as men often and fruitlessly attempt, without even seeing the end they are aiming at ; but a revelation of perfection, the Son of God descending from Heaven, the epiphany of the grace of God bringing salvation and the treasury of all things pertaining to life and godliness. We are to start with the knowledge of God the Father, Son, and Holy Ghost, and in the peaceful light of Heaven and redemption are we to view the wants, and sins, and temptations, and evil of earth.

Like all other petitions which Christ teaches, He himself offers it to the Father on behalf of His people: " I pray not that Thou shouldest take them out of the world, but that Thou shouldest keep them from the evil."

I. Evil is around us and within us. The evil that is around us may by God's grace be converted into a channel of blessing, and thus belong to the " all things which work in harmony for good;" and yet let us not forget that from this external evil also we ask to be delivered. Sickness, poverty, affliction, cannot separate us from the love of God, which is in Christ Jesus ; we must, and if we seek God's grace, can bear them patiently and even cheerfully. But let us not forget that all misery is the consequence of sin, and as such evil, which God regards with displeasure, and from which it is His purpose ultimately to deliver. Where is the mind of God clearly revealed but in Christ ? When Christ is brought into contact with disease, with the palsied, the lepers, the blind—He *healed* them. When He beheld the hungry He gave them food. When He stood before death, He attacked death as an enemy, girding Himself with a warrior's wrath, and overcame the mighty foe. He met poverty, sickness, and death, not with the assurance that these evils are channels of blessing (which is undoubtedly true), but He teaches us the greater lesson, that God takes no pleasure in evil; that sin has introduced it; that God is full of power and love; and that His will is to destroy evil. Nay, Jesus connects evil, not merely with sin, but with the evil one: " Ought not this woman, being a daughter of Abraham, whom Satan hath bound, lo, these eighteen years, be loosed from this bond ?" Such are His words concerning the woman which was bowed together and could in nowise lift up herself. In like manner He rebukes the storm as a hostile power.

The Jews were promised temporal prosperity for their obedience, and threatened with temporal calamities in case of disobedience. The godly ones among them understood the meaning of suffering, the character of divine chastisement, the joy of the soul in the midst of sorrow and trial. Not for a single moment can we forget that the religion of Abraham, Moses, David was as truly spiritual and heavenly as that of Paul and Peter: " Whom have I in the heavens but Thee, and there is none upon earth that I desire beside Thee." Why then was temporal prosperity so linked to obedience in the Books of Moses ? Doubtless to impress upon Israel that God delights in giving prosperity; that famine, poverty, and disease are consequences of sin; and that, when righteousness dwelleth in the earth, evil shall be banished.

We feel humbled in every affliction; not that we regard it as sent to us judicially, but every sensitive Christian is reminded by it of sin within him and around him. The Christian humbles himself in any national calamity, for he, like Daniel, confesses with contrition the sins of the nation.

We look forward also to the time when there shall be no evil on the earth, no cruelty and oppression, no disease brought on by transgression of God's law, moral and physical, no abject poverty and destitution, engendered by selfishness on one side, and indolence and improvidence on the other; no war and bloodshed through ambition or avarice. We look forward to the time when this righteousness, which is primarily God's righteousness through Christ Jesus the Saviour, shall manifest itself in moral rectitude, and even in the external condition of the earth, and of all creation; when Satan shall be banished into the abyss, and when the very creature, which now groans, shall feel the exhilarating and ennobling influence of holiness triumphant.

And as we thus look forward to that time, so in the spirit of this petition we ought to meet evil, not merely with pity and sighs, and comforting assurances of Divine Providence overruling all, but with the mind and purpose and energy of a *conqueror;* dissipating ignorance, healing the sick, helping the poor, driving out devils. The Church of Christ has in all ages more or less converted the prayer " deliver us from evil " into works of benevolence and charity, into warfare with the miseries of earth.

There is evil in the world. And the world is in the evil one. God declares it is a vale of tears, and the apostle describes it as "this present evil world," from which Christ, by His death, hath delivered us. It is "evil" in its character and spirit, in its habits and methods, in its aim and standard. It is not a Christian world. The Christians are strangers, sometimes persecuted, at all times only tolerated; the kingdoms of the earth are not at present the kingdom of God and of His anointed, but ruled by the god of this world. The Christian is in Babel, and often he cannot sing the song of Zion in a strange land; he is compassed with enemies, with difficulties.

Yet these "evils" are changed into good. Wood in the fire is consumed, gold in the fire is purified. The trial of our faith will be found unto praise and glory at the appearing of our Saviour. The sufferings of David and of Paul are not regarded by them now as "evil." Whence would have come David's Psalms and Paul's Epistles without them? And how can that be regarded as evil which serves to conform us to the image of Christ, and forms a bond both of similarity and sympathy between the Lord and His people? As captivity itself is led captive, so evil itself is made subservient to good and glory.

The consequences of sin are recognised by all as evil; not so sin itself. The law of God is necessary to make us see sin exceedingly sinful. The cross of Jesus Christ is necessary to reveal to us the depth of guilt and pollution. The believer is astonished at his sins, their number, their ubiquity, their insidiousness, their tenacity. And he feels the burden of sins which are known only to himself: "I hate vain thoughts."

While thus mourning over sins, we learn that we have not merely sins, but sin; that there is a fountain within us which sendeth forth bitter streams, that evil thoughts proceed out of the heart. Sin *dwells* in us, it is not a visitor but an inmate. "When I would do good evil is present with me." It is not merely an inmate, but a bold, ever-watchful, persistently-interfering *enemy*. "I see another law striving in my members." It is not merely an enemy, but it has established itself in adaptation to my organisation, mental and physical, and through long habit become a *law,* working almost unconsciously, and with a regularity and force which are appalling. No wonder the believer exclaims "Deliver us from evil!"

And it is when we thus view the evil around us, connected with the evil within us, that we see its exceeding depth and breadth. When David confesses his sin, he views it in connexion with the sinfulness of the human race, with that evil which he inherited from his parents, with that depravity which, since the fall, characterises man; not in extenuation of his guilt, but in acknowledgment of the depth and helplessness of his sinful condition.

Evil within us, evil around us, complicated and multiform as it is, has a central unity. It may be viewed as one—"*the* evil." Numerous as are our enemies, they are under the direction of one great adversary. Death is the culminating point of evil, and he who has the power of death is the devil. No doubt the Saviour thought of this great enemy when He taught us this petition. Nor can we wonder why Satan is not mentioned by name. It would be against the holy calmness of the Lord's Prayer. As in the petition " Lead us not into temptation," we look away from Satan to that only God and Guide whom even Satan must serve, so here, also, we are altogether absorbed in the thought of divine sovereignty, love, and power, which will deliver us from evil. Thus shall that great ambition of Satan finally end in his name and remembrance being blotted out in the realm of God and His children.

II. But who delivers? The evil is so great, so deep, so wide-spread, that none can deliver but God. Our Father, who loves us; our Father, who is in heaven; whose power is infinite; whose glory is above all: He is willing, He is able. Here are the hills to which we lift up our eyes, imploring help.

But how does God deliver us? He delivers *in Christ*. We have seen Christ in every sentence of the Lord's Prayer. Christ, the Revealer of God's name; Christ, the King anointed by the Father; Christ, the second Adam, who quickens us by His Spirit renewing our will; Christ, the gift of God, giving bread; Christ, the gift of God, forgiving sin; Christ, the safety and sympathy of the tempted. Christ is also the deliverer from evil. " Deliver him

from going down into the pit, *I have found a ransom.*"
Who delivers the true Israel from all evil? Who
else but the Angel, the Messenger of the Covenant.

See how the prince of the world is judged! see how
evil is conquered!

Satan's aim was to obscure the glory of God, and
to frustrate His purpose of love through the fall of
man. God's glory is the ultimate object—both of
God to reveal it, and of the enemy to obscure it.
Earth is the battle-field; man the chosen centre both
of God's wonderful plan and of Satan's design.

Sin entered, and with sin misery and death. And
the root being poisoned, the branches of the whole
tree are corrupt. The very blessing of God, " Be
fruitful and multiply," becomes, through the introduction of sin, the triumph of Satan. And when he
beheld the fall of our parents, he thought he saw
only the commencement of sin, evil, death, progress-
ing with increasing intensity and accelerating force,
a course which no power could stop, and which no
remedy could heal. Wherever he sees the children
of Adam, he thinks his triumph secure. Flesh and
blood, the carnal mind, is enmity against God. It
is there that Satan holds his easy sway.

What, then, must his astonishment have been when
one day there sounded forth the glorious and awful
message, " The Word was made *flesh;* " when the
Child was born, the Son was given, whose name is
the mighty God; when, one with us, and yet not
connected with the poisoned root, the Son of man,

and yet not Adam's sinful child, Jesus was born of
the Virgin Mary, Jesus conceived of the Holy Ghost,
the Son of the Most High, and yet partaker of flesh
and blood !

Satan was vanquished. God had come down to
deliver us from evil. And yet Satan did not give
up hope. The very fact that the Son of God was
now in the likeness of sinful flesh, in the weakness of
our nature, gave him new thoughts of victory. First
he instigated Herod to murder the child; and, when
violence was of no avail, he tempted the Son of man
in the wilderness. But though Jesus had come into
the midst, the very heart of evil, no evil could
ever enter into the heart of Jesus. And thus, in the
midst of this evil world, He lived, He loved; bringing blessing and healing wherever He went, attack-
ing Satan and evil, delivering men from sin and fear,
from bondage, and heart-consuming grief, from the
possession of devils, and from the darkness of the
grave. He, the Son of Man, showed His supremacy
given Him by the Father on earth. In our nature,
in flesh and blood, in the position of a servant,
humble, obedient, submissive, the Son of God
destroyed the works of the devil, declared him with
word and deed, and by His very presence, as the adversary of God, the usurper ; judged him, bound
him hand and foot, and announced the kingdom of
heaven come nigh unto us.

He, the Son of man, was Lord, Lord of the human
heart, whose secrets He alone can understand, and

whose longings He alone can satisfy. Lord over disease and over the storm of the sea, He rebukes fever and tempest—the enemy vanishes. Lord over death, for He is the resurrection and the life. And as He asserts that He is Lord, as Son of man, so he gives unto all poor and needy souls the blessed assurance of victory over Satan. He came to be the Head of the body, the Church, to be the second Adam of an innumerable multitude, to raise us so entirely out of the region of darkness into that region of Sonship, of union with Himself, of the Father's love and delight resting upon us, who are one with Him. He brings us unto glory. But how? Evil must be removed; sin, guilt, darkness, God's anger, the condemnation of the law, the claim and power of Satan. The very incarnation of the Son of God was a death-blow to Satan and the realm of evil; and every manifestation of the Son of man was a binding of the strong one. But Christ must enter into the very stronghold and centre of evil.

Surely He hath borne our griefs and carried our sorrow. God laid upon Him the iniquity of us all. He tasted the bitterness of death; He bore the guilt of sin — fear and sorrow, anguish and woe bodily and spiritual, darkness from above, darkness from beneath. The Father forsook Him; the sin of His people clave to Him. Behold the Lamb of God —bruised, bleeding, laden with the appalling load —going into the wilderness, into a very far land! But He has come back again, in life, in peace, in joy, in glory, without sin; for when He was delivered for our offences, He delivered us from evil. Present Christ, who was crucified, yea, rather who is risen again, to the Father when you offer this petition.

Offer it constantly; for though the victory is secure, evil is present, aggressive, deceptive. Offer it in liberty, and with thanksgiving. Though you say, " Oh, wretched man that I am!" you can praise God through Jesus Christ, and you are persuaded that nothing can separate you from the love of God. Pray it, above all, in sympathy with the Lord Jesus. His great object in delivering you from evil was God's glory, the manifestation of God through and in His ransomed people. Let this be your aim, and thus, as in a circle, the last petition leads back to the first, " Hallowed be Thy name;" and the whole prayer ends in the ascription of praise, " For Thine is the kingdom, and the power, and the glory."

The aged patriarch, Jacob, at the end of his pilgrimage, of which his own testimony was, " Few and evil have been the days of the years of my life," was blessing his grandchildren. He had passed through many sorrows, hardships, disappointments. But he could say, " The Messenger of God, the mysterious One, who condescends, who visits, who becomes visible; He who is equal to the Most High, and yet near us; a man, and yet one in whom I behold the face of God; the Angel which delivered me from all evil, bless the lads." God had redeemed Jacob from all evil. When Jacob fled from home, on account of his sinful yielding to deception, God met him in forgiving love and with gracious blessing at Bethel. God guided him during his sojourn of twenty-one years at Padan-aram. God delivered him afterwards from his brother Esau, who, instead of meeting him as an enemy, fell on his neck and kissed him. It was then that the Angel of the Covenant, even the Son of God, appeared unto him; and at Peniel Jacob became Israel. God sustained him after that amid the heartrending trials in his family, and brought him out of famine and sorrow into Egypt, to see his son Joseph, and to bless the sons of Joseph. It was a word full of meaning, very deep, very touching, when Jacob spoke on his death-bed of the Angel which redeemed him from all evil. Blessed retrospect, when Christ is beheld as the Redeemer! And while he implored the same blessing of the redeeming Angel to rest on the lads just beginning the perilous journey, he was looking forward to that perfect salvation for which he had so long waited.*

Compare with this the last testimony of a son of Jacob's favourite child, Benjamin. It is uttered not on a peaceful bed, surrounded by affectionate children. He is in bonds and lonely. "For Demas hath forsaken me, having loved this present world, and is departed unto Thessalonica; Crescens unto Galatia; Titus unto Dalmatia; only Luke is with me." At his first trial before the cruel enemy no man stood by him, but he was able to say, "The Lord stood with

---

* Gen. xlix. 18; xlviii. 16.

me, and strengthened me." And looking forward unto his near departure, he adds, " The Lord shall deliver me from every evil work, and will preserve me unto His heavenly kingdom."

Jacob and Paul experienced the answer of the petition, " Deliver us from evil."

III. Let us look, in conclusion, at the promise involved in the petition.

At the appearing of Christ our life shall be made manifest, our salvation shall be revealed, our adoption, even the redemption of the body, shall be complete. Blessed and peaceful as is our condition immediately after death, only when Jesus comes again shall we receive the crown of righteousness and the perfect glory.

More beautiful than the garden of Eden is our inheritance. The one the gift of Divine Goodness, the other the gift of His abundant mercy; the one created by Omnipotence, the other purchased with the blood of Christ; the one soon converted into a battle-field, where the tempter gained the victory, the other inhabited by Christ, and those who, through His resurrection, were begotten again by the Holy Ghost. This inheritance is incorruptible; for here is the gold of perfect righteousness; it is undefiled; for whiter than snow are the garments washed in the blood of the Lamb; it fadeth not away; Christ and Christ's saints have the dew of their youth. Here all tears are wiped away from our eyes by the hand of

God. The voice that was heard in Ramah, lamentation and bitter weeping, Rachel weeping over her children, and refusing to be comforted, is now full of joy, for behold " her children have come again to their own border." Suffering and affliction have left no trace on their countenance, except in beautifying them with a peculiar likeness to Jesus, such as no angels possess. And even the sins and falls, the evil through which grace has brought them, have left nought behind but a deeper and more fervent humility and joy in the love of God.

They are the children of the resurrection. Theirs is glory, such as mere unfallen creatures cannot possess. The incarnation of the Son of God, the atonement of the cross, the resurrection of the First-born, the indwelling of the Holy Ghost, the gift of Christ and the gift of the Spirit, have brought unto them the adoption of children, and made them joint-heirs with Christ Jesus. Sin is remembered no longer, except as magnifying the grace of God. The mystery of evil is solved unto them : * sinners saved by

---

* That Scripture teaches, both in many isolated passages, and by its whole tenor, that punishment is endless, as contrasted with the endless glory of saints, seems to be the impression of the simple reader, as well as of the most candid and learned critics. (Comp., among many others, Meyer, Kommentar, i. 529 ; Güder, in Herzoz Real. Enc. vi. 185.) Though held by men of so eminent piety and erudition as Bengel, there is, as Delitzsch says, " no doctrine contradicting Scripture in a less defensible manner," than the doctrine of the restitution of all things, while it is beset with many metaphysical and doctrinal difficulties, whether the problem is viewed from the theological or anthropological side. Bengel himself confesses

grace, that in the ages to come He might show the exceeding riches of His grace in His kindness towards them through Christ Jesus.

Is evil near us, around, within, beneath us? Look unto Jesus, and even in the valley of the shadow of death you will fear no evil. The Angel of the Covenant, who has redeemed you from all evil, will bless you, and bring you safely through all trials and sufferings to your everlasting home, to " our Father in heaven."

(*Süddeutsche Originalien*, p. 24), that this doctrine ought not to be preached, as it would produce most pernicious results. (Why, if it was true? and with what right can revealed truth be kept back?) Against the theory of annihilation we think Scripture is equally clear. For instance, in Matt. x. 28 (comp. with Luke xii. 5), Christ contr sts the destruction of the body (ἀποκτεῖναι) with the perishing of the soul (ἀπολέσαι) or being cast into hell.

17

THE DOXOLOGY

"For thine is the kingdom, and the power, and the glory, for ever."

THE doxology is wanting in the most ancient manuscripts, and yet it seems to have been used very early in the Church ; and as it occurs also in one of the oldest versions, some have thought that it must have been originally given by the Lord himself.

Such a conclusion does indeed lie in the heart of every true worshipper ; and after descending from the heavenly heights to our earthly wants and woes, we long to return, before we say "Amen," to the contemplation of God and His perfection. We could not conclude with the word "evil;" we wish to return to the sunshine of the first three petitions—Thy name, Thy kingdom, Thy will.

Whether the Lord uttered the words on this occasion, or some other, or not at all, they are a true echo as well as a real conclusion of the prayer. We do not regard the Lord's Prayer as primarily a form, but a model,—form, indeed, in the sense of outline, to be filled up as the Spirit teaches us. What if the Lord had purposely left to us, as it were, a little blank space to fill up with the response, the doxology and Amen ?   His Church, guided by the Spirit, has responded: For Thine is the kingdom, and the power, and the glory.   Amen.*

I. We take, first, A SEVENFOLD VIEW OF PRAISE.

1. Prayer ends in praise; but God, who sees the end from the beginning, sees *praise in every petition.* The keynote of every prayer is the ascription of glory to God; for all prayer is an appeal to divine love and power.   Is not God's glory revealed in His mercy ? do not all His attributes shine forth in our salvation ?   When we pray, Guide us, we magnify God's wisdom; when we implore pardon, we exalt His mercy ; when we ask deliverance, we extol His strength.   There is a doxology even in the first sup- plication of the penitent, " God be merciful to me the sinner ;" though it is inaudible to the poor and needy one, who cries out of the depths, it ascends to the ear of the Lord of Hosts, amid all the hallelujahs of blessed angels and glorified saints.   Praise is God's temple, as it is written, " He inhabiteth the praises of Israel ;" God has two heavens,—one above, and the other in broken and contrite hearts.   Out of the mouth of babes, in the first feeble accents of the newly- roused conscience, the newly-touched heart, God has ordained praise to Himself.

---

* This was the last utterance of William Burns in the comfort- less little inn of New-Chwang. What a noble conclusion of his apostolic life !

2. Praise is the language of the soul in communion with God. The spirit of man, vitalised by
the Holy Ghost, stands on his high watchtower, and
rejoicing in God the Saviour, calls upon the soul to
magnify the Lord, and upon all that is within to
bless His holy name. All our thoughts of God, all
meditation on His character and work, all new dis-
coveries in His Word, lead to praise. Thus we find in
the Epistles of Paul, that the contemplation of deep
and high mysteries filled the soul of the apostle with
adoration, and out of the abundance of his heart the
utterance of praise bursts forth in such words as
these, "Who is over all, God blessed for ever. Oh the
depth of the riches both of the wisdom and knowledge of God! How unsearchable are His judgments, and His ways past finding out. For of Him,
and through Him, and to Him, are all things!"

3. Though praise is essentially contained in
every supplication and all meditation, and the whole
inner life of the Christian is in constant adoration,
we may regard praise as the *culminating point of
prayer*. The apostle exhorts us to connect thanksgiving with prayer and supplication. And after we
have poured out our heart before God, and brought
before Him our desires, confessing our wants, we cannot but praise Him, not for His gifts only, but for
what He is in Himself. Prayer is crowned in praise.
Prayer finds its Sabbath in praise. The Book of
Psalms concludes with hymns of praise—and when
the prayers of God's beloved children are ended, the

never-ending song of praise will commence. For what is it that we seek by prayer, except the renewed assurance that the Lord is our God ; and finding again that He is good, and that His mercy endureth for ever, we rest in peaceful joy, extolling His great and holy name.

4. Let us learn, too, that the doxology is an argument. We say, " *For* Thine is the kingdom, and the power, and the glory." We expect to be heard, not on account of anything in ourselves, not because of what we are or promise to be, but our sure and only hope is in God, His character, His name, His promise. Not even our faith or our helplessness is our plea, but His own kingdom, power, and glory. With that little word " for " we plant our foot, as it were, on the step of His throne,[*] and remind the Lord that in Himself we seek the foundation for our hopes and expectations. Thus Moses, when he made intercession for the sinful and rebellious people, could find no other argument than this, " For Thine own great name." Daniel's plea was, " For Thine own sake, O my God ! "[†]

When the glory of God and our salvation, when the character of God and our blessedness, when the promise of God and the supply of all our need, are so intimately and inseparably connected, praise is not merely the efflorescence, but the very root, not merely

---

[*] Claus Harms.

[†] How remarkable was the prayer of Martin Luther, overheard by a friend at the diet of Worms.

the copestone, but the very foundation of prayer. For praise is nothing else but faith contemplating and appropriating God. He that cometh to God must believe, or, in other words, magnify God.

5. Praise is faith, and it is more than faith. It stands on the borderland—very bright, indeed; for faith itself is in light—between faith and vision, between earth and heaven. *It is an anticipation of the perfect rest and joy reserved for us.* As Jesus at the grave of Lazarus, anticipating the Father's answer, said, "I thank thee," while Lazarus was still in the bonds of death, we also, lifted above our present wants and sorrows, even above the inward conflicts and distresses of the soul, lose ourselves in God and rejoice in Him, our sure portion and exceeding great reward. It is God who fills our heart with wonder and joy. The Song of Solomon and the Book of Revelation are full of praise. In both we read so much about the Lord himself, His glory and beauty. The saints in heaven and the angels are represented in the crowning Book of Scripture as continually ascribing praise to the Father and to the Lamb. Imperfect as must be our ideas of celestial praise, we can easily understand that it employs intellect as well as feeling, that it is a many-stringed harp, that it is an ever-new song, and that it expresses itself in constant service; and as Peter said on the Mount of Transfiguration, " It is good to be here," we say, " It is a good thing to give thanks unto the Lord, and to praise His name."

6. *The great bond of union is praise.* It is the bond between man and man, between man and angel. For is not praise acknowledging that God is the centre, that His glory is to be sought, that He is the Sun whose light is our joy and whose influence is our strength? The secret of all discord is that men have gone astray, each looking to his own way, seeking their own glory. But when God is praised, self is destroyed, love begins to reign.

Self may come in various disguises, some of them sacred. It may be a form of doctrine, valuable in itself, which becomes a wall of separation between God's children. There may be a want of sympathy between the more advanced and the less instructed Christians. But all Christians understand what is meant by Hosannah, Hallelujah, Worthy is the Lamb; and in proportion as we praise, that is, think of God and Christ, we feel united. Take up a good collection of hymns, there you find the true union of believers. How peacefully Wesley's and Toplady's hymns stand together! How readily do we avail ourselves of the fervent language of Bernard of Clairvaux! High above all imperfections and errors, above the earth-born darkness and mist, is the song of thanksgiving and praise, offered by the humble and rejoicing believer to the Father and Christ. For praise is spiritually what song is outwardly. A multitude cannot easily speak together clearly and sweetly unless they sing, and men, it seems, cannot think and feel together unless they praise.

Praise binds us to the angels. In love they descend to us, in praise we ascend with them to God's throne.

Lastly, Praise is God's gift. The first song is after redemption. After God had delivered Israel from Egypt and brought them through the Red Sea, they sang a song of praise. And as praise is born of redemption, it is the work of God's Spirit. He who delivers us puts a new song into our mouth. And more wonderful than this, Christ himself, our risen and glorified Saviour, is the chief singer ; as it is written, " I will declare Thy name unto my brethren, in the midst of the Church will I sing praise unto Thee."

How precious is praise !—the gift of the Triune God, the flower of redemption, the breath of the Spirit, the voice of Jesus in the Church ! By the Spirit Jesus is in the midst of us, and He presents our praise to the Father, from whom it originally descended into our hearts.

We have thus seen praise in a sevenfold aspect: the hidden soul of prayer, the undercurrent of all communion with God, the culminating point, and the argument of all petitions, the anticipation of heaven, the bond of union between men and angels, and the gift of the Triune God.

II. Consider the threefold ascription of praise.

1. " Thine is the kingdom." It is not ours ; it is altogether His. He prepared it from all eternity. He

founded it on a sure foundation. He made His own Son the king. He has surrounded it with walls—salvation, and made the gates thereof praise. He protects and defends it against all enemies. He assigns to each of His servants a place and a work, distributing His gifts according to His own good pleasure. We may therefore rest in peace, and commit ourselves and our work in humble confidence to our great King.

The kingdom is God's. Though we read of the kingdom of darkness, strictly speaking there are not two kings and two kingdoms; there is but one God and Lord, even the God and Father of our Lord Jesus Christ; His is *the* kingdom. God's enemies are a mass, not a body; a crowd, not an organism; a collection of individuals, not a flock guided by a shepherd. There are at present many things that offend in this kingdom, but they will be cast out; there are tares and weeds, but they will be gathered and burnt; there are rebels, but they will be banished from His presence. The kingdom is the Lord's. In nature, in providence, in grace, He is sovereign; and there is a kingdom of glory, which He is preparing through these subordinate kingdoms. "The earth is the Lord's, and the fulness thereof, the world and they that dwell therein." "The Lord reigneth."

It is this light which shines in Scripture, and which explains to us that history has a meaning and an aim. We wait for the kingdom of the Son of man, and of the saints of the Most High. The kingdom of

God is over all, and God's children, watching the signs of the times, lift up their heads, for their redemption draweth nigh. They know also that He overrules all things for His glory and their good, and that all powers and influences in His vast kingdom, from the ministry of the angels down to the fall of the sparrow, are obeying His perfect and loving will.

2. As the kingdom is His, so power belongeth unto the Lord. He is able to do all things which please Him. The thought of infinite power would have in it something overwhelming and crushing, if all divine attributes did not coexist in perfect harmony, if might were not inseparably linked to wisdom, and mercy, and holiness. And how sweet is the thought, that the greatest manifestation of divine power is Christ, and Christ crucified, the Lamb of God that taketh away the sin of the world! Christ is the Word of His power. By Him all things were created, and by Him they are upheld. The power of God is manifested through His Son.

When we thus see the strong hand of the Lord and His outstretched arm in redemption, when we remember that all power in heaven and earth is given now to the man Christ Jesus, we can contemplate Omnipotence with joy, though not without awe.

Is anything too hard for the Lord? When we think of the miracle of the incarnation, when we think of the resurrection of Christ, what miracle of divine power and love can be incredible? What

future event predicted surpasses in wonder the former
mighty acts of God ?   His is *the* power—all power.
All forces and energies, however opposed to Him, are
His ; and, after many circuitous roads of their own
perverse choice, they must at last bow down before
Him.   Pharaoh, Cæsar, Satan himself; all kingdoms must serve the coming of God's kingdom.
The star shines forth to lead the wise men from the
East to Israel's King ; when the Messiah suffers,
the sun becomes dark, the rocks are rent, the earth
trembles ; and when He comes again, all heaven and
earth shall be filled with wonders and signs.

His is the power ; great things become small, and
little things become great when He wills it.   He can
send twelve legions of angels as easily as commission
the ravens to fly across the hills and bring food to His
servant.   The decree of Cæsar Augustus for all the
world to be taxed has its true reason in the ancient
prediction of Micah and the Babe of Bethlehem.
Herod's cruel designs of murder are frustrated by
the angel appearing unto Joseph in a dream.   God
has paths invisible ; His step is so gentle that no ear
can perceive it, and His power so great that no might
can resist.

It is God's delight to manifest His power so as to
abase man's pride and to strengthen the faith of the
humble.   " For the day of the Lord of Hosts shall be
upon every one that is proud and lofty, and upon
every one that is lifted up, and upon all the high
mountains, and upon all the cedars of Lebanon, and

upon all the oaks of Bashan, and the Lord alone
shall be exalted in that day." It is when men
triumph and glory in their strength that God shows
forth His power in His weakness. All human
power had combined against Jesus, and done its
utmost: a traitor among His own disciples, the
highest council and authority of the land, Herod
the king, and Pilate the judge, the people of Jerusalem, and the Roman soldiers. And what more
could they do or wish to do than to silence that un-
welcome voice witnessing for the truth, and to banish Him from the land of the living? There He lay
low in the grave, silent and dead; and so anxious
were they to keep Him in His prison, that they
placed a great stone on His sepulchre, and sealed it,
and the soldiers kept watch. Perfect was their triumph
and great their security. Death is the lowest state of
weakness; to be buried out of sight, the greatest
defeat. But the weakness of God was greater than
the power of man. He was buried—but only as a
corn of wheat, to spring up in new glory, and to bring
forth much fruit. Very early in the morning, no
human eye witnessing it, the Father raised His Holy
Child Jesus; and in the power of His resurrection He
is since going on from strength to strength, leading
captive captivity, having the strong for His spoil, and
subduing all things unto Himself.

3. His is the kingdom, and by His power will it be
established, for the end of all divine works and ways
is His glory. Let us not think of God's glory as we

think of our own. Man seeks glory because he is
selfish; but " God is love ;" His glory is the manifestation of Himself ; His glory is to fill heaven and
earth ; it is the blessedness and joy of all His children.
When man seeks glory, he seeks to make himself a
centre, and thereby destroys himself and others ;
when God seeks His own glory, it is because He is
the only centre of life and light.

There is no glory except God's. His is *the* glory.
All other glory is false, empty; nay, the very opposite
of glory—shame and misery.

Glory is brightness, and God is light; whatever
light there is, is the reflection as well as the gift
of the Lord in Christ Jesus. Separated from God,
men, even of the most brilliant genius and the most
richly-stored mind, are in darkness, and, unless they
come to Christ, they will be for ever in utter darkness.
Glory means, in Hebrew, weight, substance. God is
the great reality ; all things are shadowy, vain, mere
outlines, without fulness, unless they are connected
with God and with eternity.

Glory belongs absolutely to the Lord ; and therefore we have confidence in praying to Him ; for His
own glory He will bless, save, sanctify, and glorify
all who call upon His holy name.

III. Let us consider now the kingdom, and the
power, and the glory, *as belonging to the Triune
God.*

The kingdom is the Father's. He has prepared it

from all eternity. Therefore Christ will say, on that day, "Come, ye blessed of my Father, and inherit the kingdom prepared for you from the foundation of the world." But Christ the Son is the King and Heir, and His subjects are all who, by the Spirit, are called and renewed after His image.

As the kingdom belongs to the Father, and Christ, and the Spirit, so the power. Both in the first and second creation, the Father's power is manifested by the Word and Spirit. The renewal of man's heart is the greatest manifestation of power. "The storm can break the oak, the sun can melt ice, fire softens iron, but the heart of man can resist God for a long time." * And though strong is the fire, and strong is the earthquake, yet stronger is the still small voice when the Spirit speaks of the love of Jesus. That gentle touch which opened Lydia's heart is the great power of God.

And once this power is known to us, it takes up its abode in our souls. He is able to do exceeding abundantly above all that we ask, according to the power that worketh in us. And finally, the Spirit will raise up our mortal bodies, and then the work of divine power shall be complete. Thine, Father, Son, and Holy Ghost, is the power.

And the glory belongs to the Triune God. The Father is the Father of Glory. Jesus came to manifest, to glorify the Father. We are to confess that Jesus is the Christ to the glory of the Father ; and

---

* C. Harms.

when we abide in Christ, and bring forth fruit, the Father is glorified.

But the Father hath also glorified His Holy Child Jesus. He hath crowned Him with glory, and highly exalted Him. It is the Father's will that all men should honour the Son as they honour the Father. The Son has entered again into the glory which He had before the foundation of the world was laid. And all angels and saints worship Him, and cry, "Worthy is the Lamb."

And who is it that glorifies Christ and the Father in our hearts? Even that Spirit by whom Jesus glorified the Father, and in whom is the eternal communion between Father and Son.

We say "Thine," and find in this rest and joy. But faith is able to add, "Thine is mine," and faith can add this, because faith takes the *lowest place*, and trusts exclusively in the grace of God.

Faith says, The kingdom is mine, because Jesus said, "Blessed are the *poor in spirit*, for theirs is the kingdom of heaven;" and again, "Fear not, *little flock*, for it is your Father's good pleasure to give you the kingdom."

Faith says, The power is mine, for He maketh the worm Jacob to be Israel, and to prevail. "He giveth power to the faint, and to them that have no might He increaseth strength. Even the youths shall faint, and the young men shall utterly fall: but they that trust in the Lord shall renew their strength; they shall mount up with wings as eagles; they shall run and not be weary; and they shall walk and not faint."

Faith says, The glory is mine, for it is written, "Christ shall come to be glorified in His saints." "When Christ, who is our life, shall appear, then shall ye also appear with Him in glory."

Yet remember it is "mine" simply and solely because it is "Thine." For this is the foundation of all our hope and our joy in time and eternity: "I am the Lord thy God."

Finally, Let us take the best and simplest view of these words by remembering their paternal character.

It is a Father's kingdom into which we have been brought; a Father's power, which is not merely invincible, but tender; a Father's glory, which is fulfilled when Jesus His Son presents us unto Him: "Lo, I and the children whom Thou hast given me."

And thus the doxology leads back to the invocation. The Spirit of His Son cries in us, "Abba, Father."

IV. Dwell now on the word "For ever."

Scripture adduces no proof for the existence of God or of eternity, but rests on the testimony of conscience, and on the longing of the human heart for communion with the infinite God and for eternal life.

For Scripture does not precede or take the place of God's revelation of Himself to man: it is the record of this revelation. God, in His condescending love, and in manifold wisdom, came to His people, manifested Himself, declared His name, showed Himself in mighty acts and wonders, and Scripture narrates the revelation of God. Bringing us into communion with the living, loving God, what need is there to prove His existence, as if He was unknown, distant, quiescent ? narrating to us how His eternal thoughts were unfolded in time, what need to endeavour a definition of eternity ? God appears, and He is seen in His own light. We hear the words of God, we see the acts of the Most High, we breathe the atmosphere of eternity, and we say, " From everlasting to everlasting Thou art God."

As the perfect revelation of God is only in Christ, so in Him is the perfect revelation of eternity. God has brought life and immortality to light in the gospel. Jesus Christ is Alpha and Omega, the first and the last. In Him we are chosen from all eternity. We behold Him with God, the eternal Wisdom, the Word, the chosen Head of the Church, and Heir of all things ; and thus the realm of a past eternity is illumined with a light both clear and peaceful. And we behold Him, who was dead and liveth for evermore, the same for ever ; and believing that we are joint heirs with Him, we look forward to the ages to come, with hope and joyous adoration.

Our position is indeed one of high favour and privilege. For the true light now shineth. But when we ask, What did the patriarchs and prophets know and believe concerning eternal life ? our safest answer will be found by asking, What did they know of God ? For as we know God, so we know eternity.

The knowledge of eternity is spiritual and experimental. As the soul takes hold of God in reverence, trust, and affection, as the soul lives for God's glory and for things which are true and substantial, the soul knows the meaning of "for ever," though much obscurity may envelop the intellectual perception.

And here notice, that the possession of the soul is according to God, the Giver, and not according to man, the receiver. A child is not conscious of the various elements in the character of his parent; but the influence of that character is no less truly exerted on the child. God was dealing with the patriarchs and prophets; and though they understood only in part and dimly, it was the *true* God and the *whole* God who spoke to them, and who manifested Himself to their hearts. When Christ is born within us, it is the true Christ, it is the whole Christ, though as to our perception it is only an infant Christ. And thus we may say, it is not so important *what* we believe as *whom* we believe, for, if we look to God, all truth is virtually ours.

How spiritual were the conceptions of God's ancient servants ! *So spiritual, that they could only have been produced by the revelation of the reality.* And one symptom of their spirituality is, that they combine in practical solution contradictory elements. They knew that God is high above—that the inhabitants of the earth are as grasshoppers before Him, and yet they believed that He is near unto all that call upon Him, and that He will not despise the sighing of the afflicted and contrite. They believed that He had ordained all things according to the counsel of His will, and that His purpose standeth firm for ever, and yet they believed in the power of prayer, and that it will repent Him concerning the evil. They knew that the heaven of heavens cannot contain Him, and yet they rejoiced that He manifested His presence and His glory in the Temple, and that He dwelt in the hearts of the humble. They knew that He was not like man, that His ways and thoughts were heaven-high above us; and yet they did not hesitate to ascribe unto Him fatherly pity, and the affection, tenderness, and jealousy of a husband. They believed that God had revealed Himself unto them and made known His ways unto Moses and His statutes unto Israel, and yet they knew that God was great, unsearchable, that darkness and clouds were round about Him, that His ways are past finding out.

Whence came such thoughts of God? So elevated and grand, without being vague and cold—so reverential and so trustful—so definite and yet so humble—so abstract and yet so practical? God had visited them; they had heard His voice and seen His ways.

They knew Him, whose name is I Am. The eternity of God, the first and the last, who abideth the same for ever, who changeth not—is expressed in a most beautiful manner in the 90th Psalm.

This Psalm bears so distinctly the impress of its

authorship, that even without the superscription we ought to recognise in it the hand and experience of Moses. It seems an epitome of all the characteristics of his life, and of his position in the kingdom of God. The whole Pentateuch is condensed in it. He speaks of God as the Creator of heaven and earth. He speaks of man in his fall, frail as a flower, the heir of death ; he represents death as the penalty of the law, the consequence of sin, the expression of God's holy displeasure. He speaks of God himself revealing to us in His own light the exceeding sinfulness of sin. And he concludes with the gospel— the mercy of Jehovah, the grace which maketh alive those whom He hath killed, and bringeth joy to those who have mourned.

In this Psalm Moses dwells on the eternity of God. God is from everlasting to everlasting. Before the ancient rocks, and amid all the changes of earth and men, He is beyond and above, though also with and in time. A thousand years are but as a day in His sight.

But what is man's relation to this eternity ? So far from it appearing to him a vast and dreary wilderness, or an ocean without shore, this eternal God, and that because He is eternal, is *our home*, our dwelling-place. The flower of the field flourisheth, and then passeth away ; for this is its *nature*. Not so with man. He passeth away, not because of his nature, but because of his *sin*. His death is not an inherent necessity, but a punishment. God's anger is expressed in it ; and this itself is the pledge, that man's destiny and home is eternity ; that God's mercy, taking away sin, will know also how to bring man into the house of God, to dwell there *for evermore.*

" For ever " was the keynote thus struck by Moses. David takes up the same thought (Ps. ciii.) The whole Psalm is full of the grandeur and fragrance of eternity. In the very opening verses we read, that God not merely forgives, but redeems life from destruction, and renews our youth : he praises God for redemption of a forfeited life, for renewal and perennial youth. Then he speaks of God's mercy in outliving His anger, and dwells on the infinity of mercy. The comparisons are very striking, as showing the vast conceptions of David's mind. The height of heaven above earth, who can measure it? Such is His mercy towards them that fear Him. The distance of the east from the west—notice how truly ideal or eternal—so far hath He removed our transgressions from us. This is the length of His love. The pity of a father towards his children is its infinite depth. And then He speaks of man as finite, weak. As for man, his days are as grass, as a flower of the field so he flourisheth. But, he continues, and here is man's infinity—the mercy of the Lord is from everlasting to everlasting upon them that fear Him. He thought of us in eternity, He will be glorified in us throughout eternity. God's eternity was the sweet refuge of God's children.

The grass withereth, the flower fadeth; thus the voice crieth in the wilderness: and in that voice we may hear not merely John the Baptist, but Moses and the prophets. But the word of our God shall stand *for ever*, and this word was their life.

If the ancients knew the connexion between sin and death (revealed as it was to them not merely in doctrine, but continually embodied in the ceremonial law), did they not also know that redemption was connected with resurrection and eternal life?

One thing they knew, and that was sufficient, that Jehovah was their God. They knew and loved Him, they rejoiced in His promise, that His glory should be revealed to the very ends of the earth. Was not this eternal life? And God knew them, God loved them, God called Himself *their* God; and was not this the pledge of eternity?*

Hence Christ's argument in reply to the Sadducees. They knew neither the Scriptures, nor the power of God. They had not experienced *eternal life in time*, therefore they could not see it either in the Scripture or beyond the grave. "Have ye not read in the Book of Moses, how in the bush God spake unto him,

---

* The frequent *direct* references to the doctrine of the resurrection and the future life, contained in the scriptures of Moses and the prophets, are here *purposely* left out of consideration. I cannot refrain from quoting Ewald's testimony to the true meaning of Job xix. 23–29: "What has been demonstrated with stricter cogency, than that Job arrived at last at the eternally-true and necessary faith in immortality (Jahrbücher, ix. 30, comp. also Ewald on Job, 2d edit., p. 198).

saying, I am the God of Abraham, and the God of Isaac, and the God of Jacob.   He is not the God of the dead, but of the living."

The words " for ever " awe us by their majesty and grandeur, but they bring with them peace and rest. Whenever we pray, whenever we enter into the secret place of the Most High, we betake ourselves into eternity and find repose in the infinite power, wisdom, and love of God our Father.

Nor do we view eternity merely as contrasted with time.   The painful feeling of the brevity of life, of the fleeting nature of earth's most precious and beautiful treasures, gives way to a nobler and higher sentiment.   For apart from eternity, as viewed in God the Father and Christ the Redeemer, what influence can such thoughts and melancholy feelings exert on our character ?   The sorrow of the world is selfish, bitter, and without elevating power.   Man, enamoured of himself, like Narcissus, perishes in his very self-admiration and self-lamentation.   Whereas he who ascribes glory to God has found the secret by which things of time become of eternal value and never-fading beauty.   We can eat and drink to the glory of God ; we can combine diligence in business with fervour in spirit ; we can see the pattern of heavenly things in earthly duties and relationships.   We can love and train our children for heaven, and view in a higher light the affections and ties which God the Father has ordained, which Christ the Son has redeemed. thus finding a bond which time cannot weaken or death sever. We see in the beauty of all things around us the symbol of that beauty which will never fade. Nothing is trifling; for all duties imposed by God, all trials permitted and sent by Him, are of eternal importance, and bring with them the presence of God.

We who know the temple of Zion can understand the quarry and the workshop of Lebanon. We do not feel irritated by the din, the harsh sounds, the grating of tools, the complication of the machinery. For we know the stones are prepared here for Zion, for the temple, for heaven, where all is perfect.

We know that a moment may have eternity involved in it. The silent victory gained over sin, the word of truth spoken in faithfulness and love, the intercession for friends and enemies, for saints and the impenitent, is seed—the harvest of which shall be from age to age.

And our very ignorance is no longer an ignorance of darkness; for we know that what we do not understand now we shall see hereafter. There is a height from which all mysteries are solved, all intricate labyrinths understood, all questions answered; and this height is reached when we are with our Father in heaven, when we are in the everlasting kingdom and glory. Then shall we see that all God's dealings were according to that wisdom which knoweth all things and all times, and that love which considereth all her children.

There is one very solemn peculiarity which the present age possesses. It has been the conviction of almost all God's children that in *time* our everlasting destiny is decided; that the to-morrow of eternity is decided by the to-day when we hear His voice. Scripture throughout speaks in this wise. It does not open to us an endless vista of periods, during which sinners are converted and added to the number of God's saints. It never speaks of a renewal of those who have died without faith in God the Saviour. Scripture speaks of an end, a termination, a conclusion. Light and glory above—darkness and torment beneath.

Yet the true penitent is not so much alarmed by the *duration* as by the *nature* of future punishment, —separation from God, the fountain of all light and goodness. The soul, quickened by the Spirit of God, would not delay a moment to drink from the fountain of living water. The believer understands that in hell one moment is as a thousand years, and that in heaven a thousand years are but as a moment.

The believer knows also that life, God's gift in Christ by the Spirit, must be eternal. Even now he is one with Jesus the Son of God. And he waits calmly and patiently; the glory will come peacefully, not with overwhelming, dazzling splendour. We need not dread the darkness of the grave or the brightness of the resurrection glory. Christ is the Morning Star, guiding us now with gentle, hope-inspiring light; and when we shall see Him as He is, we ourselves shall shine forth as the sun; glory will then not only be above and around, but within us, for Christ shall be glorified *in* His saints.

Meanwhile remember that he who has found God and eternity, finds time and strength for every good work which God lays before him.   Even now is he a son of God; he has entered upon that life which never ends; he is possessed of that love which never faileth.

18

AMEN

"Amen."

MARTIN LUTHER said once of the Lord's Prayer, that it was the greatest martyr on earth, because it was used so frequently without thought and feeling, without reverence and faith. This quaint remark, as true as it is sad, applies perhaps with still greater force to the word " Amen."

Familiar to us from our infancy is the sound of this word, which has found a home wherever the nations have learned to adore Israel's God and Saviour. It has been adopted, and without translation retained, in all languages in which the gospel of Jesus the son of David is preached.[*] The literal signification, " So be it," is known to all; yet few consider the deep meaning, the great solemnity, and the abundant consolation treasured up in this word, which has formed for centuries the conclusion of the prayers and praises of God's people.

---

[*] Isa. lxv. 15, " The God Amen." " Here is a prediction that Amen, as is already the case in the Christian Church, will be the very word of the holy language used on earth."—*Stier, Jesaiah,* p. 829.

A word which is frequently used without due thoughtfulness, and unaccompanied with the feeling which it is intended to call forth, loses its power from this very familiarity, and though constantly on our lips, lies bedridden in the dormitory of our soul. But it is a great word this word Amen; and Luther has said truly, " As your Amen is, so has been your prayer."

I. IT IS A WORD OF VENERABLE HISTORY IN ISRAEL AND IN THE CHURCH.

The word dates as far back as the law of Moses. When a solemn oath was pronounced by the priest, the response of the person who was adjured consisted simply of the word " Amen." In like manner the people responded Amen when, from the heights of Ebal and Gerizim, the blessings and the curses of the divine law were pronounced. Again, at the great festival which David made when the ark of God was brought from Obed-Edom, the psalm of praise which Asaph and his brethren sang concluded with the words, " Blessed be the Lord God of Israel for ever and ever. And all the people said, Amen." * Thus we find in the Psalms, not merely that David concludes his psalm of praise with the word Amen, but he says, " And let all the people say, Amen." †

When Ezra gathered the people together and opened the book (even the law) in the sight of all

---

* 1 Chron. xvi. 36.   † Psalm cvi. 48.

the people, and blessed the Lord the great God, all
the people answered Amen with lifting up their
hands.*

And that this usage, so constant in Israel from
the time of Moses, was familiarly known in the apostolic Churches is quite evident from the remarks of
Paul, when he asks, " How, in the case of a person
speaking an unknown tongue, he that occupieth the
room of the unlearned shall be able to say Amen at
thy giving of thanks, seeing he understandeth not
what thou sayest ? "†

Amen was, then, the response of the apostolic con-
gregations to every prayer and praise, and so has it
been in the Churches of Christ, though, I grieve to
say, in some Churches the voice of the congregation
is never heard saying Amen. How different from
the description which a Church father gives, that the
Amens of the congregation were like the waves roll-
ing on the shore !

Remember for how many centuries, in how many
august and solemn assemblies, in the Temple, in the
synagogues, by God's ancient people, by the early
Church, and by almost all the Churches of Christ,
this word Amen has ascended from His worshipping
saints to the Lord our God. And were it only for
this it ought to be a word dear to us, linking us with
all the past generations of the godly, and helping us
to realise the communion of saints, the oneness of
God's family in all ages and climes.

---

* Neh. viii. 5.   † 1 Cor. xiv. 26.

II. The Word Amen announces God's Truth and Faithfulness.

Prayer is a great reality. It is speaking to the living God. The object of prayer is not that we may speak, but that God may hear. Without this faith there is no true prayer. There may be solemn and touching monologue, but prayer is essentially an address directed to God. In the word Amen we have an assurance of God's truth and faithfulness. The character and the promises of God, which form the basis of our supplications, are pillars sure and immovable. Amen assures us we have spoken to Him who is, and who is truth. God lives; faithful is He who hath called. The prophets, who declared the message and promise of God, always introduced the words they were commissioned to utter by declaring, "Thus saith the Lord." And all who received this in faith knew that whatever God had spoken was Amen. And in wonderful condescension God gave us the assurance of His favour in the form of an *oath*. God's truth is so essentially connected with Himself, His holiness and His love are so inseparably connected with the word of His promise, that His covenant is sealed and confirmed by an oath; and seeing there is none above Him, God appeals to Himself.* Zachariah, in the name of all Israel, expresses this

---

* "As I live, saith the Lord, the earth shall be filled with my glory. As I live I have no pleasure in the death of the wicked. The Lord hath sworn, and will not repent; thou art a priest for ever after the order of Melchisedec."

ground of confidence, when he says in his song of praise, " To perform the mercy promised to our fathers, and to remember His holy covenant, *the oath*, which He sware to our father Abraham." And Paul says in his Epistle to the Hebrews, " God willing more abundantly to show unto the heirs of promise the immutability of His counsel, confirmed it by an oath, that by two immutable things, in which it was impossible for God to lie, we might have a strong consolation who have fled for refuge to lay hold upon the hope set before us." The answer to our petition, Amen, is secured to us by all the holy and blessed attributes of a covenant God.

III. AMEN IS THE NAME OF CHRIST.

All the promises of God are Yea and Amen in Christ Jesus. For Christ is the Amen of God. In Him are fulfilled God's thoughts and purposes of peace concerning us, as all our desires and longings towards God find their fulfilment in Him.

Jesus often prefaced His sayings by the solemn words, " Amen, amen, I say unto you." Not like the prophets did He say, " Thus saith the Lord;" for He himself was Jehovah, the Word of God; and therefore revealing His divinity, He said with infinite authority and majesty, " Amen, amen, I say unto you." For He was able to say of Himself, " I am the Truth," not I declare truth, I lead you to truth, I illumine truth—but I am Truth. For He was the revelation of God. And He is the Truth; for all the thoughts and words which have been uttered before imperfectly, in fragments, and separately, are contained in absolute perfection in Him. And He is the Truth in the sense of substance and fulfilment. God's promises are fulfilled in Him. The law was given by Moses; it contained requirements and shadows, the one revealing guilt, the other inspiring hope; but grace and truth came in the person of Jesus Christ. All divine gifts and promises are in Him.

And thus is He the true Amen, revealing to us the God of truth, and the truth of God, speaking with absolute authority and clearness, confirming and fulfilling to us the love and promises of the Father.

Yet in another sense is He the Amen. For not only is the covenant confirmed by the blood of His atonement, but the gifts and blessings of God are secured to us by His intercession, and they are treasured up for us in Him, that out of His fulness we may receive, and grace for grace.

In the Book of Revelation the Lord Jesus Christ says, " These things saith the Amen, the true and faithful Witness, the Beginning of the creation of God." From all eternity He was the Amen of the Father's thought and will—the response and the realisation of the Father's purpose. And as the eternal Amen, the Word equal with the Father, Light of light, He became the Witness, true and faithful. For who but He could testify of things known only

to the blessed Three? It was the Spirit of Christ
which testified in the prophets, and finally the Lord
came into the world to witness of the truth, and to
seal the covenant by His death. And this Witness
is the beginning of the creation, which sprang from
Him as a fountain. Thus He is the channel as well
as the seal and pledge of all divine love and power.

IV. WE VIEW AMEN AS THE SEAL OF PRAYER.

Since Christ is the Amen, the conclusion of the
prayer is as great and weighty as the beginning.
We commence by lifting up our hearts to our Father
in heaven, we conclude by sealing our petitions with
Christ, the Eternal Word. It is as if we said, " for
Christ's sake." And we know that whatsoever we
ask in His name will be granted unto us.

What is meant by praying in Christ's name? It
cannot mean simply mentioning the name of Christ
at the end of our petitions, or appearing before God
with faith in the mediation of the Saviour. When
the disciples asked Jesus to teach them to pray, He
gave them no rules about the manner of prayer, but
He supplied them with petitions. They were not so
much ignorant how to pray, as what to pray for. And
afterwards Jesus said to them, " Hitherto have ye
asked nothing in my name." Until the Spirit came
the seven petitions of the Lord's Prayer lay as it were
dormant within them. When by the Holy Ghost
Christ descended into their hearts, they desired the
very blessings which Christ as our High Priest ob-

tains for us by His prayer from the Father. And such petitions are always answered. The Father is always willing to give what Christ asks. The Spirit of Christ always teaches and influences us to offer up the petitions which Christ ratifies and presents to the Father. To pray in Christ's name is therefore to be identified with Christ as to righteousness, and to be identified with Christ in our desires by the indwelling of the Holy Ghost. *To pray in the Spirit, to pray according to the will of the Father, to pray in Christ's name, are identical expressions.* The Father himself loveth us, and is willing to hear us ; two intercessors, Christ the Advocate above, and the Holy Ghost the Advocate within, are the gifts of His love.

This view may at first appear less consoling than a more prevalent one, which refers prayer in Christ's name chiefly to our trust in Christ's merit. The defect of this opinion is, that it does not combine the intercession of the Saviour with the will of the Father, and the indwelling Spirit's aid in prayer. Nor does it fully realise the mediation of Christ ; for this mediation consists not merely in that for Christ's sake the holy and loving Father is able to regard me and my prayer, but also in that Christ himself presents my petitions as His petitions, desired by Him for me, even as all blessings are purchased for me by His precious blood.

For this reason the Lord's Prayer, given us by Christ, is, in the strictest sense of the word, prayer in Christ's name; by which all other prayers must be judged.

Is, then, the Lord's Prayer a limitation of our petitions? In one sense it certainly is. Petitions which are selfish, which are contrary to God's name, kingdom, and will, are excluded; for God can and will give only good gifts.

But is it exclusive of individual and minute petitions? By no means. All blessings, spiritual and temporal, are included, and whatever our wants and difficulties may be, they are mentioned here. But it is an exercise of the conscience to know what individual wish and desire, connected either with temporal blessings or difficulties on our path, are in harmony with the spirit of this prayer and each petition.

Jesus himself tells his disciples to pray that their flight be not in winter, or on the Sabbath-day; the apostle exhorts us in *everything* by prayer and supplication to make our requests known unto God; and how numerous are the examples of answers vouchsafed by God to the minute petitions of His people? Yet in all prayer the one essential condition is, that we are able to offer it in the name of Jesus, as according to His desire for us, according to the Father's will, according to the Spirit's teaching. And thus, praying in Christ's name is impossible without self-examination, without reflection, without self-denial; in short, without the aid of the Divine Spirit.

But when we do pray in Christ's name, what power

is in Amen ! It is the seal of God. Be our faith ever so feeble, our words imperfect, our desires languid, be the blessings we implore ever so great, Amen covers all defects, and secures all good gifts.

V. AMEN IS THE VOICE OF FAITH.

We must offer up true petitions, but we must offer them up in faith. The promise is, that whatsoever we ask in faith, believing that God will hear us, shall be given us. Our Saviour often lays great stress on this point, and throughout Scripture we see the connexion between faith and the blessings of God. Faith and prayer are not merely inseparably connected, but we may view them almost as identical. Prayer is faith vocal. When we pray, we are to believe that God hears us ; and we express this faith by saying Amen. For, believing God's promises, and praying to God for things He promised, how can we doubt His faithfulness ? If we ask, we shall receive ; if we approach God as suppliants, in humility, without claim or merit of our own, but simply ask, God will give; if we seek with diligence and earnestness, we shall find ; if we knock with persevering importunity, it shall be opened to us.

Our faith is weak, because our view of prayer is not simple and childlike. Prayer is a great reality in God's mind. He does not regard it as a mere form, or as wholesome discipline for our hearts ; but it has pleased Him in His eternal wisdom and love to connect His blessings with the petitions of His children, and He has so ordered it, that our prayers should be a power and an influence, moving His will and directing the course of human life.

God hears prayer. This is the revelation of God's word. The eternal purpose of God has thus fixed it, that prayer is to be the link in the chain, and that the blessing is to wait on our petition. At the beginning of our supplication, as in the case of Daniel, the commandment goes forth from the throne of Heaven. Angels are sent by the Father to minister to the heirs of salvation, but they wait until the cry of need and faith has reached the Hearer of prayer, and then in faithfulness to His promise, He sends deliverance from His high sanctuary.

Blessed assurance, that God is a Father who hears the prayers of His children, who gives because they ask. Blessed condescension of the Eternal, that He will live with us, the children of time, and answer us day by day. Blessed peaceful sunshine, which gladdens every childlike heart. Think not of prayer as a duty, regard it not as a mental and moral discipline, but let your prominent idea be that prayer influences God. Prayer is as much a power or cause as any other law which God has established in nature or history.

If we believed that prayer is a real influence with God, our prayer would be earnest, direct, definite, expectant. It would give concentration to our thoughts and desires. Prayer would not be a reverie, but a transaction. Faith is the life and strength of prayer. The prayers of God's saints recorded in Scripture are prayers of faith. This is their excellence, and for this reason they possess all excellencies. This gave them reverence, simplicity, intense fervour. He who speaks to God has no thought about trifles; he does not mirror himself with complacency in his pious and devout sentences; he may be speaking before men, but he is not speaking at or to them; he is not anxious to express his views, but his feelings; to explain his doctrines, but his wants.

When we say Amen we express our faith in the prevailing power of prayer. God sometimes answers in a way different from what we expect. Instead of removing the difficulty, he increases our strength to overcome it; He gives purity of heart when we ask Him to place the temptation out of sight; He shows us love in what appeared judgment, and sweetness in that which was bitter. Sometimes God gives more than we ask. Solomon asked for wisdom, and God gave him not merely wisdom, but also riches and honour. Again, we may not live to see the answer to our prayer. So Manasseh was brought in repentance to the Lord after Hezekiah's death, and to Stephen's prayer the Church attributed Paul's conversion. God often hears even while we are speaking, and sends help while we are praying. But, however various God's methods are, God hears prayer; and Amen is the voice of faith. All our life we exercise faith, even as Jacob said on his death-bed, "I have waited for my salvation;" and as Simeon only before his departure saw the Amen to his prayers, when he beheld the child Jesus, and took Him in his arms.

All blessings which visit earth are brought down by prayer, and by the faith of prayer, by our Amen. And the constant Amen of the Church, " even so come Lord Jesus, come quickly," will bring down the Lord of glory and the kingdom of blessedness. Faith sees all petitions sealed with Amen. Has not God promised that He will sanctify His name before all nations? therefore His name will be hallowed. Has He not promised to establish His kingdom, and to write His law in our hearts, and put His Spirit within us? There will be one flock and one Shepherd. God has promised to give us food and raiment; He has promised to pardon our iniquity and to receive us graciously; He has promised not to allow us to be tempted above what we are able to bear, and to give with the temptation a door of escape; He has promised to deliver us from all evil, and, finally, to bruise Satan under our feet. We say Amen to every petition, for God, by His promise in Christ, has sealed every petition "Amen." Amen sees the fulfilment of all prayer, the time when we no longer need daily bread and daily pardon, when temptation is past and evil banished, when the true and faithful Amen shall say again, as He said on the cross, " It is finished."

VI. Amen is the Answer of a Good Conscience. Amen is the test and mirror of sincerity. Do we really desire the blessings we ask? Do we ask these blessings in the spirit of the Lord's Prayer? Are we willing to remember and observe the precepts connected with promise and petition? These three questions are answered by the good conscience with Amen. To dwell only on the last test, if we sincerely ask blessings, we shall place ourselves in the true position for receiving them in the way of God's commandments. The precepts connected with "Hallowed be thy name," are—Acquaint thyself with God; search the Scriptures; meditate on these things; consider the great High Priest of our profession, Jesus Christ. The precept connected with "Thy kingdom come" is—Pray for the peace of Jerusalem; pray the Lord to send forth labourers into the harvest; preach or send forth the gospel into all the world. The precept connected with the third petition is—Prove (by experimentally trying it) what is the good and perfect and holy will of God; submit yourself to God; if any man will follow Me let him deny himself and take up the cross; let every one please his neighbour unto edification; seek not high things; present yourself a living sacrifice unto God. The prayer for our daily bread implies many precepts. Work—not slothful in business, providing things honest in the sight of all men. Contentment—having food and raiment, let us therewith be content; beware of covetousness, which is idolatry; haste not to be rich. Charity—give and it shall be given you; I was an hungered and ye gave me to eat; minister to the necessities of saints; hide not thyself from thine own flesh. Giving up anxiety—take no thought for your life, what ye shall eat, or what ye shall drink; nor yet for your body, what ye shall put on; trust in the Lord, and verily thou shalt be fed. The prayer for pardon has most especially the command annexed —Forgiving one another, and forbearing one another; seventy times seven forgive him; as much as lieth in you live peaceably with all men; love your enemies. The sixth petition involves commandments such as these—consider your ways; enter not into the path of the wicked, and go not in the way of evil men, avoid it, pass not by it, turn from it and pass away; make a covenant with thine eye not to look on vanity; be vigilant, be sober, be filled with the Spirit. And when we ask to be delivered from evil, the command is—Abhor that which is evil, cleave to that which is good; avoid the very appearance of evil; keep yourselves unspotted from the world; love not the world; resist the devil; abide in Christ.

If we love the petitions we shall also love the precepts, as the channels through which promises are fulfilled and prayers answered; and when we say Amen, we express our willingness to receive God's answer in the appointed way.

Is it not true, then, that Amen is the answer of a good conscience?

VII. IT IS A RENEWAL OF OUR DEDICATION TO GOD.

As God gives Himself to us, we give ourselves to

God. God's gift comes first, ours comes not merely second, but is itself the consequence of His grace and the influence of His Spirit. God gives perfectly, joyfully, constantly; our surrender to God is full of imperfections, interruptions, and repinings. Yet it is a real surrender to God. Every child of God yields himself unto God, and offers himself, body, soul, and mind, for time and eternity, to the Lord.

God has bound Himself to us by oath, and every time we say Amen we swear by the God of truth, by Jesus the Amen, that we are the Lord's. "Thy vows are upon me." Christ crucified is God's Amen to us; and our heart crucified to the world, and devoted to Him, is our Amen to God. With truth did the ancient Church speak of sacraments, confirmations by oath, pledging us to the love and service of God. And when the Spirit of God is poured out, "One shall say I am the Lord's, and another shall call himself by the name of Jacob, and another shall subscribe with his hand unto the Lord, and surname himself by the name of Israel."

When judgment of death was pronounced on the great teacher of the Church, Cyprian, because he worshipped the Lord Christ, the sentence of the proconsul having been read with a loud voice, "Thascius Cyprian is to be put to death by the sword," Cyprian lifted up his voice and said, "Amen." Was not this a great *Amen?* Can you not hear in it all the petitions of the Lord's Prayer, "Our Father which art in heaven, hallowed be Thy name, Thy

kingdom come, Thy will be done on earth?" Did it
not express his faith that God would give him that
day his daily bread, strength to suffer? Did it not
manifest the meekness and forbearance of a forgiven
soul, and the bright hope of safe conduct through all
temptation and deliverance from evil? It was a great
Amen, and the soul of that Amen was Christ, whom
Cyprian worshipped, and in whom all truths and hopes
were to him Amen. So let us learn to say Amen,
that we may reach that end, which is better than the
beginning; that end which itself is endless, where we
join the song of praise, which, according to the testimony of the beloved disciple, is enclosed with the
twofold Amen: Amen, blessing, and glory, and wisdom, and thanksgiving, and honour, and power, and
might, be unto our God for ever and ever, Amen.

When life ends we can commit our souls, as we
constantly do our prayers, to Christ, the Amen, to
bring them safely to the God of glory, *our Father
in Heaven.*